O. Leontine Tuttle, U. C. '97.

MUNICIPAL GOVERNMENT
IN GREAT BRITAIN

MUNICIPAL GOVERNMENT
IN GREAT BRITAIN

BY

ALBERT SHAW
AUTHOR OF
"MUNICIPAL GOVERNMENT IN CONTINENTAL EUROPE"

NEW YORK
THE CENTURY CO.
1895

PREFACE

ANY account of living institutions, whether chiefly critical and comparative, or chiefly descriptive and statistical, has always to contend with the difficulty that life means growth and change, and that everything is in motion. This difficulty, quite formidable enough as regards the United States and its social and political organisms, is perhaps even greater in Europe, where innovation and change have in recent years been more marked and bold than in America. When, however, as in the present volume and its successor, the discussion is limited to those particular forms of organization that we may agree to call City Government,—although the word " government" would seem ill adapted to embrace at once the mechanism and the varied tasks of modern municipal corporations,—Europe affords a simpler and more satisfactory field of inquiry than the United States. And the reason may be given in a word. In no European country are the principles, purposes, or essential mechanisms of municipal government under serious discussion. Each country has worked out for itself, or borrowed from a neighboring country, a practicable system of municipal organization; and the system is strong enough and elastic enough to endure the double test of a marvelous new growth of city population and a fast increasing list of administrative undertakings.

If one should attempt to describe exhaustively the current activities of European city governments, his narrations and his statistics might have grown obsolescent before they could be printed, so rapid is the expansion of municipal life. But, fortunately, the structure of European municipal government possesses principles of a permanent nature. With all the differences of detail that the American inquirer may find in different countries, he discovers that in the whole range of municipal institutions, from Great Britain to Southeastern Europe, there are not nearly so many important variations, either of principle or of method, as in the United States alone. The primary difficulty in the way of a general study of American municipal government lies in the lack of any logical system, or of any guiding principles, and in the capricious and arbitrary nature of the legislative changes that one State or another is constantly making. I am strongly impressed with the belief that municipal reform proceeds haltingly in the United States because, for one reason, many citizens who desire sincerely to aid in the regeneration of their town life and neighborhood affairs have formed no definite municipal ideals. They have neither learned what

in the experience of the world has come to be regarded as a sound constitution or framework of
municipal government, nor have they made up
their minds to what positive tasks and public services a municipal government may wisely apply
itself. I have no intention to prescribe European
remedies for American maladies, nor to suggest
any degree whatsoever of imitation. We must deal
with our own problems in our own way. But we
must be willing to gain all possible enlighten-
ment from the experience of others who have been
dealing with kindred problems and have found
solutions that are satisfactory under their own circumstances.

In the present volume I have sought to give such
an account of the working of municipal institutions in Great Britain as would supply the information that American readers might find most
suggestive and useful for their purposes. A second
volume will treat, somewhat similarly, of municipal
government in the chief countries of Continental
Europe. The British system and its developments,
particularly in the great manufacturing and commercial towns, would seem to be worthy of the
practical attention of our ambitious American cities
of corresponding rank as regards population and
commercial importance.

The chapters upon Glasgow and London have
made free use of my articles upon the governments
of those cities that have appeared in "The Century
Magazine"; and the chapter upon the practical

working of the British system has in like manner drawn upon an article contributed to the "Political Science Quarterly" several years ago. But the book is in no sense a reprint of such studies, and it is designed to present a fairly symmetrical account of the British municipal system, its methods and its results, as in operation in the present year.

New York, January, 1895.

CONTENTS

MUNICIPAL GOVERNMENT
IN GREAT BRITAIN

MUNICIPAL GOVERNMENT IN GREAT BRITAIN

CHAPTER I

INTRODUCTORY: THE GROWTH AND PROBLEMS OF MODERN CITIES

THE nineteenth century is closing upon a race that is destined, for the great majority, to live in cities, or under conditions more or less strictly urban. This fact has only recently forced its way into the general consciousness. Circumstances of an obvious kind compelled its recognition in England and western Europe somewhat sooner than in America; and sterner necessities led to a speedier and more complete adoption of means to lessen the disadvantages and dangers, and to secure the possible benefits, of the massing of population in large towns. For a quarter of a century the cities of the United States have taken an undisguised pride in their buoyant growth. Most of them have eagerly welcomed the evidence of large yearly or decennial additions to their numbers. But at length they are discovering that the city element begins to preponderate in a country whose whole fabric of civilization had been wrought upon a foundation of agriculture and rural life; and that the future safety

The new preponderance of cities.

I.—1   1

CHAP. I.   of our institutions requires that we learn how to adapt
city life to the promotion of the general welfare.   The
manner in which the principal nations of Europe have
of late dealt with these new problems of community
life, under conditions of dense inhabitancy, is highly
Value of   instructive.   The problems to be solved are so similar
European
experience. in all their essential characteristics, regardless of national distinctions, that they afford an important field
of comparative study both descriptive and critical. An
inquiry into the experiences and the present status of
the great municipalities of several other countries can
but result in a clearer perception of the nature of the
practical problems of municipal government that con-
front our American cities — while also aiding, through
the processes of comparison and induction, to establish
certain fundamental principles and methods that must
have place in the wise and permanent ordering of the
affairs of any modern industrial community, in whatever portion of the world.

It is the purpose of the present volume and its
successor to perform this service of a comparative account of municipal administrations — their methods
and their results — in the chief capitals and the typical industrial and commercial towns of Europe. The
chief aim is to present significant facts in the spirit of
Aim of pres- impartial interpretation ; and there has been no desire
ent volume.
to construct an argument or to defend a thesis. Nevertheless, certain fundamental views have undoubtedly
exercised so strong an influence upon the mode of inquiry pursued, that a preliminary statement or two
may be permitted as furnishing the key to all that follows. Since life in cities, under new and artificial
conditions, is henceforth the providential lot assigned
to the majority of families, it is to be accepted as a
permanent fact for this generation and its immediate
successors ; and the inevitable order is not to be re-

belled against as an evil, but welcomed as if it were the most desirable of destinies. For the present evils of city life are temporary and remediable. The abolition of the slums, and the destruction of their virus, are as feasible as the drainage of a swamp and the total dissipation of its miasmas. The conditions and circumstances that surround the lives of the masses of people in modern cities can be so adjusted to their needs as to result in the highest development of the race, in body, in mind, and in moral character. The so-called problems of the modern city are but the various phases of the one main question, How can the environment be most perfectly adapted to the welfare of urban populations? And science can meet and answer every one of these problems. The science of the modern city — of the ordering of common concerns in dense population-groups — draws upon many branches of theoretical and practical knowledge. It includes administrative science, statistical science, engineering and technological science, sanitary science, and educational, social, and moral science. If one uses the term City Government in the large sense that makes it inclusive of this entire ordering of the general affairs and interests of the community, and further, if one grasps the idea that the cheerful and rational acceptance of urban life as a great social fact demands that the City Government should proceed to make such urban life conduce positively to the welfare of all the people whose lawful interests bring them together as denizens of great towns, he will understand the point of view from which this book has been written.

It is not, as has been said, with the purpose of maintaining a thesis, or of provoking controversy, that these preliminary propositions have been laid down. They would seem to rest so palpably at the bottom of all that is encouraging and inspiring in the recent

CHAP. I.

Evils of city life remediable.

A science of the modern city.

progress of municipal life in Europe, that a discussion from any more restricted point of view would be well nigh useless. It would fail to perceive clearly and to grasp solidly the dominating principle. I may be pardoned, then, if I venture to elaborate somewhat further these introductory considerations. For it is of consequence that the distinctive nature of the modern city should be comprehended, and that the logic of its origin should be made to throw some light upon the problem of its destiny.

All the important economic and social problems of the age have presented themselves in a perfectly rational and predicable manner. Some time ago,— not to look too closely at dates, let us say a century ago,—following the French and American Revolutions, there began an era of the most extraordinary progress. The economist views it as an era of industrialism. The perfection of the steam-engine, the rapid invention of machinery and its adoption in manufactures, the building of railroads — all these innovations enormously increased production. The accumulation of capital and the world's progress in opulence were now at a rate many times more rapid than had ever been known before. Political economy became the science of this new era of capital and production; and the idols of this science, naturally and properly enough for the time being, were production and capital. Human society does not advance in symmetrical fashion, but rather by tangents and zigzag lines. It was inevitable that economic production and the development of capital, under the new industrial forces, should be the dominant ideas of the nineteenth century until its last decades. But it was equally natural and necessary that the social problems which grew out of the new facts and conditions of wealth-production should, in the fullness of time, have forced themselves to a front place and won universal attention.   Those who have observed the economic writing and discussion of the last quarter of the century cannot have failed to note how almost exclusively men are wrestling with the problems of wealth-distribution.   The social and ethical aspects of industrialism are now prominent.   Having to so great an extent conquered the forces of nature and made them vastly productive of material goods, men are raising the question in its logical order how this good fortune can be made most conducive to the welfare of all members and classes of the social body.

Chap. I.

Emergence of social questions.

But these resistless forces of modern life have not merely resolved society into distinct elements as regards production, thereby creating all the hard problems that we discuss under such heads as capital and labor, profits and wages; but they have had other and revolutionary effects upon the grouping of population-masses.   They have in the first place prodigiously stimulated the growth of population.   In the second place they have concentrated all this increase of population in large towns.   Under old conditions, country life was the rule and town life the exception.   But under the new conditions, urban life becomes the necessary lot of an ever-increasing proportion — a proportion that in several countries has now reached preponderant dimensions, while in all civilized lands a like result is only a matter of a few years.   The same general causes are in operation everywhere, with similar consequences.   The hundred grave and distinctive problems that the new era of town life brings with it are of universal, simultaneous moment.   The essential questions pertaining to administration, and to social and economic arrangements, affect all the cities of the civilized world.   We are accustomed to think and speak of the rapid evolution of American

New grouping of population-masses.

I.— 1*

cities as incidental to the growth of a new country, and to overlook the significant fact that the European cities are growing nearly or quite as fast as our own, in spite of the tide of emigration that is always ebbing from European shores. The great towns have sprung up with magical rapidity everywhere, but not with magical order and completeness. Nobody had wisely anticipated their development, and they came into being as great hives of industry, sufficiently organized for temporary purposes of industrial production, but ill-organized, even chaotic, as regards comfort, health, and the various amenities of civilized life. New organs of administration had to be devised. Common regulations, and centralized services of several kinds, became necessary. How to minimize the evils and, at length, how to maximize the advantages of urban life were questions that took practical form under many successive emergencies and incentives. And thus, in the working out of a series of complex problems, having their economic and financial, their political and administrative, their sociological and ethical, and their technical and engineering aspects, there has been evolved a knowledge which, as I think, might now be systematized as the science and art of modern city government.

Universality of the great industrial town.

The new art of city government.

It is evident that we are entering upon a period of notable transformations. The social life of the world is adapting itself to the new conditions. Yet it does not follow that new principles need be invoked. Only let it be remembered that old principles if retained must have novel applications. Thus, superficially regarded, the activities of the modern city would seem to have a strong and rapid socialistic trend, because so many subjects of common interest are passing under the direct control of the municipal authorities. But in point of fact, when strictly analyzed, modern

Municipal collectivism.

municipal collectivism does not so very seriously trans- gress the valuable old principles of individual free- dom and private initiative, and the household basis of economic and social life. To speak in a popular and unscientific way, the word socialism, as relating to the increasingly complex functions of the large modern town, might be defined to mean the sum total of all those governmental activities which have been super- imposed upon the negative or strictly necessary func- tions. But in practice it is extremely difficult to clas- sify public functions and activities upon any logical scheme which proposes to set individualism over against socialism. The former "ism" holds it to be the duty of government to secure to the individual the largest liberty and immunity compatible with the reasonable liberty and immunity of other individuals. The means, Old doc- trines — new applications. however, by which this protection is to be made effi- cient cannot be the same in the simple agricultural community and in the great and densely peopled city. The most extreme advocate of the doctrine of individ- ualism, if we except the anarchist, has always stoutly upheld the police authority of the State or commu- nity, as necessary to safeguard the individual in the exercise of his freedom. Organized society must main- tain an environment of order. In the jostling throngs of the city, a careless or vicious member of society has a hundredfold more opportunities to disturb the com- fort and endanger the health and well-being of his fellows than in the country. How many of the new activities of municipal government — the activities often regarded as socialistic — are but the application to changed conditions of the venerable principles of the individualists? The most strictly defensive war has its offensive operations. A close analysis would Individual- ism justifies a limited socialism. reveal the fact that a very large part of the list of modern undertakings commonly deemed socialistic

might properly be regarded as extensions of individualism.   These are logical distinctions, it is true; yet
their recognition would clarify many a fruitless argument, and set at rest many a groundless apprehension.
Thus the doctrine of individualism itself, extended to
meet existing conditions, may be invoked to justify
and sustain that ever-broadening basis of collective
municipal activity upon which the individual stands to
play his private rôle.   If that rôle is of necessity restricted in certain directions, it gains in others much
more than it surrenders to the central actor, the
municipality.

In the theory and art of modern city-making, we
must frankly acknowledge, collectivism has a large
and growing place.   The municipal corporations, until

Rapid
growth of
municipal
functions.
recently rather passive as political and social organisms, are now becoming highly conscious of their
organic entity, and highly active in extending old
functions and assuming new ones.   No short-cut
method of proving this would be more conclusive
than a few comparative data on the increase of municipal taxes and the growth of municipal indebtedness.
The English statistics on these lines are, for example,
especially instructive.   They point to an aggressive
demand upon the resources of society that has increased in a ratio far higher either than the relative
growth of town populations or than the development
of the national wealth.   But I am not willing to de-
duce any pessimistic conclusions from this general
tendency, whether exhibited in England, in Germany,
or in America.   I do not for a moment believe that
modern cities are hastening on to bankruptcy, that
they are becoming dangerously socialistic in the range
of their municipal activities, or that the high and ever
higher rates of local taxation thus far indicate anything detrimental to the general welfare.   It all

means simply that the great towns are remaking themselves physically, and providing themselves with the appointments of civilization, because they have made the great discovery that their new masses of population are to remain permanently. They have in practice rejected the old view that the evils of city life were inevitable, and have begun to remedy them, and to prove that city life can be made not tolerable only for working-men and their families, but positively wholesome and desirable. Are the magnificent activities and material achievements of our century an evil thing? It is a false, unhealthy philosophy that so characterizes them. They are to be the basis of a high and widely diffused civilization. These activities have populated cities and industrial towns; and in the sudden, haphazard, fortuitous concourse there have been serious evils. But cannot the same energy that has won great achievements in the field of production solve the social problems that have sprung up in the wake of those achievements, when once it fairly grapples with them? Modern society, having learned how to produce abundantly, can also find a way to distribute the product equitably, and to overcome the ills of irresponsible private wealth and undeserved poverty. And modern production having stimulated the increase of population, and massed men in cities, can it be so great an evil that men must live where it is ordained that they must work? Those whose circumstances permit a free choice of environment are not primarily concerned. But the cardinal fact remains that the majority of families must henceforth, in increasing areas of the earth, live under urban conditions. Those conditions since the opening of the new industrial era have been upon the whole vicious. They must be so improved that for the average family the life of the town shall not per-

CHAP. I.

The permanent remaking of great towns.

Possibilities of the ideal city.

force be detrimental. The race must not decay in city tenements, but somehow it must, under these conditions of dense neighborhood, find a higher and better life. Infection, disease, a high death-rate must surrender to the science of public sanitation, so that the health of children and the longevity of the mature shall be better assured in the town than in the country, urban death-rates falling below those of the nation at large. The moral and educational environment must be made such as to produce the best results, and to preserve the virtue, intelligence, industrial capacity, and physical stamina of the race.

City life must become positively good.

It is most encouraging, from this point of view, to note the recent and now progressing transformations of old European cities to meet the needs of their multiplied population — a new population that refuses to rest content with the unwholesomeness of old conditions, and demands broader and better streets, more scientific drainage, better water-supplies, better public cleansing, better sanitary protection against infectious diseases, better illumination, better housing, better urban transportation facilities, better educational facilities, better parks and opportunities for recreation, and all the other improvements that modern science can suggest. We find the transformation further advanced in some places than in others, and as yet complete nowhere. But everywhere in Europe we behold the struggle fairly entered upon, and great undertakings bravely instituted. With the war-cloud continually hovering over these European nations, and vast armaments draining the resources of the people, while emigration transfers to the New World so much of the accumulated capital and expensively trained working energy of the old countries, it is astonishing to note the costliness and magnificence of the municipal improvements of recent years, and to

Present-day transformations of European cities.

observe the effort they are universally making to improve the social and sanitary conditions of town life. It requires no peculiar discernment on the part of the traveler to discover that large towns are becoming alike the world over.   There is something to be regretted in the loss of picturesqueness, quaintness, and distinctive flavor.   But if our observer be public-spirited and humane, the spread of modern improvements will not greatly vex him.   He will consider the fact that these changes redound to the convenience and welfare of the people now on earth, who cannot live on medieval picturesqueness or accommodate the hundredfold greater business of the present-day city in the narrow thoroughfares that sufficed for the limited traffic of other centuries.   He will sympathize with the efforts of the present generation of Italians to make Rome, Naples, and many another historic city the fit abiding-place of hopeful communities whose gaze is forward rather than backward.   He will be delighted with the resurrection and out-blossoming of Hungary's aspiring, twentieth-century capital, Budapest.   He will be impressed and gratified as he notes the renovation and development, on the scientific lines of the modern city-making, of Athens and Bucharest, Belgrade and Sofia.   And he will find food for optimistic reflection rather than for disappointment in the discovery that even Constantinople, Alexandria, Cairo, Jerusalem, and Damascus are beginning to take on the municipal forms and appointments of the western European nations.

It is of great importance for our present purpose that we should hold in clear remembrance the fact that, except for its ancient core, its immemorial nucleus, almost every European city of our time is altogether of recent construction.   Not to anticipate here in any fullness of detail the statistical data that may belong more properly to subsequent chapters, a few general statements regarding the growth of European towns may help to illumine the propositions of this introductory discussion. It is in Great Britain that modern industrialism has attained its highest development, and it was there that the new phenomena of the rapid expansion of town populations first became apparent. In Scotland and the north of England, especially, the change from rural to urban conditions has been revolutionary. At the beginning of the nineteenth century (census of 1801) the total population of Scotland was 1,600,000, and only a small proportion was made up of town dwellers. Rural influences played a dominant part in the forming of those characteristics — physical, intellectual, and moral — that are deemed most distinctive of the Scotch people. But the proportions are wholly changed. The Scotch have become an urban people. The social effects of altered industrial conditions are nowhere else more strikingly exemplified. According to the census of 1891, the total population had grown to more than 4,000,000, of which only 928,500 was strictly rural. The town population was 2,631,300, and the villagers, forming an intermediate class, numbered 465,-800. The rural population had declined absolutely in the ten years from 1881, the decrease being $5\frac{1}{3}$ per cent., while in the previous ten years, from 1871 to 1881, there had also been a loss of 4 per cent. The town population, on the other hand, had increased 18 per cent. from 1871 to 1881, and 14 per cent. from 1881 to 1891. The village population shows a slight growth. As against the Scotland of other days, when there were three country dwellers to one citizen of a town, there are now three townspeople for every one who lives in the country. This does not count the half-million villagers in either category. Even if they are regarded as living under conditions that belong to the country rather than to the town, it still holds true that practically two thirds of the Scotch people now live as townsfolk; and the reversal signifies so much that it amounts to a social revolution of prime magnitude. The change is all the sharper because town and country life are in more violent contrast in Scotland than in other English-speaking countries by reason of the extraordinary density of the Scotch population, even in towns of moderate size. It is evident that if the Scotch people are to sustain their high traditions, they must learn the art of living well in cities. What progress they have made toward the mastery of that art, for their own preservation and for the instruction of other communities, I shall endeavor to set forth in a chapter devoted to their chief center of population and industry.

The growth of urban population in the midlands and north of England has been no less remarkable than in Scotland. The old English seaports, cathedral cities, and county towns, that were the important population-centers two hundred or even one hundred years ago, have been left hopelessly behind in the race for greatness by the new manufacturing towns. Of twenty-eight large cities and towns included by the Registrar-general in a list for the publication of mortality rates, fourteen had no corporate existence prior to the Municipal Reform Act of 1835, and these fourteen contain much more than half the total population, while the other fourteen also have had their chief growth within sixty years. Manchester, beginning to grow rapidly only toward the end of the eighteenth century, had attained a population of 250,000 when in 1838 it was granted a municipal charter. So enormously have the manufacturing interests of this great spinning and weaving district expanded, that within a radius of twenty miles from the Manchester town-hall there is now a population of more than three million souls, assigned to a number of almost contiguous municipal corporations. Birmingham, another of the new manufacturing towns, has half a million people of its own. Sheffield, Bradford, Salford, and many other large towns are of still more recent incorporation than Manchester and Birmingham. And not a few of those whose charters are of earlier date, as Liverpool, Leeds, and Nottingham, are just as essentially modern, their earlier municipal history having little or no importance. The Reform Act of 1835 dealt with 178 municipal corporations in England and Wales, and since that time, under Queen Victoria, 125 new charters of incorporation have been granted. By the census of 1891, the 178 old corporations had a total population of 5,483,000, and that of the 125 new corporations was 5,512,000. The population of England and Wales in 1891 was 29,000,000; and 11,000,000 people were living in 302 cities and towns possessing full municipal governments. This does not include approximately 6,000,000 inhabitants of the "Greater London," or several million people who are in the suburban districts of large towns, or in communities living under urban conditions but not embraced within the present boundaries of municipal corporations. The administration of the English public-health acts divides the country into urban and rural sanitary districts; and this line can best be taken to distinguish the town dwellers from the country dwellers. The urban sanitary districts number somewhat more than one thousand, and by the last census they contained a population of 20,800,000. The population of the rural districts was 8,200,000. The inhabitancy of the urban districts — nearly 72 per cent. of the total — had increased 15.3 per cent. from 1881 to 1891. That

Growth of
the recent
corpora-
tions.

of the rural districts had grown only 3.4 per cent.
One third of the whole population is now in towns of
over 100,000 inhabitants, and nearly another third is
in towns having from 10,000 to 100,000 people. For
twenty years the growth of the towns having from
10,000 to 250,000 people has been at the average rate
of 2 per cent. a year, or 20 per cent. a decade. Thus
town life will soon prevail for three fourths of the
English people

If in France the tidal movement toward the towns
appears less strong, it is only because of the lack of
surplus population to be mobilized. The multiplicity
of small farms with peasant proprietorship has been
favorable to the kinds of rural industry that occupy
many hands, while the total population remains almost stationary. Nevertheless, the urban tendency
is exhibited very strikingly in the fact that while the
entire increase of the French nation from the census
of 1886 to the census of 1891 was less than 125,000,
there was in those five years a growth of 340,000 in
the aggregate population of the fifty-six largest cities
and towns—those having more than 30,000 people.
For many years it has, in like manner, been true that
the towns were absorbing more than the total increase, and that the country districts were absolutely
declining. Nothing but the low birth-rate that prevails in France has prevented the rapid development
of a great urban population. The body of country
dwellers has for half a century maintained itself at
about 25,000,000 with a slight but steady decline,
while the townsfolk have increased from a body of
about 7,000,000 to one of 13,000,000. Paris has had
the principal growth, and is more than five times as
large as it was a hundred years ago in the Revolutionary period. Lyons and Marseilles had rather more
than 100,000 people each at the opening of the present

century, and they have now more than 400,000 each. The other large French towns have for the most part grown to about three times their size at the beginning of the century, and nearly all of this growth has been in the last half of the period. Taking the ten largest towns of France, including Paris, we find that their average population was about 100,000 in 1801, 160,000 in 1835, and nearly 450,000 in 1894. At a very early day the town population of France will be 40 per cent. of the whole.

In Germany. In Germany, until lately a country of farms, forests, and mountains, with a predominantly rural population, the recent movement toward the towns has been almost unexampled in its rapidity. Since the Franco-Prussian war the German town population has been growing at the rate of 20 per cent. a decade, while the rural population has been at a standstill. Berlin is seven or eight times as large as it was in 1831, and the large towns of all parts of the new empire have expanded astonishingly within twenty years. The German census classifies as "large" towns those having more than 100,000 people; as "middle-sized," those of 20,000 to 100,000; as "small," those of 5000 to 20,000; and as villages or "country towns," those of 2000 to 5000. The large towns had 7.24 per cent. of the whole population in 1880, 9.5 per cent. in 1885, 12.1 in 1890, and will undoubtedly have 15 or 16 per cent. in 1895. The towns of the other three classes have not grown nearly so fast, but the census of 1895 will show that just half the German population is living in towns and villages of 2000 people or more, and that nearly 40 per cent. are in places having more than 5000.

Holland and Belgium. Urban population grows apace also in Holland and Belgium. One third of the Netherlanders live in towns of 20,000 people or more, and a quarter of the

Belgians are similarly grouped. In the twenty-five years from 1868 to 1893, the Holland towns of this class advanced from possessing exactly one fourth to exactly one third of the whole people. In both Holland and Belgium the commercial and manufacturing towns continue to develop at a rate that shows no signs of abatement. The Italians, until very lately, had not been affected in a marked way by the new forces that are centralizing population in urban groups, and the agricultural phase is still greatly predominant. Nevertheless, the new municipal spirit has begun to stir itself almost as strongly in the chief Italian towns as anywhere else in the world; Italy. and their growth in population and in the appurtenances of the modern city constitutes a chapter of progress well worth a place in the record. I shall endeavor to present its outlines and salient features in a succeeding volume. In thirty years Rome and Milan have more than doubled their population; Florence has come little short of the same achievement; Turin and Genoa are about 70 per cent. larger than in 1864; overcrowded Naples has gained a hundred thousand people; Palermo has added nearly as many; and numerous large communes have gained 50 per cent. In future chapters on Vienna and Budapest some indications will be given of the urban developments in the Danubian valley that bear so new and striking Southeastern Europe. a character.

The growth of our American cities is not a subject that I shall discuss in detail in a series of comparisons intended primarily to acquaint American readers with the municipal problems of Europe. Yet I may be allowed to reassert that there is nothing peculiar to our country in the conditions of our urban development. Except in the newest regions, it is true here, as in Europe, that rural population does not grow at all.

I.— 2

CHAP. I.

Decline of
rural popu-
lation in the
United
States.

Lessons
from Euro-
pean towns.

For twenty-five years the older farming districts even
of Western States like Iowa and Minnesota have been
declining absolutely in population, and the towns are
receiving all the new increments, besides drawing
from the country.   Farm machinery has lessened the
number of people required to cultivate each square
mile of farm-land, and diversified industry creates
employment in the towns.   And thus we are facing
the same kind of problems having to do with the
amelioration of town life that Europe has been and is
still compelled to meet.   We shall solve our problems,
and in the end we shall do many or most things in
our own way, which also will probably be the best
way.   But we cannot wisely continue to ignore the
lessons that European cities have to teach.   The present costliness of their past negligence might well stimulate us to greater precautions.   For example, within
recent years many of the European cities of second
and third as well as all of those of the first rank
have been widening old thoroughfares, cutting new
ones through solid masses of buildings, making open
spaces and breathing-spots, admitting air and sunlight
to dark and densely crowded neighborhoods, and making room for the movement of traffic.   To lay out
new towns, or new additions to older ones, with narrow streets and insufficient provision for playgrounds,
open squares, and park room, is in our day an un-
pardonable offense against civilization.   Yet we find
numbers of our American towns, even in the far
West, which are making an ill beginning in these respects, and are unquestionably subjecting posterity
to great trouble and expense.   The art of making and
administering modern cities happens not to have engaged the attention of the same order of talent in
America that it has commanded in Europe.   In the
official life of the European municipalities one contin-

ually finds men who have a high ideal of the municipality, and a large conception of its duties and possibilities, besides possessing great technical knowledge and experience. A general familiarity with their attempts and achievements might save our American cities from some mistakes, and might stimulate them to adopt broader and more generous municipal programs.

CHAPTER II

THE RISE OF BRITISH TOWNS, THE REFORM ACTS, AND THE MUNICIPAL CODE

IN our more particular survey of European municipalities, those of Great Britain will claim first attention. The English towns had been governed upon a popular plan by the whole body of the freemen in the Saxon days; and while under the Norman sovereigns they became fiefs of the crown, "royal boroughs," they retained for a long time most of their old privileges of self-government. At length, however, their character was changed. In the fifteenth century they began to secure charters of incorporation, usually by purchase from the crown, or by pledge of generous annual contributions to the royal exchequer.

Rise of the boroughs. The boroughs, as they were entitled, had representation in Parliament, and they played no small part in the overthrow of the feudal system and the development of the modern political order. Having helped to reform Parliament, in due time Parliament returned the favor and reformed and modernized them.

The most active and influential elements in the medieval town life were the associations of the craftsmen and merchants of a like trade. These societies or guilds were at the outset voluntary organizations for social purposes and mutual benefit — for the regulation of apprenticeships and the protection of the interests of the particular craft. They served a very useful purpose in the period when industrial life and municipal citi-

zenship were repressed and obscured by feudal government. And it was their effective organization,
and their united action through their central delegate
bodies,— the merchants' house and the trades' house,
— that availed in many, if not in most, instances to
secure charters of self-government for the towns. Inasmuch as all reputable men in these towns exercised
some useful calling, and were supposed to be connected with the guilds, it became the custom to vest
the control of the town affairs in the hands of the
members or "freemen" of these companies. The municipalities, or boroughs, had previously been mere
local aggregations, with no assured institutions or
permanent character. Now they became corporations,
legal personages, with vested rights subject to the interpretation of the courts. Assuming that the members of the trades guilds were the freemen or burgesses
named in these charters of incorporation as the governing body of the community,— which was usually,
though not invariably, the case,— it is interesting to
consider how well adapted their government was to
the existing condition, and what was the state of municipal life in those old times. It is easy to praise too
glowingly the system of that period, and also easy to
disparage it with too little qualification. Its chief
merit, perhaps, lay in the fact that it was indeed a
system. Every man had his place and status in the
industrial and commercial world, and by virtue of
that place and status he had his position fixed for him
in the public life of the community. Feudal institutions had subjected the many to the few, but had at
least provided a place and a relationship for every
one. The rise of town life, which dignified mercantile
pursuits and handicrafts, had opposed the system of
leagued and equal freemen, of burgesses, of incorporated citizenship, to the feudal military system of lord-

I.— 2*

CHAP. II.

ship and vassalage. And this was a great preparatory step toward modern institutions and conditions. We know that there was a certain dignity and form about municipal life that appears well in the retrospect. We have surviving, here and there, a fine old medieval town-hall, or guild-hall, with its banqueting-chamber and its council-room. There was much stateliness in the office of mayor; and the old maces of mayoral authority survive to this day. Then there was impressiveness in the liveries that the freemen of the guilds disported on formal occasions. As for municipal conveniences, those were times when life was simple, and "modern improvements" not so much as dreamed about. The streets were narrow, with the houses built close upon them. The paving was of the rudest character. There was simple surface drainage, and no garbage removal or cleansing system.

Medieval town life.

Water was supplied from a few town fountains or public wells. Street-lighting had not been invented, and early hours were prescribed. Most towns had a skirting of common lands where the cows were pastured, and where, in many cases, fuel was procured. The houses were, in large part, built of wood; and in spite of vigilant "watch and ward" and compulsory hearth precautions, destructive fires were not infrequent. The death-rate, of course, was high. There was infection in the wells, and no means of checking the spread and fatality of the frequent "plagues" that swept the towns. But the science of public sanitation being undiscovered, these things were accepted piously as inscrutable visitations of God. There are, to-day, certain big villages in the interior of Ireland, remote from the railway lines, that, as I strongly suspect, retain many of the characteristics of old English borough life. There is more squalor and poverty, doubtless, in these Irish villages, and less of dignity and order in

the local government and institutions. But the standard of living and the character of town conveniences
are probably similar.

However fairly representative of the people of the
towns these municipal corporations may for some time
have been, they fell an easy prey at length to great
abuses. Their character as parliamentary constituencies tempted the arbitrary Tudor sovereigns, and
still more their successors the Stuarts. It was for the
interest of these sovereigns to restrict the corpora,
tions to the smallest membership, to make them as
close and non-representative as possible, and to bring
them by every available means under royal influence
and control. The course of their degeneration is a
long story, the details of which are different for each
town. But the principle at work was usually the
same. The immediately governing body in most towns
gradually became a handful of men forming a close,
self-perpetuating corporation. In many instances the
crown packed the town-governing bodies with honorary, non-resident freemen. The corporations of men
chartered to rule the communities became less and less
representative of the mass of the town dwellers, and
more and more irresponsible. As old public properties grew in value, and as old charitable trusts waxed
remunerative through the appreciation and accumulation of investments, grave financial abuses grew up
in the administration of these now scandalous municipal corporations. Through the eighteenth century the situation grew from bad to worse. Scores
of the corporations were held as " pocket boroughs "
by the crown, the ministers of state, and the great lords,
who used them to dictate their representation in Parliament. The municipalities became in large part a
great vested interest, held in a few hands and used
corruptly and wickedly to demoralize politics and mis-

CHAP. II. govern the nation. As for the towns themselves, in their local management, they were neglected and in a disgraceful state.

The aggravated ills of this situation were rendered
Decay of the old indus-trial system. intolerable by the rise of modern industry. The old organization of crafts and trades had become hopelessly obsolete, so that the earlier industrial society of the towns was now disordered beyond recognition. To add to the confusion, there came pouring into the centers of the new industry the surplus population of the rural districts and of the small villages, whose household crafts and industries had been superseded by the development of the factory system. It is not for me here even to summarize that chapter of misery and degradation. There are novels that depict the horrors of early factory life — the long hours of labor for women and children as well as men, and the vice and turpitude that prevailed among the industrial population. The economic writings of Ricardo and Malthus have the color of that period. But while the industrial society of England in the first three decades of this century has been described with some fullness, we have fewer graphic and accessible accounts of the life of the towns, distinctly considered. The old corporations were still existent, continuing their careers
Degradation of the fac-tory towns. of scandal and misgovernment; while, as for the new towns,— the simple hamlets and villages that had expanded into centers of manufacturing activity,— they had no municipal government of any character, and no representation in Parliament. They were merely populous parts of the counties — Lancashire or Yorkshire or some other — in which they happened to be. Their town life was of a kind that beggars description. Improperly constructed tenements were hurriedly provided to house the working population, and the evils of overcrowding were beyond belief. These structures

teemed with human life from cellar to garret — one family, two families, or even three families in a single room being common. The mortality became a fear- ful thing. Epidemic diseases could not be controlled, and cleanliness, which was no part of the habits of the people, was, under the circumstances, in any case a physical impossibility. The streets were abominable. There was almost nothing to break the monotony and meanness of the domestic architecture. Efficient common services of water, drainage, or illumination were, of course, wholly lacking. Religion lost its hold, except as Methodism came partly to the rescue with an uncurbed enthusiasm that seemed to fit the conditions of the people. Drunkenness, prizefighting, dog- and cock-fights, such were the prevalent diversions. There was no pretense of a good society in the industrial towns. There were no schools worth mentioning, no libraries, almost no civilizing agencies whatever. Those were the days of Robert Owen's despair of the industrial society, and of his attempts at Utopian reform.

The whole political structure, general as well as local, had become so vicious that the national spirit awakened in stormy protest, and it became plain that the alternative was reform or a revolution. Of necessity the reform began with Parliament itself. The great act of 1832 reconstructed the boroughs for the purposes of the parliamentary franchise. The "rotten" and "pocket" boroughs were deprived of their seats in the House of Commons. Small places that had previously been entitled to separate representation in Parliament were merged for that purpose with the counties. The large new towns, many of which were not yet incorporated, were designated as parliamentary boroughs with representation adjusted in some measure to their size and importance. With a .

reformed parliament duly installed at Westminster, it became possible to attack successfully the abuses and anomalies of local administration.   Commissions were appointed to study exhaustively the condition of the municipal corporations of the three kingdoms.   The Scotch towns, being fewer and less complicated in their traditional structure and corporate claims than those of England, were reformed first, their case being met by the Scotch Municipal Government Act of 1833.

Work of the municipal government commission.

The commission found its task, as regarded the English cities, a colossal one, but the work was performed in monumental fashion.   It must be remembered that each corporation had sheltered itself behind its accretion of old charters, alleged prescriptive rights, immemorial customs and self-created usages, and that no two were governed in exactly the same way, while none was accountable to any central authority or held to any duty of making public its expenditures or transactions.   What the investigation of Parliament proved beyond any possibility of contradiction is summed up in the most moderate terms by a distinguished authority [1] as follows:

> The municipal corporations were, for the most part, in the hands of narrow and self-elected cliques, who administered local affairs for their own advantage rather than for that of the borough; the inhabitants were practically deprived of all power of local self-government, and were ruled by those whom they had not chosen and in whom they had no confidence; the corporate funds were wasted; the interests and improvements of towns were not cared for; the local courts were too often corrupted by party influence, and failed to render impartial justice; and municipal institutions, instead of strengthening and supporting the political framework of the country, were a source of weakness and a fertile cause of discontent.

Local self-government was the primary object that the reform measures sought to secure.   In ancient times the householders had been the voters, and their

[1] Sir J. R. Somers Vine, F. S. S.

representatives had governed. Return was made to
this principle. What had been close corporations
became open to the citizens. It remained for later
enactments to grant the suffrage to the laboring
classes; but the municipal reform of 1835, following
the lines of the parliamentary franchise of 1832, admitted to the burgess right all property-owners, and
all occupiers of rented property that was rated as
worth £10 per annum. That is to say, the occupant
of a residence or a shop that rented for a dollar a
week was now entitled to vote, and the voting citizens
became the corporate body. The new system retained
the titles of mayor and aldermen, as well as that of
common councilors. But in reality it provided for a
municipal government exercised by an elected committee of the burgesses or citizens. The act provided
that common councils, varying in size according to
the population, should be elected; that these councils
should add to their own body by selecting a certain
number of aldermen; and that this chamber of councilors and aldermen should appoint the mayor from
its own number, who should act as its presiding officer. The one body of mayor, aldermen, and councilors was constituted the full municipal governing
authority. It is not necessary at this point to explain
the differences of detail between the Scotch and English systems, for their main features are similar, and
their practical operation is harmonious.

Lord John Russell, in introducing the Municipal
Reform Bill of 1835, remarked:

I have no doubt that when this new constitution of the municipal boroughs comes into effect, we shall find not only that it
will be productive of great improvements, not only that many
defects will be remedied and many abuses corrected, but that
the working of the bill itself will point out how the whole system
may be perfected.

His observations have been justified by the results.
The bill reformed and assimilated the government of
178 existing boroughs (about seventy in Scotland had
been reconstructed by the act of 1833), and provided
an intelligible system under which 125 more English
and Welsh towns have come into the enjoyment of
corporate privileges. From time to time new enactments applying in general to all municipal corporations were made by Parliament, modifying at some
points the structure of town government, but affecting more usually the scope and functions of the municipal administration. The chief outlines of the act
of 1835 had remained unobscured. Considered as a
system, the municipal government of England had acquired a permanent foundation and a stanch framework. But nearly half a century of experience and of
growing institutional and social life had placed several scores of additional laws upon the statute-books
when, in 1882, it was decided to consolidate and revise all existing statutory provisions relating to the
incorporated towns into a lucid municipal code. The
law of 1835, together with nearly sixty other statutes,
which it was proposed to recast into the simplest and
most orderly series of codified statements, constituted
a body of law the purport of which has been well
summarized by Sir J. R. Somers Vine as follows:

*General re-
sults.*

*Consolidated
code of 1882.*

(*a*) To constitute a corporation composed of a mayor, aldermen, and burgesses, acting by a council in which the general
body of burgesses were represented by from twelve to sixty-four
members thereof. The burgesses, by which term is indicated
those individuals enjoying the privileges of voting, consisted
of householders within the borough (residents within seven
miles of it, and payers of borough and poor rates) ; an occupancy of not less than twelve months being necessary, and
non-payment of rates or acceptance of poor-relief entailed de-
privation of the franchise. The register of voters, or "burgess
roll," was prepared annually, and, in boroughs both municipal

*The munici-
pal frame-
work.*

and parliamentary, settled by a revising barrister; in boroughs municipal only, that duty devolved upon the mayor, aided by two annually elected assessors. The burgesses elected the councilors by ballot, on the first of November in each year, and the council chose the aldermen bi-annually (one for every three councilors), and the mayor annually. The qualification for a councilor or alderman was £1000 property or £30 rating, if the borough was, before the year 1869, divided into four or more wards, or £500 property or £15 rating in other cases, and residence within fifteen miles of the borough; but by a very recent act (43 Vict. c. 17) this restriction was modified in a very important sense, as any person qualified to be a burgess was thereby qualified to serve as alderman or councilor. The property qualification then applied only to burgesses living beyond seven but within fifteen miles of the borough. In such boroughs as were divided into wards the councilors were apportioned among, and separately elected in, the several wards. A person might be chosen an alderman although he had not been elected a councilor, but the mayor had to be selected from the aldermen or councilors. By virtue of his appointment the mayor became a justice of the peace for the borough during his tenure of office and one year after. There were certain monetary penalties, limited in amount, for the non-acceptance of office.

(b) To provide for the performance of the following functions (amongst others of a minor character):

Functions of English municipal government.

(1) Administration of justice in local criminal and civil courts.

(2) Appointment and supervision of police.

(3) Administration of public property and the levy of rates when such property is not sufficient to meet the public expenses.

(4) The enactment of by-laws and appointment and dismissal of public servants.

(5) Execution of sanitary regulations under the public-health acts.

(6) Paving, lighting, supplying water, cleansing, and maintenance and improvement of thoroughfares and sewerage.

(7) Establishment and maintenance of public buildings, works, museums, and libraries.

(8) Making and maintaining harbors, docks, and navigations.

(9) Administration of special charitable trusts.

(10) Superintendence and enforcement of educational regulations where there is no school-board.

The Code groups its topics into thirteen parts, and
contains altogether 269 sections. It may be worth our
while to devote some space to an analysis of its arrangement and provisions. Part I is preliminary,
and sets forth in detail the division and section titles
of the entire act, lists the enactments that are superseded and repealed, declares the act applicable to all incorporated cities and towns existing and hereafter to
be created, except in Scotland and Ireland, and defines
and construes terms and phrases. Part II is the most
essential one, inasmuch as it prescribes the constitution
and government of municipal corporations. The burgesses are declared to be those entitled to be so en-
The
franchise.   rolled because, being of full age and having lived for
twelve months in the borough or within seven miles
of it, they are also occupants of premises of some kind
inside the town limits, have been rated for the poor-
relief fund on account of such occupancy, and have
paid all rates within the proper period, having meanwhile received no public alms themselves. This means
every man of family living in the town, every woman
who is the head of a family or a business, and every
man or woman living outside the limits (within seven
miles) who occupies business property inside. Thus
the municipal franchise is broad enough to include
every family that lives or does business in a town, except those who are paupers. The acceptance of public
relief disfranchises only for the following election.

The whole substance of British municipal government is condensed in the following clause:

The council
exercises
all powers.
The municipal corporation of a borough shall be capable of
acting by the council of the borough, and the council shall exercise all powers vested in the corporation by this Act or otherwise.

All that the burgesses have to do is to elect the councilors, and they do the rest. Any burgess is eligible

to the council. In addition, certain property and ratepaying qualifications admit to eligibility for the council those suburbans who live beyond seven but within
fifteen miles from the limits, yet have their business
interests in the town. The councilors are elected for
three years, and one third of them retire annually.
The aldermen and mayor are an integral part of the
council, the law stating specifically that " the council
shall consist of the mayor, aldermen, and councilors."   Mayor, al-
The aldermen " shall be fit persons elected by the coun-   dermen, and
cil." They hold their office six years. They are one   councilors.
third as many as the councilors. The act declares :

A person shall not be qualified to be elected or to be an alderman unless he is a councilor or qualified to be a councilor. If
a councilor is elected to, and accepts, the office of alderman he
vacates his office of councilor.

Half the aldermen retire every three years. When
the council confers aldermanic rank upon its own members, special elections in the wards fill the vacant coun-
cilorships.

The clause relating to the choice of a mayor is as
follows :

The mayor shall be a fit person elected by the council from
among the aldermen or councilors or persons qualified to be
such.

The law of 1835 made it necessary for the council
to put one of its own number into the mayor's chair,
and the honor was generally accorded to an alderman
of long service. The revision of 1882 makes it possible to elect any citizen; but the practice remains as
before. The mayor is elected for a year, and is eligible to reëlection. He appoints an alderman or councilor to act as deputy mayor. He presides at council
meetings, but has no veto power, and no authority as

CHAP. II.

an appointing officer; but he is *ex officio* a magistrate of the rank of justice of the peace.

Municipal appointees.

The council appoints two important standing officers, the town clerk and the treasurer, outside its own membership, and makes appointment of such other officers and department heads as it finds necessary, and all such officers must report to the council.

Conduct of business.

Frequent council meetings may be called, but the law makes obligatory at least four quarterly meetings for general business. The law authorizes the council to appoint from their own body general or special standing committees "for any purpose which, in the opinion of the council, would be better regulated and managed by means of such committees; but the acts of every such committee shall be submitted to the council for their approval." The council is authorized to make by-laws, for the good rule and government of the borough, in meetings at which at least two thirds of the members are present, and forty days must elapse after its publication before a by-law can take effect, the central government of the kingdom having the power to postpone or disallow the by-law.

Anditors.

The mayor names an auditor from the council, and the burgesses elect two others (usually expert accountants) from outside the official ranks, and these three audit the semi-annual accounts of the treasurer, who is obliged by law to print annually a full abstract of accounts. The town clerk must also make a yearly return to the Local Government Board — one of the executive departments of the national government — of the receipts and expenditures of the municipal corporation.

Wards.

The division of a town into wards, or the rearrangement of existing wards, is accomplished by a petition to the Queen, two thirds of the council having agreed to the plan. The council, of course, is the real actor,

but nominally the Crown, acting through the Local
Government Board, effects the change.   The number
of councilors assigned to a ward must be three, or a
multiple of three.

For non-acceptance of office — certain exemptions
being allowed — the law provides that the council may
fix a penalty, not to exceed £100 in the case of a mayor,
or £50 in that of an alderman, councilor, auditor, or
revising officer.   In the absence of any by-law, the
statute prescribes fines of half the amounts named
above.

Part III of the Code is devoted to municipal elections — from the preparation of the burgess lists to the
selection of mayor.   The revised burgess rolls are
completed before October 20 each year, and the town
clerk is obliged to print the names of all persons enrolled or claiming the right to be.   The safeguards
that protect registration are many and well devised.
The danger is that the registration machinery may
interfere with a full enrolment, rather than that any
improper names will be admitted to it.   Election day
is November 1.   At least nine days before the election
the town clerk must post notices on the town hall,
and in the wards where councilors are to be elected.
Nominations are filed with the town clerk.   All that is
necessary to a valid nomination is the signature of a
proposer, a seconder, and eight other citizens, all of
the ten being enrolled as voters in the ward.   The
nominations must be filed at least seven days before
the election.   All valid nominations are printed on
the official ballot-paper.   If only one nomination is
filed in a ward where one councilor is to be elected,
the polls are not opened and the nominee is declared
elected.   In like manner in a small town which is not
divided into wards, where there are several councilors
to be elected and the nominations do not exceed the

number of places to be filled, the candidates are declared elected. The election of aldermen occurs on November 9 at the quarterly meeting of the council immediately following the election of the mayor. The admission of women householders to the municipal franchise is not attended with eligibility for office.

Corrupt practices.

The next portion of the Code (Part IV) contains very elaborate provisions for the punishment of corrupt practices in municipal elections. It has been superseded by the still more detailed enactment of 1884 covering the whole subject. It is enough, perhaps, to say that these bristling regulations, which hedge about the election of town councilors with as formidable defenses as those that guard parliamentary elections, are absolutely efficacious.

Municipal property.

Part V of the Code deals with corporate property and liabilities, and defines the powers of the council with respect to the purchase and sale of land and buildings, and the borrowing of money for public purposes. The subject is treated with much detail; but in general it may be said that for every important step it proposes to take the council must go through the form of obtaining the sanction of the Treasury, or other departments of the general government, under a prescribed system.

Charitable trusts.

The object of Part VI was to bring under the uniform control of the council various charitable and other trusts of earlier periods, and also to make the council the trustees in the case of matters of local administration that had, under earlier acts of Parliament, been committed to some other agency. Concentration of local authority in the immediate hands of the one central council is the key-note to this part of the Code, as, indeed, to the whole instrument.

Part VII has to do with revenues and expenditure. It begins with the " borough fund," which consists of

the income derived from corporate property, from
fines, and from other sources than a levy of rates, and
which is to go as far as may be toward public expenses. Its insufficiency is to be met by the ordering
of a "borough rate." The method of assessment is prescribed with much particularity. It is enough to say
that the rate is levied against the occupiers of houses
and real property, upon the annual rental value.

The title of Part VIII is "Administration of Justice."
Mayors are borough justices while in office, and for
a year afterward. In the smaller towns and cities
the county justices have jurisdiction, and hold quarter-
sessions. In the larger ones, on petition of the council, a separate "commission of the peace" is granted
by the Queen, and her Majesty proceeds from time to
time to commission persons to act as justices. The
justices for a borough appoint a clerk, and the council makes provision of proper accommodation for the
business of the justices. The council may make petition for the appointment of one or more "stipendiary
magistrates" (salaried police-judges); and the large
towns have availed themselves of this provision. To
the large towns is also accorded a judge, called a "recorder," who holds "quarter-sessions" as a court of
record with jurisdiction in criminal matters. He also
holds a "borough civil court." The large towns, being
counties of themselves, have each its sheriff, appointed
by the council, and its coroner, whose selection is also
in the council's hands. Every burgess is presumably
liable to duty as a grand juror, or to serve on juries
for the trial of issues, in either the quarter-sessions or
civil court.

Part IX is concerned with the police. It authorizes
the council to appoint a committee from its own number who, with the mayor, shall be the "watch committee," and control police affairs. The committee

CHAP. II.

Police
control.

The granting
of charters.

Local Gov-
ernment Act,
1888.

appoints policemen (borough constables), and makes
regulations for the service. The absolute power of
dismissal is in the hands of the committee, but any
two justices who have jurisdiction in the borough may
suspend a policeman. The intent of the Code is to
vest full police authority in the council, to be exercised by a large committee, generally consisting of
one member from each ward, with the mayor as an *ex-
officio* member, and presumably chairman.

The next portion of the act relates to the privileges
of "freemen," and is designed to protect certain rights
of individuals existing prior to 1835. It has no practical significance. Part XI is devoted to the granting
of municipal charters. This right has always been,
and still is, exercised as a prerogative of the Crown;
but there is nothing arbitrary in the methods that are
pursued. Any populous place that desires to become
incorporated as a municipality petitions the Queen,
notifying the County Council and the Local Government Board. The Privy Council hears the facts, and
if the petition can properly be granted, a charter is
issued which defines the boundaries and ward divisions of the new municipal borough, and which places
it under the provisions of the Municipal Corporations
Act. Part XII of the Code is entitled "Legal Proceedings," and while highly important in practical administration, it involves no principles that require
explanation here. The final portion of the act is devoted to many miscellaneous topics, none of which
bear importantly upon the general character of the
municipal constitution.

The great statute of 1888, known as the Local Government Act, had chiefly to do with the giving of representative councils to the English counties; and its
provisions affect at few points, and not vitally at any,
the scheme of government provided in the Municipal

Code of 1882. The enactment of 1888 does, however, specifically provide that cities and towns having 50,-000 inhabitants shall be distinct counties for administrative purposes, the municipal councils assuming all duties which would otherwise devolve upon county councils. The special result achieved for municipal government by the act of 1888 was in the separate treatment of the metropolis, which was erected into the administrative County of London and given an elected County Council whose functions are in many respects analogous to those of the municipal councils possessed by the other great towns, and which will in due time acquire the full range of municipal authority and privilege. But this subject will find place in the chapter devoted especially to the government of London. Other general enactments since 1882 have affected in some respects the details of municipal government, but they have had to do far more extensively with the ever-expanding functions and undertakings than with the essential nature or structure of the town corporations.

The London council.

CHAPTER III

THE BRITISH SYSTEM IN OPERATION

IT has been a comparatively easy task to describe the British municipal system as it stands to-day, written in the law of the land. To describe it, or some parts of it, in actual operation in the large towns is more difficult, but also more profitable. It is especially true of British institutions that they are to be examined in their practical workings rather than in their theoretical aspects. The first question to be asked and answered in an inquiry on the ground into the character of municipal government would relate to the franchise. The essence of British municipal reform has consisted of the investiture of all authority in a council, which has been made directly representative of a burgess body nominally composed of all the householders. It is important to ascertain what limitations in practice there may be upon the exercise of the elective franchise. At the risk of a slightly tedious explanation, let me proceed to some analysis of the electorate.

The franchise in practice.

While the general course of the franchise in Great Britain has been toward freedom and popularity, it is as yet so full of anomalies and distinctions that the citizen who can explain it is exceptional; and the foreign inquirer must be diligent and alert, or some important proviso or detail will escape his notice. For purposes of illustration let us begin with Glasgow—

the largest municipal corporation in the British empire, "greater London" not having as yet attained a unified corporate existence. The qualified voters of Glasgow go to the polls at various times to elect (1) members of Parliament, (2) members of the town council, (3) school-boards, (4) parochial boards for the care of the poor and for other administrative work, and (5) members of the Clyde Navigation Trust. For each of these purposes the franchise is different. The parliamentary list includes male householders who have lived within the limits of the town a year, have paid their rates, and have received no relief from the parochial authorities. This list also admits lodgers who occupy quarters worth £10 a year. It also includes all occupiers of non-residence property, provided they live within seven miles and provided the premises are worth £10 a year. Finally it includes owners of town property worth £10 a year, provided they reside within seven miles of the limits. But there are several parliamentary constituencies — or districts, as we should say — in any large town, and a man who owns property in the different constituencies has a vote in each. Thus one man may have a number of parliamentary votes, though he may not cumulate them, but must visit the different districts where he is enrolled as a property-owner. The roll of municipal voters is the same as the parliamentary roll, with the important exception that women who are occupiers and ratepayers are allowed to vote, and with the further qualification that no man may vote in more than one ward, no matter how large an owner in other wards he may be. Very different still is the voting system for the election of parochial boards — all Scotland being divided into parishes, and Glasgow comprising three. The size of the board varies with the population of the parish; but we will take for

CHAP. III.

Parochial
voters.

Plural vot-
ing non-
cumulative
for parish
boards.

School vo-
ters — the
cumulative
plan.

illustration a large city parish of 200,000 people, that
has a board of twenty-five members. The entire
board is renewed annually, five members being chosen
in each one of five subdivisions or "parish wards"
(not to be confounded with the municipal wards).
Poor-rates in Scotland are divided between owner and
occupier, and the voting is based upon the ratepay-
ment. The ratable property in the particular parish
I am citing for illustration is owned, let us say, by
5000 persons, and occupied by 45,000 tenants and
their families. The owners and the occupiers alike
are entitled to from one to six votes apiece, according
to the value upon which they pay rates. All who pay
on a yearly value of £20 or less have a single vote,
while all who pay on £500 or more have six votes, the
values between £20 and £500 being graded, and en-
titling the ratepayers to two, three, four, or five votes.
Ratepaying is the sole qualification, and residence and
allegiance are immaterial. Let it be noted that the
parochial vote is non-cumulative. That is, if A has
six votes, and there are five men to be elected, he may
cast six votes, and no more or no less, for each man
he votes for — and he may vote for five, although he
may restrict himself to a smaller number if he chooses.
Women ratepayers, of course, are parochial electors.
And now as to the school-board franchise: all persons
are school-board electors who are on the assessor's
valuation roll for £4 and upward, that is, who are
either owners or occupiers of property of the annual
value of £4. The entire school-board retires every
three years, and the new board is elected upon a general ticket, with the cumulative plan. The Glasgow
board numbers fifteen; and from all the persons nominated the voter may select fifteen, or he may bestow
fifteen votes upon one candidate, or he may apportion
the fifteen votes as he likes among two or more nomi-

nees. The electorate for the Clyde Navigation Trust needs no further explanation than this, that it is limited, so far as the ratepayers are concerned, to those whose valuation exceeds £20.

This discussion of the franchises other than the municipal is, in strictness, a digression; but it is entirely germane to our main purpose. Which of these electorates is the broadest and most popular? The reader will naturally think it to be the municipal, which differs from the parliamentary by its inclusion of women, while it also includes the humble occupiers of premises valued at less than £4 who are excluded from the school-board electorate. But in practical effect the school-board franchise is the broadest of all, and this because it does not require that the rates shall have been actually paid. Rates are levied upon all householders; and for the exercise of the municipal and parliamentary franchises it is requisite that those rates shall have been paid at a date some months prior to the elections. The £4 clause in the school law really disfranchises almost nobody who would think of caring to vote, for only paupers and vagrants would be rent-payers in a smaller amount than $1.66 per month. But the provision that municipal and parliamentary voters must have paid their rates before a certain "qualifying date" so operates as to keep about fifty thousand householders off the registration roll which it is the business of the Glasgow assessor and his canvassers to make up every year. This is a very important fact. The Glasgow parliamentary voters' roll in 1891 included 78,738 names. The municipal roll simply added the names of 15,448 women, making a total municipal registration of 94,186. But the number of enrolled school-board electors in 1891 was 141,152, while the census of 1891 found 126,422 separate families living in Glasgow. Thus, while the

Which electorate is largest?

A sweeping disqualification.

CHAP. III.

One third of
the Glasgow
house-hold-
ers practi-
cally non-
voting.

municipal franchise is theoretically and apparently
broader than the school franchise, the registration for
the latter was the greater by 47,000 voters in 1891,
which amounts to an excess of exactly 50 per cent!
At least one third of the householders and theoretical
voters of Glasgow never appear on the municipal or
parliamentary registration lists. Their enrolment as

Scotch
slums self-
disfran-
chised.

school-board voters is involuntary. The slums evade
the tax-collector and sacrifice the franchise. Household enfranchisement in the Scotch towns therefore
means, in reality, ratepayers' enfranchisement. It is
a significant thing that the whole body of men who
are ignorant, vicious, and irresponsible is practically
outside the pale of politics in Glasgow and Edinburgh,
Dundee and Aberdeen.

If the stranger happens to have examined municipal
institutions in Glasgow or Edinburgh before prosecut-
ing his inquiries in the large English towns, supposing
also that he has preferred to observe and investigate
things on the ground before looking closely into the
distinctions of the law, he will probably go from Scotland to Liverpool, Manchester, or Birmingham expect-
ing to find that there also the ratepaying qualification
— which he knows is existent there as well as in the
North — will operate to diminish the burgess roll. In
Glasgow it makes the roll vastly smaller than the
number of householders, and it has the same effect in

Wholly dif-
ferent in
England.

Edinburgh. But in point of fact it has no such consequences in the English towns, for a reason that is
very readily explained. In Scotland, rates are divided
between owner and occupier, and are collected directly
and separately from each. Collection from the poorer
sort of tenants in the great towns is a very difficult
matter. In England the agitation for such division
of rates is as yet unsuccessful, and the entire burden
falls upon the occupier. But a number of years ago

the extreme difficulty of collecting from the occupants
of small tenements was met by the adoption of a plan
of composition with the landlords, by which they ad- How pre-
payment by
vance the rates on all tenements of less than £10 value, landlords
affects the
whether actually occupied or not, and get a discount voting lists.
of 30 per cent. They collect from their tenants by
charging these public rates into the rents. All the
householders who are thus arranged for consequently
find their names upon the parliamentary and municipal rolls; and the defection among the class of
tenants occupying houses worth £10 or more, while
considerable, is not enough to make the ratepaying
qualification affect the registration lists in any such
vital manner as in Scotland. I find in Birmingham
about 95,500 inhabited houses, and the burgess roll
contains 92,700 names. Of these, 11,600 are women,
leaving 81,100 parliamentary voters. Leeds is fairly
representative, with 78,000 inhabited houses, 67,500
municipal and 57,600 parliamentary voters.

In comparing the English franchise with the American, the practical exclusion of unmarried men is to be
taken into account as an item of great importance.
Here again the actual working of the British system
is not to be inferred from the law. The so-called
lodgers' franchise (parliamentary) gives a vote to men Lodgers'
franchise.
who occupy apartments worth £10 a year. The number of young men in any American city who occupy
lodgings at a rent of $4 a month would constitute a
very considerable element of the voting strength, and
I should not hesitate to estimate it as high as 15 per
cent. In many American cities it is certainly a much
larger proportion than that, in some cases reaching 30
or 35 per cent. Young men of this class are not, perhaps, so numerous in the English towns, but that they
form a very large element of the population is obvious. One may well be surprised, therefore, at the net

CHAP. III.

Exclusion of
unmarried
men from
municipal
voting lists.

Occupants
of small
shops
admitted.

results of the lodgers' franchise. The parliamentary
borough of Birmingham, several years ago, out of a
registration of 72,000, had only about 400 "lodgers"
on the list, where one might have expected to find ten
or twenty times as many. Manchester in 1894 had
1086 enrolled lodger voters in a parliamentary roll of
64,227. And Glasgow, with scores of thousands of unmarried men above the voting age, has only about one
thousand of them on the voting roll as "lodgers." In
Scotland the qualified lodgers have also the municipal
franchise. In England they have only the parliamentary. But in both countries they are obliged to appear
and make good their claim at each annual revision
of the registration lists; and this may mean a delay
of hours in the court of a "revising barrister." The
other classes of voters are put and kept on the lists
in spite of themselves in practice if not in law. But
the lodger in English cities is in effect disfranchised
by the burdensome conditions that attach to his registration as a parliamentary voter, and has never
been admitted at all to the burgess or municipal
suffrage.

The municipal franchise has remained substantially
unchanged since the "household" extension of 1868,
the more recently granted "service" franchise affecting the parliamentary enrolment only. But this, like
the lodgers' list, turns out a very insignificant thing in
practice, adding only a few hundreds of names to the
parliamentary enrolment of a borough of half a million people.

There is another class of municipal voters in the
English towns of which account should be made. It
is the class of men who are occupiers of small shops
worth less than £10 a year, and who are not qualified
to vote as householders. The occupation of shops or
business premises worth £10 entitles to the parliamen-

tary vote, while for municipal purposes this limit is
wholly removed. In Birmingham there are large numbers of mechanics who occupy diminutive shops or
work-stalls to which power is distributed from a common center, and who pay very trifling rents. Several
thousand of them are on the municipal or "burgess"
roll. Not to prolong my discussion of these exasper-
ating distinctions, it may simply be stated that the
municipal enrolment in English towns will average
about twenty per cent. larger than the parliamentary, and that the difference is accounted for chiefly
by the municipal enfranchisement of women who are
ratepayers.

To make comparison again with the American electorate, which includes all male citizens of legal age, Comparison
the English municipal electorate excludes in practice with Ameri-
nearly all the unmarried men, all floating laborers rate.
and lodging-house sleepers, and nearly all the serving
class. Furthermore, in judging of the political effects
of the extension of the franchise to the humblest householders, it must be borne in mind that the exploitation
of the votes of the ignorant, vicious, and indifferent in
English cities by demagogues or party agents is so extremely difficult that it does not count for anything at
all in election results. The extraordinarily severe laws
against bribery, direct and indirect, apply to muni- British poli-
cipal elections; and it is next to impossible to get a not exploit
British voter to the polls who does not contemplate vote.
the contest with some glimmering of interest and intelligence. In Scotch towns the slums do not vote
because they evade the rate-collector and are not registered. In English towns, although registered by
canvassers, they do not care about voting, and are
a neglected field so far as political missionary work
goes. The organized working-men vote, of course;
and they seem to vote with more intelligent and dis-

CHAP. III.

Women in
municipal
elections.

tinct purpose than any other class in the community. Of the women ratepayers nothing is to be said except that their voting is variable, sometimes being high in proportion to their numbers, and sometimes low, depending upon their interest in particular candidates or special issues. Their disposition to espouse party causes seems very marked, but it is not to be relied upon as unthinking or as oblivious of the qualities of candidates. Obviously, the franchise needs simplification, although for municipal purposes it is difficult to see what desirable end would be gained by changing the principle from that of a household franchise to a personal one. No public or private interests require the participation in municipal elections of unattached or floating elements of the population.

Structure
of the
council.

The largest English towns are as a rule divided into sixteen wards, each of which sends three members to the council for terms of three years, one councilor being elected in each ward every year. The council of such towns further contains sixteen aldermen, who sit for terms of six years and who are chosen by the council itself, making a total body of sixty-four. The mayor is elected by the council. The "burgesses," or registered citizens, have therefore no ordinary direct responsibility in municipal government except for the choice of one councilor in each ward on the first of November of every year.

Easy mode
of nomina-
tions.

The English methods of nomination and balloting as applied to parliamentary elections have attracted no little attention in the United States; but the working of these methods, and their advantages in municipal affairs, have not become so familiar to American readers. Let me first state the essential features of the nominating system. At least nine days before the election, the town clerk causes notices to be conspicuously published, explaining what vacancies are to occur and how the nominations are to be made. The names of candidates must be left at the clerk's office, inscribed upon official blanks, a week before the election. Accompanying each name must be the signature of a "proposer," a "seconder," and eight other citizens. Only such persons as have been nominated in this way may be voted for. Nominations being all in, the list is at once printed and conspicuously bulletined. The announcement contains the full names, residences (street and number), and occupations of the nominees, and the names of the proposer and seconder in each case. If only one nomination has been made in any ward, the nomination is itself the election, and the polls will not be opened in that ward. This is a good and sensible system upon its face; but experience alone can tell us how any piece of political machinery will actually work. Ought this system to be productive of many nominations or of few? The most natural inference would seem to be that its adoption would increase the number of candidates, since any ten men may secure for an eleventh man, without expense, the official announcement of candidacy and the placing of the candidate's name upon the ballot-papers.

But this inference is not justified by the facts. In recent municipal elections, although party issues have been introduced to a quite unprecedented extent and the number of ward contests has been materially increased by the unwonted employment of the occasion for a testing of strength on the Home Rule question, it is nevertheless true that contests have been confined to a minority of the wards, taking all the towns together. This must seem to the American observer a remarkable state of things. It means that, in a majority of the wards, public opinion had in ad-

The system does not multiply candidates.

vance agreed so decisively upon a particular man that nobody was nominated against him, and the entire ex-

pense and distraction of a contest at the polls was thus obviated. Closer inquiry will reveal the fact that by far the greater number of these cases have to do with the reëlection of men already in the council. There is every year a considerable list of towns which, in spite of the exceptionally acute condition of party feeling throughout the country, renew one third of their councilors without a single ward contest, all the new members obtaining their seats by virtue of unopposed nominations. There were not less than fifty such fortunate towns in November, 1893. These are not often the large towns, though I happened to note among them on one occasion such examples as Rochester, Windsor, Colchester, Lincoln, Newark, Taunton, Burton-on-Trent, Reading, Halifax, and other places of from ten thousand to seventy-five thousand people. In Cambridge, Salisbury, Derby, Worcester, Great Yarmouth, Plymouth, Cardiff, Newcastle-on-Tyne,

Wrexham, Carnarvon, and several other places, there were contests in only one ward. Except for contests in two wards each, all nominations were equivalent to elections in Bristol, Oxford, Winchester, Coventry, Sunderland, Stockton-on-Tees, Weymouth, Durham, and several other towns. When it is remembered that Bristol is an active commercial city of a quarter-million population, it is decidedly interesting to learn that it can choose councilors from fourteen out of sixteen wards by unanimous consent and without the work and cost of holding an election, while its stirring

and growing rival, Cardiff, escapes with only one contested ward. By way of comparison it should be added that in November, 1893, six of Bristol's sixteen wards, and four of Cardiff's ten wards, were contested.

Referring again to notes of an election several years

ago, I find that even in the eighteen great wards of
Manchester there were only three contests, those turning upon political issues chiefly, while in Liverpool
there were but six contests. The party men pretended
to fight the Liverpool contests upon strictly political lines; but the situation seems to have been in the
hands of the "ratepayers' association," composed of
men who advocated municipal economy and ignored
party lines in local affairs.

The most numerous and exciting contests of that
year occurred in the great inland towns of the Midlands and the North, that have long been the home of
advanced Liberalism, and where the Liberals have heretofore maintained a large preponderance of strength
in the municipal councils. It is in these towns that
the split in the Liberal party is most keenly felt; and
the municipal elections of that November were made
a series of battles between the Liberals and the Conservatives as reënforced by the Dissentients. Birmingham was the chief point of interest, and contests
were waged in nine of the sixteen wards. In eight of
the nine wards the retiring members were candidates
for reëlection, and in six of the eight cases they were
successful. Thus, although in Birmingham that municipal election was probably unprecedented for the
number and severity of its contests, the next council
contained only three new men. Thirteen out of sixteen retiring councilors were reëlected — seven of them
without opposition. In Leeds there were five contests,
the town having sixteen wards, and the issues in every
case were political. Curiously enough, a sixth contest was averted by the oversight of the Liberals, who
failed to file a nomination-paper for their expected
candidate, the retiring member. The result of this
inadvertence was that a Conservative stepped into the
place without a contest. The Bradford politicians

I.— 4

CHAP. III.

contested twelve of fifteen wards, while Nottingham had nine contests and Sheffield six. It is an unusual year when Glasgow or Edinburgh has more than four or five ward contests; and there, as in all the British towns, a very considerable proportion of the contests occur when retiring councilors decline to stand for reëlection.

Contests and results in the election of 1893.

Manchester has lately been enlarged, and has now twenty-five wards, in seventeen of which there were contests on November 1, 1893. In twelve of these wards the retiring members were actually reëlected, and only two who were candidates for another term were defeated. Thus in a council of 104 members, the election made barely half a dozen changes. In 1893 Birmingham's wards, eighteen in number, witnessed only six contests, these being waged upon local and municipal rather than upon party lines. This was a milder municipal season than usual for Birmingham; but in Leeds, fourth in size of the great English towns, there was a trial of strength on national political lines, and fifteen wards out of sixteen were contested. In Liverpool, also, the party men invaded the municipal field and contested twelve of the sixteen wards. In Sheffield, on the other hand, there were only three contested wards, in Nottingham only six of sixteen, in Huddersfield only three of thirteen, and in Hull, Newcastle-on-Tyne, and Wolverhampton — all large places — the elections went practically by default. In a number of large towns of from 25,000 to 100,000 people, the contested wards were not more than half of the whole number.

Third-party and independent nominations.

As regards nominations by third parties or special interests, one might well expect to find them more numerous than they are. In only one of the nine contested Birmingham wards, at the election already referred to, were there more than two nominations. In the one ward there were four, the Socialists having a candidate, and a fourth man standing as an Independent. In one of the Leeds wards there were three candidates, as was also the case in one of the Manchester wards. In only two of the seventeen contested Manchester wards of 1893 was there a third-party Labor candidate. Taking the elections of 1893 as a whole, the number of Socialist and Labor candidates making three contestants on the ward ballot-paper was greater than in previous years. But at best the triangular contests are exceptional rather than common.[1]

The preliminary selection of party candidates usually rests with ward committees, candidature being accepted and ratified by the voters in open ward meetings, where municipal questions are discussed. The American primary election or party caucus system is quite unknown, and in ordinary cases the distinctions of party are not strenuously emphasized. The councilor from a decidedly Liberal ward is likely to be a Liberal; but he is in most cases as entirely acceptable, so far as

Party politics in municipal elections.

[1] The municipal elections of November 1, 1894, were marked chiefly by the increased aggressiveness of the Independent-Labor and Socialist groups, which presented candidates in various towns where otherwise there would have been few contests or none at all. This was the case in Liverpool, where it was agreed between the two regular parties not to contest a single ward. The Labor party precipitated conflicts in five wards, though all their candidates were defeated. In Birmingham old political lines were drawn in six wards, while twelve escaped without any contests whatever. In seventeen of Manchester's twenty-five wards there were no contests; but the Labor party won two out of eight disputed seats. The Labor men contested six wards in Bradford, without success. In Salford and Bolton, as in Liverpool and Bradford, harmony was disturbed by numerous Labor candidates, none of whom were successful. Leeds had fourteen contests, Nottingham eleven, Huddersfield and Leicester each eight, Rochdale seven, Oldham six, Bristol four, Sheffield three, many towns only one or two, and at least fifty places none at all.

The elections of 1894.

municipal matters are concerned, to the Conservatives as to the Liberals, and he will never in any case be opposed by a nominee of the other party who is brought forward for the sole purpose of maintaining party organization in the ward. An Englishman is not often willing to be put up for a place merely to be sacrificed. The extension of the franchise is resulting in more elaborate and more democratic forms of party organization in England; and it is not unlikely that the future may see party lines more closely drawn in municipal elections than they have been up to the present time — a prospect not by any means welcome.

Freedom of nomination a constant safeguard.

Meanwhile, however, the freedom of nomination is a great safeguard. So long as ten citizens of a ward can place a candidate on the official voting-paper, there is no great danger from party machinery. It is the nominating even more than the balloting features of the English and Australian systems that deserve American attention, and we have unduly emphasized the official ballot.

Registration system.

The English voting machinery is perhaps sufficiently well known. The overseers of the poor in the several parishes, who are the rating officers, are also the registration authorities. On the 1st of August of each year, copies of the new list of electors are posted upon the doors of all churches and chapels and public buildings, and they must be kept exposed for a period including two Sundays. The party agents are particularly minute in their scrutiny of the lists. Before the 20th of August, all claims and objections must be filed with the parish authorities, who make out a list of them and post copies of it in the same manner as the original lists and for the same length of time. The claims and objections are then submitted to a revising barrister appointed by the High Court, who sits in open court and passes upon them one by

one.   The list thus revised is ready for the November
election.

The voter at the polls receives a ticket upon which
are printed the names of the candidates.   The ticket
is torn from a book which retains a counterfoil or
stub, upon which is written the registration number
of the person voting.   The voter is instructed to take
the ticket into an alcove, where he will find pencils,
and to mark a cross in the blank space at the right,
opposite the name of the man for whom he desires to
vote.   He folds his ticket in such a manner as to ex-
hibit the official mark on the back, when he drops it
into the box in the presence of the election officers.
His mind is not confused with a multiplicity of issues,
for he has nothing whatever to do but to indicate his
choice of a man for councilor from his ward.   The
municipal election is kept separate from all others,
and this conduces to wise and harmonious action.

To be a member of an English town council is to
hold a position of honor — a position which no man
affects to despise.   As a corollary observation, it is
also to be remarked that the councils are almost universally in high repute.   Yet if the stranger asks
whether or not the councilors come from the best
classes he will generally be answered in the negative,
his informer having in mind the English distinctions
which place tradesmen and manufacturers below the
aristocracy of land-owners.   The councilors, as a rule,
are representatives of the best elements of business
life.   They are men of intelligence and character, and
of practical conversance with affairs.   The idea of rotation in office seems utterly foreign to the British mind
except as regards the office of mayor.   And that office
is one of dignity and honor rather than of responsibility.   The aldermen are almost invariably chosen
from the membership of the council, and the mayor is

I.—4*

a man who has served his town with ability and zeal as councilor and alderman. No salaries attach to these offices, and by the common consent of the community none but men of worth, who have made their way to a good standing among their neighbors, are regarded as eligible for the council. This, of course, is an attractive view, against which numerous individual facts might be arrayed. But it seems to me

a just view. The whole system is favorable to the selection and retention of capable and honest men. Once seated in the council, faithful and efficient service may reasonably be counted upon to make a man's place secure from term to term for as long as he is willing to serve, and he has before him the prospect of aldermanic honors, and of his crowning year of dignity in the mayor's robes.

It is to be remembered, moreover, that while the honors of public position are perhaps nowhere so highly esteemed as in Great Britain, the town-councilorships are the most important places in the gift of the people except the parliamentary seats. The difference between England and the United States in this respect is so marked, and is a matter of so much practical consequence, that I am somewhat surprised that it should so generally have escaped attention. In an American State, the legislature affords places for about one hundred and fifty ambitious citizens. Then the elected executive officers of the State are a considerable group — governor, lieutenant-governor, secretary of state, auditor, treasurer, superintendent of education, commissioners of railways, labor statisticians, and still others in some of the commonwealths — and

there is a further group of appointive offices open to politicians of the same rank as those who go to the legislature and fill the elective offices. The American counties, since they also include the towns in their jurisdiction,— as county governments ordinarily do not in England,— offer another group of elective positions to the same classes of place-seekers; for they all have their boards of commissioners and their sheriffs, treasurers, recorders, clerks of courts, and auditors to be elected. Finally, the city itself has its elective places, the mayoralty included, which are independent of the council; and as a rule there are places on park boards, police boards, and other commissions, that rank quite as high in honor as seats in the council. With all these other positions of as high or higher rank in the common estimation, the American town council competes for good men at a great disadvantage. But few corresponding places exist in England; and the capable citizen with a taste for affairs may be elected an overseer of the poor for his parish, a member of his town school-board, or, last and greatest, a member of the municipal council. Surely this condition of things affords one of the reasons why municipal government has more dignity, and attracts better men on the average, in England than in America.

Another reason may, perhaps, be found in the fact that the English municipalities within the past generation have had problems of a more serious and pressing nature to deal with than the less crowded American cities have had, while they have also had a larger number of men with leisure and trained ability to bestow upon those problems. Again, there is much less in the English system of municipal organization to tempt unworthy men into the council for purposes of gain. There are no salaries to receive, and very remote chances of profit through contracts or jobbery of any sort. A high proportion of the English councilors will be found to be men who have wholly or partly retired from the activities of successful business life, who are glad to devote their time to the affairs of

Our town councils at a disadvantage.

In England the council next in honor to Parliament.

Additional reasons why English municipal government secures good men.

CHAP. III.

their communities, and whose motives are as honorable as their services are intelligent and efficient. Let it be remembered that the councilors are the fully empowered trustees through whom all the affairs of the municipal corporation are managed. In American cities the council is usually limited on all sides; and the smaller its responsibilities, the less are its attractions for men of the highest fitness.

Long service of men in the aldermanic rank.

Upon inquiry several years ago, I learned that not one of Manchester's aldermen had attained the superior rank without having served several terms as an ordinary councilor. One had served continuously for forty-five years, and had held the aldermanic rank for thirty-five. Another had served for forty-two years, another for thirty-seven, another for thirty-two, another for twenty-seven, seven more for from twenty to twenty-four years, and all the rest for from thirteen to eighteen years. The ordinary councilors are less venerable, and fully half of them had come into the office within five years, while only ten had seen ten years or more of continuous service. Great average stability is characteristic of all the municipal councils of Great Britain, few of which are without their Nestors of from twenty to fifty years of continuous service.

Aldermen are promoted councilors.

The act of 1835, which specified that the aldermen should constitute one fourth of the whole council, and that they should be elected by the council for terms of six years, made any burgess eligible for the position. It seems to have been thought that the councilors would go outside their own numbers, at least very frequently, to choose distinguished and especially qualified fellow-townsmen for aldermen on the 9th of November of every third year, when half the aldermanic places become vacant. But that expectation was not realized. It has come to be almost the

universal custom to promote to the rank of aldermen,
when vacancies occur, the councilors whose service
has been longest and most efficient. At present there
is one Manchester alderman who had not served as an
elected councilor; but his case is a rare one. An interesting discussion in the House of Commons, which
I happened to hear, on the question of aldermen in
the new county councils, brought to light some instances of the appointment of municipal aldermen
from outside the council; but the general testimony
of members from the boroughs who had especial *Arguments against the aldermanic distinction.*
knowledge of municipal affairs was to the effect that
they had never known any such appointments. The
Liberals argued strongly against the aldermanic rank
for the county councils, principally on the ground
that it might enable a majority greatly to increase
and perpetuate itself. In some of the large towns, it
is well known that the preponderating party in the
council organizes for the purpose of choosing aldermen and mayor, although it does not follow that the
selections are upon strictly partisan lines. While the
aldermanic rank has not been positively objectionable
in practice, it has none of the advantages that were
anticipated for it, and is as needless as a fifth wheel.
If the system were to be constructed anew in the light
of experience, it is hardly probable that provision
would be made for any other class of councilors than
the directly chosen representatives of the wards. As
matters stand, it is quite common to confer the aldermanic rank upon the senior councilor from each
ward, thus creating a vacancy to be filled by the elec-
tion of a new councilor. In effect this gives each *Virtually a fourth ward representa- tive.*
ward four representatives, the alderman being a sort
of ward "father." In some councils it is customary
to give the chairmanships of committees exclusively
to aldermen.

CHAP. III.

The ward system in English municipal government
is relieved of one great objection to ward representation in American cities from the fact that there is no
rule, tradition, or practice that makes the council candidate a resident of the ward. In this regard the customs of England and America are totally different.
If ward representation in councils meant " ward politics" and strictly local candidates, as in American
cities, the English would at once adopt the general
ticket plan of electing councilors on some such principle as they have adopted in the election of school-
boards.

Residence in
ward not
required.

The great consolidation act of 1882 did somewhat
more than revise and "codify" the existing statutes.
It introduced changes here and there, the most important of which, perhaps, is the addition of the words
italicized in the clause which declares that the mayor
shall be elected "from the aldermen or councilors, *or
persons qualified to be such.*"   In the old days of close
corporations the mayor was chosen from the aldermanic rank. The Reform Act of 1835 limited the range
of selection to the membership of the body of aldermen and councilors, by whom he was to be designated.
The act of 1882 gave the council permission to elect
any qualified citizen. Since that date there may have
been several deviations from the time-honored custom
of selecting the mayor from the council; but at least
they have been rare. I can cite one instance. The
city of Cambridge in November, 1893, by agreement between the political parties elected ten councilors, five
Conservatives and five Liberals, without contest; and
by unanimous agreement of the forty members, the
mayoralty was conferred upon Mr. E. H. Parker, who
was not in the body. This is the only instance of
which I am aware. Aldermanic vacancies are filled
on the 9th of November immediately following the

Selection of
mayors.

Rare in-
stance of
mayor
chosen out-
side of
council.

election of mayor, and outgoing aldermen are eligible for the mayoralty; but the cases where an outgoing alderman is elected as mayor without being at the same time reëlected as alderman, are very exceptional. In any case, the mayor would by virtue of his office be the presiding officer of the council. He votes by right of membership, and if necessary he gives a second or casting vote as presiding officer. He is a justice of the peace during his incumbency and for the year following. He is eligible for reëlection indefinitely, and there are several smaller towns which have made the same man mayor from six to ten times. Birmingham in fifty years had forty-one different mayors, and only six of them were honored with more than one term, a third term as an extraordinary honor having been accorded Sir John Ratcliff (1856–58), Mr. Joseph Chamberlain (1873–75), and Mr. T. Martineau (1884–86). Manchester on the other hand had only twenty-seven different mayors in fifty years, and all but eight of them served for more than one term. Of two hundred and eighty-four municipal corporations of England and Wales, eighty reëlected their mayors on the November 9 of a recent year. But these reëlections were almost invariably in the smaller places, Bristol being the only one of the large towns which continued the mayor in his office.

Generally speaking, the mayoralty is conferred as an honor, and it is regarded as the fair thing to keep passing it along. The mayor is not elected so much to render new public service as to be rewarded for past service. The office confers dignity and influence, and a sort of recognized leadership in municipal affairs that may enable the incumbent to accomplish a great deal. But it confers no important administrative responsibilities. During his year of office the mayor will be expected to devote much of his time to the

Mayor as presiding officer.

Reëlection of mayors.

Significance of the mayoralty.

public welfare. He will be allowed such remuneration as the council may choose to grant for the maintenance of his official dignity. He is the presiding officer of the council, and has certain routine powers and duties that would naturally fall to a presiding officer. He may at any time call a meeting of the council, in a manner prescribed by law, and so may any five members of the council. He is a returning-officer, and has various duties in connection with the holding of elections; but these are merely formal matters.   His commission as a justice of the peace is intended to enhance his dignity and authority rather than to give him added work or responsibility. He has no appointive power, except as regards the designation of polling-officers, or some such occasional and incidental matters.   Nor has he the right of nomination to any positions whatever in the municipal service. He has no veto upon ordinances or by-laws of the council, and no more power than any councilor except that he may, in case of a tie, give a determining vote. He is, then, to be regarded simply as the presiding officer of the council, with special dignities attached to his office. He serves on council committees, and commonly holds a chairmanship or two. When his term in the chair is over, he usually goes right on with his duties as alderman, probably continuing at the head of the committee for the work of which he is best qualified. Thus there were, at a time when I inquired into the matter, at least half a dozen ex-mayors in the aldermanic rank of the Manchester council; and all the mayors that Birmingham had had for twenty years remained in the town council with four exceptions, three of which were accounted for by the promotion of Messrs. J. and R. Chamberlain and Mr. Jesse Collings to seats in Parliament; and over against these exceptions were to be placed two ex-mayors of earlier

Formal
duties.

No appointing power.

No veto.

A host of
ex-mayors
in the
councils.

dates who still served as aldermen. The ferreting out
of such facts might involve labor more curious than
profitable but for the light thus thrown upon the continuity of English municipal administration, and the
amount of ripe experience it is able to command.

The foregoing description of the English mayor
will have been very insufficient if it has failed to show
how entirely different an official he is from the American mayor. Except as regards what we may call the
"dignity business," the two officials are not even analogous. When essentials are considered, the American
functionary who corresponds to the English mayor is
the president or chairman of the common council.
And even that comparatively unpretentious officer has
greater power than the English mayor, for in many if
not in all of the American cities he makes up the
council committees according to his own fancy, and
thus exercises a far-reaching influence upon the work
of administration in the various departments; while
the English law obliges the council itself to appoint
its own committees. This is a matter of no trivial
importance, as anybody at all conversant with municipal affairs will instantly understand.

The typical American mayor is no part of the council or its organization. He is elected directly by the
people. He is an independent, coördinate authority.
He bears somewhat the same relation to the council
that the President of the United States sustains toward Congress or the governor of a State toward the
legislature. The analogy falls short, however, in the
very important practical fact that the work of Congress and the State legislature is principally that of
legislation, while the work of municipal councils is
of necessity principally that of administration. The
theoretical independence and distinct executive responsibility of the President and the governors is ex-

English and
American
mayors
wholly un-
like.

As to ap-
pointment of
council com-
mittees.

The typical
American
mayor.

CHAP. III.

No logical distribution of power between council and mayor in United States.

tremely difficult to maintain in practice, for the line between legislative and administrative work and authority is not at all distinct. Still more difficult is it in practice to apportion duties and responsibilities between an American mayor and the common council in such a way as to secure real efficiency on both sides. It is not easy to see where in the nature of things the proper functions of one authority end and those of the other begin. In the dispersion of authority, definite responsibility too easily disappears. The mayor's veto upon ordinances passed by the council divides responsibility for the by-laws. The council's power of rejecting appointees nominated by the mayor very considerably diminishes his responsibility for the proper exercise of the appointing power. Where the control of the police is not taken out of the hands of both these coördinate authorities, and vested by the State in a separate board of commissioners, the police administration is likely again and again to be a bone of contention between the mayor and the council.

Evils of divided responsibility.

The embarrassments and opportunities growing out of this divided responsibility are among the principal causes of the comparative failure of city government in the United States. Many earnest and intelligent municipal reformers, especially in New York and the Eastern States, have advocated the plan of greatly increasing the authority of the mayor, so that he may be held more definitely responsible for the administration of the various executive departments. It is

The mayor as dictator.

the plan of a periodically elective dictatorship. As a remedy for the evils that grow out of interferences by the State, and the farming out of certain departments — such as parks or water-supply — to special boards or commissions not responsible to the mayor or the council or the people, and further as a temporary measure of defense against untrustworthy and

corrupt councils, this somewhat heroic plan of making the mayor a dictator, or, to use the Cromwellian
euphemism, " a protector," seems to have a great deal in
its favor.   But it is unrepublican, and it does not at all
solve the difficult problem of harmonizing the authority
of the mayor and the authority of the council.   The relation between the two cannot at best be other than that
of a shifting, unprofitable, and illogical compromise.

It would seem a little strange that the one school
of reformers should not have been earlier opposed by
another which would advocate the concentration of   Why not try
authority and responsibility in the council.   Logically,   an all-power-
ful council?
the mayor must eventually swallow the council or the
council must swallow the mayor, if political forces
are to be accorded some degree of natural play; and
the one-man power is on the decline everywhere in
this age.   Municipal governments, elsewhere than in
the United States, after having constituted a ruling
body, do not erect a separate one-man power and give
it the means to obstruct the ruling administrative
body and to diminish its scope and responsibility.
The mayor elsewhere is an integral part of the council.   English, Scotch, and Irish municipal government
is simply government by a group of men who are to
be regarded as a grand committee of the corpora-
tion—the corporation consisting of the whole body of   Government
burgesses or qualified citizens.   In Glasgow it is a   by a citizens'
committee.
committee of seventy-eight; in Edinburgh, of forty-
one; in Manchester, of one hundred and four; in
Birmingham, of seventy-two; in Liverpool, Leeds,
Sheffield, and most of the large English towns, of
sixty-four; in Dublin, of sixty; in Belfast, of forty;
and in the other incorporated towns of the United
Kingdom it varies from twelve to sixty-four, according
to their size.   So far as these bodies have authority to
pass by-laws at all, their authority is complete, and

How it
works in
practice.

nobody obtrudes a veto. They appoint and remove
all officials. They have entire charge of municipal
administration, distributing the work of departmental management and supervision to standing committees of their own number, which they organize
and constitute as they please. If such a local government cannot be trusted, the fault is with popular institutions. It is quite certain to be as good a
government as the people concerned deserve to have.
The location of responsibility is perfectly definite.
When the Glasgow city improvement scheme became
unpopular with the voters because it was proving
more expensive than its projectors had promised, the
chairman of the committee was retired by his constituents at the end of his term. The taxpayers hold
every member of council responsible for his votes.
The system is as simple, logical, and effective as the
American system is complicated and incompatible with
harmonious and responsible administration. City government in America defeats its own ends by its "checks
and balances," its partitions of duty and responsibility, and its grand opportunities for the game of hide-
and-seek. Infinitely superior is the English system,
by which the people give the entire management of
their affairs to a big committee of their own number,
which they renew from time to time.

The town
clerk and
other
officers.

The most important official in an English municipal
corporation is the town clerk. He has a large salary,
and is expected to hold his office for life. He is the
council's recording officer, the custodian of records,
deeds, and charters, the council's legal adviser, the
medium through which communication is had with
the Local Government Board, the publisher of registration lists and election announcements, the drafts-
man of bills which the council desires Parliament to
pass, the general secretary of the borough, and a high

authority on points of municipal law, precedent, and history. The only other officer which the Municipal Corporations Act requires all town councils to appoint is a treasurer. The clerk and the treasurer must be different persons, and must not be members of the council. As for the rest, the law declares that

the council shall from time to time appoint such other officers as have been usually appointed in the borough, or as the council think necessary, and may at any time discontinue the appointment of any officer appearing to them not necessary to be reappointed.

There must be three auditors, one appointed from the council by the mayor and the other two elected by the burgesses; but they are not regarded as city officers in the ordinary sense, being merely called in twice a year to examine the treasurer's accounts and vouchers.

But while the organization of the working departments and the creation of municipal offices are left to the discretion of their respective councils, there is a general similarity among the towns. It is the almost uniform practice to appoint as permanent chiefs or superintendents of departments the most thoroughly qualified men who can be secured, and to hold them responsible to the council, through the standing committees, for the ordinary operation of their respective branches of the municipal service. These towns have, as a rule, undertaken so extensive a range of public activities that the number of their employees is great. But the average of efficiency is also very high. At the head of the police, fire, water, gas, sanitary, park, engineering, and other departments are to be found men of special fitness and training, who are selected for administrative ability as well as for expert knowledge, and whose security of tenure, for so long as they deserve it, adds to their faithfulness and usefulness.

Expert department chiefs.

I.—5

Nothing in British city government will be more likely to impress the American who observes it closely than its indebtedness for a large part of its success to the superiority of the appointive heads of departments.

It is everywhere earnestly claimed in England and Scotland that party considerations weigh nothing in appointments, and that regard is had to efficiency alone; and the claim on the whole seems to be justified. In American cities it is generally thought necessary to choose municipal servants from local applicants or candidates; but there is no such limitation in England. It is usual to advertise a vacancy; and the committee most directly concerned make their choice from the applicants, and then recommend to the full council for action. If a chief of police is wanted for a town even of moderate size, there are likely to be applicants by the score or hundred from all parts of the United Kingdom. Offices are held so permanently that promotion is not very rapid, and a vacancy at the head of a department will therefore be sought by the men of lower rank in the corresponding departments of other towns; and clear merit usually wins. There are no competitive examinations either for the higher or the lower walks of the municipal service in England or in Scotland, other means of ascertaining men's qualifications being preferred.

In filling up the ranks,— selection being left in a very considerable measure to the responsible departmental head,— the English towns have of course a great advantage over those of America. Good men are so much more numerous than good positions, and the competitive struggle for existence is so terribly severe, that a place in the public service, even though humble and poorly paid, attracts men of a class who in America could not be induced to give up the chances of success in business or professional life

The municipal civil service.

Selections for merit.

An ample supply of good officials.

for a small clerkship or inspectorship in a municipal department.

Englishmen are not indifferent about their municipal matters, and they know very well how to grumble;
and it is therefore a significant thing that one rarely
encounters a charge of favoritism or unworthy use of
patronage in municipal appointments. The number
of unsuccessful applicants is so large that if frequent
abuses of the appointive power occurred there would
be no lack of persons to complain and to make the
facts known. It would be easy to give instances of
the appointment to responsible places of men who
applied as strangers from distant towns, without acquaintance or other influence than their testimonials
and proofs of fitness and of good work already done.

A particularly valuable test of the fairness and
purity of any municipal administration is the estimation in which the police department is held by good
citizens. The complaints and suspicions so commonly
directed against the police authorities of American
cities are almost unknown in England. At least they
exist only in a very slight measure. Every precaution is taken to keep an English police force up to
a high standard. Control is vested in a council committee, of which the mayor is a member, but a quasi-
military discipline is maintained by the head constable
(chief of police), who in many cases has held a commission in the army. Half of the expense of maintaining the police force of every city or district of
Great Britain is paid by the general government.
But this payment is made on the report of government inspectors, who must find that the force is
adequate in numbers, well organized and disciplined,
and in general respects up to the high standard that
the statutes and the Home Office require. The inspection of the government tends to produce some-

CHAP. III.

Relation of
municipal to
central
government.

Advantages
of central
supervision.

thing like uniformity in the organization of police forces, and is an altogether salutary influence.

Indeed, the relationship that now exists between the municipal administration and the central government at many points is advantageous rather than hampering to the local corporation. It is no hardship to make regular annual or semi-annual reports to the Local Government Board, or the Treasury, or the Home Office, touching all matters of corporate income and outgo, and the results of the administration of sanitary and other public statutes. Through the medium of the Local Government Board,— its regular publications, its permanent staff in the London offices, and its expert visiting inspectors,— the officials of one town are supplied with knowledge of the doings and experiences of other towns, are deterred from harmful experiments, and are instructed in the best methods. At times it appears a needless interference with local affairs that compels a well-governed city to submit to the central authorities for inspection and approval every scheme whatsoever that necessitates the borrowing of money. If there were any lack of system in the methods by which local projects are passed upon by Westminster, or if there were any serious taint of partisanship, favoritism, or arbitrary judgment upon the processes employed, the mechanism would break down speedily, and a more complete local autonomy in matters involving municipal outlay and indebtedness would have to be accorded. But the system works in the interest of justice, and its costliness in money and in time is counterbalanced by the benefits which accrue from the more thorough preliminary sifting that every scheme receives in preparation for the searching ordeal at Westminster, and from the valuable emendations which so often result from the advice that expert central officials can give.

CHAPTER IV

A STUDY OF GLASGOW

THE methods and results of British municipal government may best be studied in the concrete. I have therefore chosen Glasgow as a type, for a somewhat full analysis and description. The illustrative account of its institutions may involve some repetition of matters already discussed in preceding chapters; but there are obvious advantages in rehearsing the rules and principles of a general system from the point of view of their working in a particular instance.

Glasgow's rank among British cities.

The people of Glasgow are accustomed to claim for their city the second place in the British empire. If by the words "city," "burgh," or "borough," there is meant merely a populous place,— an aggregation of houses and people with a concentration of various commercial, industrial, and social interests,— then metropolitan London would assuredly rank first and without rival. But if by these words is meant a distinct and complete municipal organism, the people of Glasgow may claim not the second, but the first place among the communities of Great Britain. London as a municipal corporation is but a mile in extent and has less than forty thousand people —" larger London" having no unified corporate existence, although the new London county government must be regarded as the beginning of a metropolitan administration.

Will soon
contain a
million
people.

Glasgow in 1891 had a population of 565,700 within a compactly inhabited area of 6111 acres; and its vigorous development had caused so generous an overflow that the whole community, including the continuously built-up suburbs, numbered more than 800,000 souls. The annexation of 5750 additional acres was accomplished by act of Parliament on November 1, 1891, some months after the census was taken, and nearly a hundred thousand people were thus added. There are other populous and immediately contiguous suburbs that should be brought within the corporate limits at an early day. The end of a half-decade after the census of April, 1891, will easily justify an estimate of 750,000 residents within the existing boundaries, and 150,000 more in the unannexed suburban districts. And the next census, in 1901, may find that the "greater Glasgow" contains approximately a million souls.

Merits study
as a modern
type.

As a type of the modern city with highly developed and vigorous municipal life, and with complex, yet unified, industrial and social activities,— in short, as one of the most characteristic of the great urban communities in the English-speaking world of the closing nineteenth century,— Glasgow may well repay study. It combines in itself most remarkably all that is significant in the history of city government among peoples of British origin—that is to say, to study Glasgow is to study the progress of municipal institutions in every stage. Like all modern commercial cities Glasgow has exhibited the phenomenon of rapid growth, and has had to meet the various problems that rapid growth under new industrial and social conditions has forced upon the attention of all such cities. In 1750 the population was less than 25,000. In 1800 it was approximately 75,000. In 1811 it was 100,000; in 1831, 200,000; in 1851, 329,000; and in 1871 it was

478,000. In 1881 it had reached 488,000, with 186,000
more of overflow into the immediate suburbs, making
a total of 674,000. And to-day within a district six
or seven miles long and three or four miles wide, containing less than 15,000 acres, there is a population of
not less than 800,000.

Whether originally due in greater or less degree to
the danger of raids from Highland clans and attacks
from invading English armies, it has from a very
early period been the custom of Scotch townsfolk to
build compactly and to house the population in tene-
ment-flats. Aberdeen, Dundee, and Leith illustrate
this custom quite as well as do Edinburgh and Glasgow. Rapid growth in the nineteenth century has
given most serious reality to all the latent and lurking
evils of a tenement-house system, and Glasgow has
been compelled to study and apply modern remedies
— indeed to be a leader in the invention and trial of
remedies — for the ills that spring from the overcrowding of the poor. The regulation of house-
building and of occupancy; provision for domestic
cleanliness; methods of street-cleansing, of garbage
removal, of epidemic-disease prevention; improved
" watching and lighting" arrangements, with a view
to the lessening of crime; provision of shelter for
floating population; a differentiated and adequate
system of sanitary inspection; the establishment of
baths and various conveniences to improve the health,
comfort, and moral condition of the people : all these
features of recent municipal activity may be studied
to special advantage in Glasgow.

Like Liverpool in England, or Chicago in America,
Glasgow is an excellent instance of what I may call
the " self-made," or rather self-located, modern commercial city, as contrasted with great urban communities like London and New York, which have as-

sumed vast proportions and importance in spite of themselves, and without the application of any organic municipal energy. More than a hundred years ago Glasgow entered deliberately upon the herculean task of making itself an important port by deepening its shallow river into a harbor and an ocean highway. Following the gradual improvement of the Clyde navigation came first a large American trade in to-
Results of Clyde improvement. bacco, cotton, and other staples. The development of the coal and iron mines of the Clyde valley in the immediate neighborhood followed; and when the day of iron ships had its dawning, Glasgow was prepared to make them for the nations. Meanwhile, textile and chemical manufactures had been growing in importance, and the community found that its courage and energy had resulted in its expansion to the rank of one of the greatest centers of industry and commerce in the entire world.

An integral community. In all this expansion Glasgow's character as an integral community has been exceptionally well sustained. The people have been disposed to live inside the circle of their work, and that must obviously signify a high degree of centralization; by which I mean something more than mere density of population. The same families send workers to the ship-yards, or iron-works, and to the textile factories where women and children are employed. All the great industries belong essentially to the one working community. It is peculiarly interesting to observe a city which, having made itself prosperous and mighty by well-directed, organized municipal energy, at a later time applies that same energy to the solution of the dark social problems which seem the inevitable concomitant of the new material progress of communities.

The early history of Scottish "burghs," like that of English "boroughs," has many points of interest; and it would be easy to yield to the temptation to dwell in detail upon the ancient charters of Glasgow and the rise to municipal power of the merchants' guildry and the incorporated bodies of tradesmen. To do more, however, than merely allude to the historical development of the municipality would not be in keeping with my present purpose. In very early times Glasgow was made a bishop's seat and erected into a " burgh of barony," governed by a provost and bailies or magistrates, who derived their offices from their patron the bishop, and who associated councilors with themselves. Without attempting to record any of the fluctuations of several centuries of charters altered and renewed, of ecclesiastical authority now dominant and now abdicated, of royal interventions sometimes in favor of the bishops, sometimes of the barons, and sometimes of the citizens, it is sufficient to say that the sixteenth century was well advanced before the citizens, organized in guilds for the regulation of their various trades, became strong enough to wrest away any considerable share of municipal authority from their ecclesiastical and baronial rulers. A royal charter granted in 1611 specifically gave the burgh to the "magistrates, council, and community"; but there were still reserved to the archbishop certain rights of nomination.

It was not until 1690, when William and Mary gave a new charter, that the city was fully empowered to choose and elect its own provost, bailies, and other officers. Originally the burgesses were the members of the merchants' guild; but the handicraftsmen, separately organized according to their crafts but federated in a "Trades' House," afterward attained the right to share with the "Merchants' House" the government of the city. Gradually in Glasgow, as in all the British towns, the municipal corporation be-

came self-perpetuating. Down to 1801 the executive
council of Glasgow was composed of the lord provost,
three bailies or magistrates, the dean of guild (head
of the Merchants' House), the deacon-convener (head
of the Trades' House), and the treasurer. The dean
of guild and deacon-convener, as the elected presi-
dents of the Merchants' and Trades' bodies, were *ex-
officio* members of the council; while, as regards the
other members, the council itself filled all vacancies
in its own number by selection either from the Merchants' order or the Trades' order. From its own membership it appointed the lord provost and treasurer.
The town clerk and chamberlain were standing officers
of the corporation, outside the membership of the
council. In 1801 there were added two more bailies,
one from each order, making a total of nine. It may
be here remarked that the course of municipal development in the other Scottish towns had been quite like
that of Glasgow. The abuses which had grown so
scandalous in most of the English towns before the
municipal reform laws of this century were passed
seem to have been less marked in Scotland, although
they must have been serious enough.

It has already been remarked that the parliamentary reform bill of 1832 made municipal reform inevitable, and that Scotland, with a smaller number of
towns than England, and with fewer extraordinary
and anomalous conditions to be dealt with, received
its municipal reform act first, the Scotch bill having
been passed in 1833, while the English bill was delayed until 1835, and municipal reform in Ireland
came as late as 1840. The Scotch Municipal Reform
Act, 1833, made the municipal franchise the same as
the new borough parliamentary franchise, and provided for the election of councilors in all the larger
towns by wards, empowering the council thus chosen

to select a provost and bailies from its own numbers. In Edinburgh and Glasgow the dean of guild and deacon-convener were allowed to remain in the council as *ex-officio* members, while in other large towns, as Aberdeen, Dundee, and Perth, the dean of guild was similarly retained as a municipal councilor. The "Dean of Guilds' Court" was also preserved, with authority over such matters as street-lining, the width of highways, the safe construction of buildings, etc., the court consisting of the dean, with four assistants from each of the incorporated orders. In 1846 the boundaries of Glasgow were greatly extended, and at that time the number of wards, and the size of the council, were much increased, while the functions of the body were enlarged by Parliament; but the general form established by the act of 1833 remained. While popular and modernizing in its spirit, that act showed great wisdom in retaining as many old names, customs, and official posts as could without harm be wrought into the new system, thus preserving the continuity of the municipal life, and minimizing prejudiced and selfish opposition against what was really a reform of the most sweeping character.

A difference or two might be profitably noted be- tween the Scotch, English, and Irish reform bills — all of which were alike in making the council the full governing body. The English bill provided for a certain number of aldermanic members of the council, to be selected by the council from the whole body of qualified citizens (although in practice quite invariably selected from their own number, thus creating vacancies to be filled by ward elections), and to sit for six years, while ordinary councilors were to be elected for only three years. The Irish act authorizes the council to choose a certain number of aldermen, but only for terms of three years. Aldermen are simply

CHAP. IV.

Scotch
bailies.

Provosts
and mayors.

The Glasgow
municipal
council.

a dignified rank of councilors, elected by an elected body, and in England (though not in Ireland) enjoying longer tenure than ordinary councilors. The Scotch bailies, on the other hand, are always first elected from wards as ordinary councilors, and they continue their duties as such, although selected by their fellows as citizen magistrates. In this magisterial capacity they try police cases; they also sit as a licensing court; and they have various minor duties placed upon them outside their functions as councilors. Inside the council-chamber they are simply the elected representatives of their wards, although there as elsewhere they are regarded as persons of superior dignity. The provosts in Scotland, also, are chosen for three years, while the mayors in England and Ireland are elected annually — in all cases alike being chosen by the council. At the risk of some slight repetition I shall now describe more particularly Glasgow's constitution.

The present municipal organization of Glasgow is simple and easily understood in its main features, although somewhat anomalous and complex in certain minor respects. The whole government may be said to be exercised by a grand committee of seventy-five men chosen by the qualified electors, together with the provost and two other *ex-officio* members, making a total body of seventy-eight. There are twenty-five [1] municipal wards, each of which elects three members of the town council. The election is for a term of three years, and one man from each ward retires annually. The two *ex-officio* members of the council are the dean of guild, who represents the venerable Merchants' House, and the deacon-convener, or chairman of the associated trade-guilds; these two

---

[1] The number of wards was increased from sixteen to twenty-five when the boundaries were extended in 1891, the elected councilors being increased from forty-eight to seventy-five.

functionaries representing the bodies which before the Scotch Municipal Reform Act of 1833 were in sole control of the municipal government. This allowance of a small share in municipal government to the old-time trades' and crafts' corporations is not practically objectionable, and it unites the present with the past in a manner peculiarly British.

In the preceding chapter I have discussed minutely the conditions of the municipal franchise in Glasgow. *Town politics and the franchise.* I have shown that, in considering the effect of the franchise upon city government, it is to be borne in mind that not only is the mass of unmarried working-men excluded, but also all others who have failed to pay their rates. About one third of the householders enfranchised by the act of 1868 evade the rates and never vote. If it were possible to secure reinstatement by payments of arrears, as an election approaches, there would be a tempting field of activity opened up to corrupt politicians. But this cannot be done. The better class of working-men in Glasgow pay their rates, take an active interest in public affairs, and do not fail to vote. But there is a very large population of the degraded poor which does not in fact participate in elections, and is not of the slightest service to "ward politicians"— genus which, by the way, is rarely found in British cities. What I have called the self-disfranchisement of the slums is an important consideration in Glasgow's municipal government.

The councilors of Glasgow come chiefly from the *Character of Glasgow's councilors.* ranks of men of business, and are upright, respected, and successful citizens. No salaries attach to such offices anywhere in the United Kingdom, and it is deemed an honor to be selected to represent one's ward. Party lines are seldom very sharply drawn in municipal elections. An efficient councilor may, in general, expect reëlection for several terms if he is willing to serve. The seat of a satisfactory man who asks reëlection is in a majority of cases not contested at all. No other candidate will appear, and he will be awarded the seat without the actual holding of an election. It may be said that in the twenty-five wards of Glasgow it is unusual to have more than from five to ten contests for seats in any one year.

From their own number the councilors choose a "Provost," usually called the "Lord Provost," and the "Bailies" or magistrates. The provost in Scotch towns corresponds to the mayor in English towns, while the bailies are in some respects analogous to the English aldermen. The provost presides over the council, serves on council committees, and personifies the pomp and dignity of the municipality; but except in his capacity as a member of the council, he has no important executive responsibility. He has no appointments to make, and has no veto upon enactments of the council. Like the bailies, he is, however, a magistrate, and has his share of judicial work to do, mostly in the exercise of ordinary police jurisdiction. The bailies sit as citizen magistrates, in certain districts of the city upon a plan of rotation, each being assisted by a paid legal adviser technically called an "assessor." To relieve them somewhat, there has been employed a "stipendiary," or salaried police judge, sitting constantly in the central district. The provost and bailies are designated for three years. It is important to make clear to American readers that the lord provost is in no sense an administrative head as the American mayors are, and that there is not in British cities any disposition whatever to concentrate appointing power and executive control in the hands of one man as an effective way to secure responsible administration. There is nothing in British organization or experience to sustain the propo-

Functions of the provost.

Judicial work of the bailies.

The provost not an executive.

sition of many American municipal reformers that
good city government can be secured only by making the mayor a dictator. American conditions differ
so widely, however, from English conditions that the
success of administration by town councils in Great
Britain is not quite a conclusive argument against the
practical wisdom of the American reformers.

All appointments, as I have said, are made by the
council itself. Heads of departments are selected
with great care, and their places are practically permanent. In the minor appointments the responsible
heads are allowed to use large liberty of suggestion,
the council ratifying such selections as are agreed
upon by the departmental head and the supervising
council committee. Although the number of persons
in the employ of the Glasgow departments is large,
there is no examination system in use. The best
men are selected from among the applicants, and
there is little or no complaint of favoritism. Those
conditions under which an examination system might
be very desirable happily do not exist.

While the full government of the city is vested in
the seventy-eight members of the town council constituting a body officially known as "the lord provost,
magistrates, and council," they exercise their powers
under various acts of Parliament, which make them
(1) water commissioners, (2) gas trustees, (3) market
and slaughter-house commissioners, (4) parks and
galleries trustees, (5) city-improvement trustees, and
(6) a board of police commissioners. These distinctions are chiefly matters of bookkeeping. The essential fact is that the powers are all vested in the common council. Each of these departments is organized
separately, and its work is carried on under the supervision of standing committees of the council.

The town clerk attends the council's meetings as

CHAP. IV.

Duties of
the clerk.

its constant legal adviser. He drafts measures desired from Parliament, and takes charge of them while
pending. He is the city's conveyancer, the custodian
of its title-deeds and charters, and its attorney in all
civil actions. Glasgow's present clerk, James D. Mar-
wick, LL. D., is a high authority upon questions of
municipal history and law.

The
chamberlain.

The chamberlain, whose office, like that of the town
clerk, is very ancient, is the treasurer of the corporation proper; and the present incumbent has been appointed as the treasurer of several of the newer departments or "trusts." He has also, in Glasgow,
gradually assumed the function of a compiler of municipal statistics. He joins the provost and town
clerk in arranging for special occasions and "doing
the honors" of the city to distinguished guests. The
nominal treasurer of the city is a member of the council; but the chamberlain is actual custodian of the
funds, while the cashier is still a different official.

The assessor.

Upon the assessor there devolves the important
work of valuing "lands and heritages" from year to
year for rating purposes, and also that of making the
registration lists of parliamentary and municipal voters. Of other officials enough will be said in the
descriptions of the working departments.

Sanitary
motives
dominant.

Considerations of the public health have been predominant in determining the most important lines
of action entered upon within the last quarter-century
by municipal Glasgow. I shall find it convenient,
therefore, to begin an account of the several departments with a sketch of the organization and work of
the sanitary administration. These new municipal
undertakings find their true center in the bureau of
the medical officer of health, who furnishes the vital
statistics, and the deductions from those statistics,

which incite and direct municipal activity, and who gives constant advice and authoritative judgment as to general methods and particular cases. A council committee of eighteen supervises the entire sanitary administration of the city, with subcommittees on cleansing and hospitals. The Sanitary Department is a model of good work and thorough organization. Its ultimate authority is the medical officer of health, while its executive head is the chief sanitary inspector. The department is in some sense double-headed; yet there is no conflict of authority, and the arrangement works admirably in practice. The medical officer is relieved from the details of administrative work. His office-room adjoins that of the sanitary inspector, and the two officials are in constant communication. The entire force of inspectors is at the service of the medical officer, yet he has no responsibility for their routine work.

The department was established in 1870 upon a broad and wise basis. It was at that time proposed by the new incumbent of the office of sanitary inspector: (1) that the city should be divided into five main districts for sanitary purposes; (2) that a subinspector should be appointed for each main district, having under him ordinary or "nuisance" inspectors, epidemic inspectors, a lodging-house inspector, and a lady visitor; and (3) that a central office should be established, with the necessary clerks. This plan was accepted by the council, and went at once into operation. The population at that time was 450,000, and the average inhabitancy of the main districts was therefore 90,000. The work began with an out-of-door force of forty inspectors, of whom five were the district chiefs, five inspected lodging-houses, seven were occupied with the detection of infectious disease, eighteen were "nuisance" men, searching for ordinary

I.—6.

Chap. IV.

Organization of Health Department.

As established in 1870.

insanitary conditions in and about the houses of their
districts, and five were "women house-to-house visitors." In essential features the organization was retained unaltered until the city was enlarged in 1891.
There remained the five main districts in which sanitary inspection was carried on, although their boundary lines had been altered in order to make each one
of them precisely inclusive of a certain number of the
twenty-four areas into which, for purposes of vital
statistics, the medical officer had divided the city.
There were employed eight epidemic inspectors, sixteen nuisance inspectors, and six female inspectors
under the immediate supervision of five district inspectors. In addition to these there were six night
inspectors, two food inspectors, a common lodging-
house inspector, and a vaccinator.

By legislation in 1890, extending the scope of the
Sanitary Department's work, and by the increase of
municipal area in 1891, there was rendered necessary
a further addition to the little army of inspectors.
At present Mr. Peter Fyfe, F. R. S. E., the efficient
chief inspector, commands the services of about one
hundred and fifty competent people, whose duties are
highly specialized and most methodically performed.
There are now seven general districts, over each of
which there is a foreman inspector. The nuisance
inspectors number more than a score, and there are
half as many men constantly occupied in making the
"smoke test" to discover defects in drain-pipes for
the protection of the people against bad plumbing.
On constant duty are twelve or more infectious-dis-
ease inspectors, and following in the wake of their
discoveries is a staff of disinfecting officers and another of whitewashers, together numbering about
twenty-five men. Protection against improper food-
supplies requires the services, besides analysts in the

municipal laboratory, of three meat inspectors, seven milk and dairy inspectors, and four inspectors of other food-supplies. So greatly have the common lodging-houses improved that whereas five or six special officers were formerly kept at work inspecting them, only two are now necessary. Six night inspectors continue to make the rounds of the tenement-houses, and six women inspectors pay visits in the interest of domestic cleanliness. A workshop inspector represents the demands of new laws touching the hours and the general conditions of factory operation. There is also a peripatetic vaccinator who fulfils relentlessly the requirements of law. In the commodious central offices of the Health Department there is a skilled indoor force of clerks and assistants. The chief sanitary inspector reviews his men daily. The seven district chiefs are in conference with him every morning, and the individual inspectors who perform special duties are also in personal daily communication with headquarters. Thus the sanitary organization is kept at the height of efficiency.

It must be remembered that the prime necessity for Population-density in Glasgow. all this vigilance grows out of the density of population, which is not equaled by that of any other British city except Liverpool. The density of London, according to the census of 1881, was 51 to the acre, while that of Glasgow was 84, which was increased to 92 by the census of 1891, the annexed suburbs not being included. The average density of sixteen of the twenty-four sanitary districts, moreover, is above 200, and the average density of five districts is 300. Localities are not few where single acres contain a thousand or Tenement-house system. more people. The tenement-house is almost universal. The best as well as the worst of the laboring class, and the large majority of the middle class, live in the " flats " of stone buildings three or four stories high. In some cases two or three hundred people use a common staircase, and much greater numbers may be found using common passageways, or "closes," as they are called in Scotland. For no other English-speaking city, as far as I am aware, are the statistics of house room and inhabitancy so complete as for Glasgow. To quote Dr. Russell, the distinguished medical officer of the city, " 25 (24.7) per cent. (of the inhabitants of Glasgow) live in houses of one apartment; 45 (44.7) per cent. in houses of two apartments; 16 per cent. in houses of three apartments; 6 per cent. (6.1) in houses of four apartments; and only 8 per cent. in houses of five apartments and upward." This simply means that 126,000 of the people of Glasgow lived in single-room housekeeping quarters in tenement buildings, and 228,000 in two-room quarters, at the time of the census of 1881. In Scotland the word "tenement" is usually applied to the entire building, and the word "house" to the one or more rooms arranged for the occupancy of a family; thus the ordinary "tenement" contains many "houses." The census of 1891 shows a cheering improvement. Dr. Russell informs us that whereas in 1871 the Glasgow population living in houses of one room amounted to 30.4 per cent. of the whole, the proportion had fallen to 24.7 per cent. in 1881, and to 18 per cent. in 1891. The proportion of two-room dwellers, on the other hand, had greatly increased. Thus in 1891 there were only 100,000 people living in one-room houses, while nearly 264,000 were in two-room houses, this class of dwellers constituting 47.5 per cent. of all the people within the city limits at the time of the census. A population thus housed might well give employment to an army of sanitary inspectors. Glasgow's extra-ordinary rapidity of growth filled the tenements with Irish and Highland laborers from the huts of the ru-

Census of house room.

One-room and two-room families.

Need of inspection.

ral districts, where they had known nothing of the
relations of cleanliness to health, and where, moreover, their insanitary modes of life were not a menace
to thousands of other people. Their uncleanliness in
the great city of Glasgow has tempted epidemics and
kept the death-rate high.

Among these overcrowded tenements the epidemic
inspectors are constantly at work ferreting out cases
of infectious disease. Until lately the law did not
make it obligatory upon medical practitioners in Scotland to report cases of such disease; but their voluntary coöperation with the Glasgow department was
quite general, and 5230 cases were reported at the office in 1887, making a total of 9000 cases registered.
In 1892 there were 12,171 cases reported at the office,
and 3708 other cases were discovered by the inspectors. Scarlet fever and measles were accountable
for the vast majority of these cases. The epidemic
inspectors are trained men who have usually served
in the higher ranks of the police force. The nuisance
inspectors are practical men who understand plumbing and the building trades, and who reported in 1892
nearly 30,000 "nuisances," practically all of which
were in consequence remedied. These had to do with
defective drains, matters of water-supply, garbage accumulations, offensive ash-pits, and all sorts of struc-
tural defects, decays, and unwholesome conditions.

The work of the night inspectors is done under the
authority of a clause in the Glasgow police act which
provides for the measurement of all houses and the
ticketing of those which have less than 2000 cubic
feet of space. The tickets posted on the doors show
the maximum number who may occupy the house, and
the night inspection is to prevent overcrowding. For,
small as these abodes are, great numbers of them take
lodgers in addition to the regular family. Fourteen

Right margin notes:

Epidemic
inspectors.

Nuisance
inspectors.

Night in-
spectors of
"ticketed"
houses.

I.—6*

per cent. of the one-room houses and 27 per cent. of the two-room houses take lodgers. In a recent public

Lodgers in one-room houses.

address, entitled "Life in One Room," Dr. Russell, the medical officer, remarked, "Nor must I permit you, in noting down the tame average of fully three inmates in each of these one-apartment houses, to remain ignorant of the fact that there are thousands of these houses which contain five, six, and seven inmates, and hundreds which are inhabited by from eight even to thirteen." A recent report of the department shows 16,413 ticketed one-room houses, and 6617 ticketed two-room houses. Of these one-room houses, 3285 contained less than 900 cubic feet of space. The inspection of these houses is of immense public benefit; but the undeviating enforcement, by the use of pains and penalties, of the rules regulating overcrowding, is obviously impossible. The inspectors and the police magistrates are obliged to use discrimination, and to deal leniently in one case and severely in another.

A change in the law has now made it obligatory, in

Air-space of "ticketed" houses.

ticketing the houses, to increase the minimum airspace allowed for each adult by 100 cubic feet, and for each child by 50 feet, above the allowance made by the law up to 1890. Mr. Fyfe explains that "the disturbance of population caused by the new clause amounts to $17\frac{1}{2}$ per cent. That is to say, the 24,000 ticketed houses, instead of being legally able to accommodate 98,400 persons (adults) are now only capable of legally accommodating 81,180."

Inspector of lodging-houses.

It is the business of the common lodging-house inspector to secure the registration of all establishments of the sort everywhere known as lodging-houses, to visit them frequently, and to enforce public regulations which have wholly transformed these places in Glasgow. But I shall have occasion on a later page to refer again to lodging-houses.

The work of "female visitation," as it is called, among the poor families is doubtless productive of great good. Statistics cannot adequately express the extent and significance of the work done by these lady inspectors; but it is worth recording that in the last year for which report has been made (1892) they paid some 75,000 visits to the domiciles of their poor constituents. Their suggestions as to cleanliness and household reform seem to carry weight by virtue of their official position. It is hardly necessary to say that in the selection of ladies for this work care is taken to obtain the services of those who have tact, discretion, and sympathy.

For its great vigilance, excellent system, and general thoroughness, the work of food inspection in Glasgow is to be commended. Its efficiency is somewhat hampered by the law (applicable to Scotland) which requires the evidence of two sales of an adulterated article instead of one. The milk-supply has the constant attention of the department. All dairies and milk-shops are registered, and their arrangements are subject to approval and inspection. On the present list are about 1200 places where milk is sold. The health officer has long desired authority to regulate all the sources of milk-supply, in order to prevent the bringing of infection into the city. To some extent this is now done. The farms whence the city is supplied are all listed, and many of them have been visited for inspection of their sanitary conditions. But the laws do not as yet give the power that should be given to the sanitary governments of all cities to refuse the admission of milk not produced under approved conditions. About two hundred cases of typhoid fever at one time in Glasgow a few years ago were traced directly to milk from a certain farm where the cows drank polluted water.

CHAP. IV.

Infectious
disease.

But I must pass on to a description of the means
used by Glasgow for the isolation and treatment of
infectious disease; for the health authorities long
ago discovered — what some American cities seem so
slow to learn — that epidemics are not inevitable visitations, but are preventable. Glasgow had suffered
from typhus and smallpox and cholera and other
plagues from time to time, and had depended upon
the parochial authorities and the privately managed
hospitals to make special provisions at such times for
the epidemic cases. At length, in that series of health
acts passed by Parliament, some for Scotland as a
whole, and some for the local authorities of Glasgow,
which began about 1855 and which is yet far from
ideally complete, it was provided that the Privy Council might, by order, in special emergencies, confer
upon the local authorities temporary powers for dealing with epidemics after their acknowledged outbreak;
these powers including the right to provide "such
medical aid and such accommodation as might be
required." Serious prevalence of typhus in 1864 com-

Beginning of
epidemic
hospitals.

pelled the health officer to look to the authorities for
accommodation; and a temporary pavilion hospital
was accordingly opened. Its usefulness was so great
that when, in 1866, the Glasgow police act was revised, a new clause compelled the local authorities to
maintain the existing hospital, and empowered them
to open others for the reception of infectious cases
and the protection of the public against epidemics.
In 1869 typhus compelled the enlargement of the
original hospital to 250 beds, and in the next year
"relapsing" fever not only filled these quarters with
patients, but forced the authorities to make additional
provisions.

They acted with a most commendable wisdom. On
the extreme eastern edge of the city was a private

estate, called Belvidere, containing rather more than thirty acres, and sloping beautifully down to the Clyde. It was purchased, and the mansion-house was enlarged and transformed into quarters for the attendant physicians and nurses. Wards were hastily built of wood in the detached-pavilion form. These have gradually been replaced by permanent pavilions of brick and stone, each containing two wards. The establishment is now the most attractive and complete in its appointments and in adaptation to its particular purposes, and the most satisfactorily administered, of any in the United Kingdom, if not in the world. It has accommodations for 1000 patients, without overcrowding of the spacious wards. A technical description of the arrangements of this institution is not compatible with the scope of my inquiry, and I must not digress in that direction. Thoroughly compatible, however, is a discussion of the policy of the Glasgow authorities in giving this place the semblance of a lovely village, with its trees and lawns, its playgrounds and beautiful flower-gardens, with its separate and home-like private apartments instead of common dormitories for the eighty nurses, and with convalescing-rooms and every convenience attached to each sick-ward — when it would have cost much less money to build a big, repulsive "pest-house" and inclose it with a grim wall, "a place for sick paupers to die."

I am not dealing with sentimental considerations when I commend this policy. The difference between popularity and unpopularity in a public hospital for infectious diseases may well mean all the difference between a terrible epidemic and its easy prevention. What, for instance, is the extra cost of a spacious and attractive hospital where it is actually a privilege for a poor child to be ill, compared with the frightful

CHAP. IV.
The institution at Belvidere.

Its great attractiveness.

Consequences of this policy.

cost, direct and indirect, entailed upon a city by the prejudices which so frequently lead to the secretion of epidemic patients by the ignorant poor? In a densely populated city everything depends upon the discovery and isolation of such forms of disease at the earliest possible moment. An epidemic destroys valuable lives, and it also paralyzes trade and industry and causes immense pecuniary loss. It is the endeavor of Glasgow to treat infectious cases with such care and tenderness, and such affluence of all that modern invention and science can suggest, as to secure ready coöperation from all classes in the work of isolating infection. The plan is growingly successful. After the average sojourn of six weeks at Belvidere, patients

A popular hospital.

are reluctant to leave; and they carry wonderful tales back to the tenement-rows. The Belvidere nurses are ladies; and the city gives them such accommodations as, in their arduous and necessarily secluded work, they might reasonably desire. The smallpox wards are built separately, and in fact the smallpox hospital is entirely distinct in all its departments; but when there are no smallpox patients, some of the wards are used for scarlet fever, measles, or other diseases, and the whole group of buildings is administered as one

Patronized by rich as well as by poor.

great fever hospital. It should be said that the rich as well as the poor may, and do, avail themselves freely of the privileges of this hospital, especially for scarlet fever and measles. The average daily number of patients in 1887 was 332, and the total number received in the year was about 3000. Dr. Allan, the accomplished medical superintendent, agrees with Dr. Russell, the health officer, in regarding the establishments at Belvidere as large enough for the highest efficiency. In 1892 there were 5282 infectious cases removed to hospital, and a temporary establishment was fitted up to relieve Belvidere in a season of unprecedented epi-

demics of measles and scarlet fever. Meanwhile, the
city had acquired land at the opposite end of the city
for its second permanent epidemic hospital; and it is
now under construction. No effort will be spared to
make its appointments even more perfect if possible
than those of Belvidere. Glasgow will now have invested more than a million dollars of capital outlay
in municipal hospitals for infectious diseases, and no
expenditure could have been more advantageous and
profitable.

Not the least important feature of the Health Department's work in Glasgow are the sanitary wash-houses.
A similar establishment should be a part of the municipal economy of every large town. In 1864 the
authorities found it necessary to superintend the disinfection of dwellings, and a small temporary wash-
house was opened, with a few tubs for the cleansing
of apparel, etc., removed from infected houses. For
a time after the acquisition of Belvidere, a part of the
laundry of the hospital was used for the purpose of a
general sanitary wash-house. But larger quarters being needed, a separate establishment was built and
opened in 1883, its cost being about $50,000. This
place is so admirable in its system and its mechanical
appointments that I am again tempted to digress with
a technical description. The place is in constant communication with sanitary headquarters, and its col-
lecting-wagons are on the road early every morning.
The larger part of the articles removed for disinfection and cleansing must be returned on the same day,
to meet the necessities of poor families. I visited the
house on a day when 1800 pieces, from 25 different
families, had come in. In 1887, 6700 washings, aggregating 380,000 pieces, were done. The quantity, of
course, varies from year to year with the amount of
infectious disease in the city. Thus in 1892 more than

700,000 articles were washed. Very recently, in 1894, there has been opened at Ruchill, at the west end of Glasgow, a new and still larger sanitary wash-house, the buildings and machinery costing not less than $75,000. It occupies two acres of the 38-acre tract which had been secured for the new infectious-diseases hospital. The establishment has a crematory, to which all household articles whatsoever that are to be burned after a case of infectious disease must be brought by the vans of the Sanitary Department. The carpet-cleaning machinery and the arrangements for disinfection by steam, by chemicals, and by boiling I cannot here describe.

The Health Department's disinfecting and white-washing staff is operated from the wash-house as head-quarters. A patient being removed to the hospital, the authorities at once take possession of the house for cleansing and disinfection. It is a point of interest also that the city has provided a comfortable "house of reception" of some ten rooms, with several permanent servants, where families may be entertained for a day or more as the city's guests if it is desirable to remove them from their homes during the progress of the dis-infecting and clothes-washing operations. This house is kept in constant use, and it is found a very conve-nient thing for the department to have at its disposal.

As net results of the sanitary work of the Glasgow authorities may be mentioned the almost entire ex-tinction of some of the worst forms of contagious dis-ease, and a mastery of the situation which leaves no ground for much fear of wide-spread epidemics in the future, in spite of the fact that Glasgow is a great seaport, has an unfavorable climate, and has an extra-ordinarily dense and badly housed working popula-tion. The steady decline of the total death-rate, and its remarkably rapid decline as regards those diseases

Increased facilities.

Crematory for infected articles.

Disinfection staff.

A novel kind of hos-pitality.

Suppression of certain diseases.

at which sanitary science more especially aims its weapons, are achievements which are a proper source of gratification to the town council and the officers of the Health Department.

In close affiliation with the Sanitary Department, and under the superintendence of the same general committee of the common council, is the Cleansing Department. While for administrative purposes it is a distinct service, it seems to me important to make conspicuous the fact that the street-sweeping, garbage-disposal, street-watering, and other work of this important public department are a part of the sanitary government. Health considerations come first. It is the business of the Superintendent of Cleansing not merely to manage his department to the greatest possible economic advantage, but to manage it primarily in such a way as to satisfy a fastidious medical officer of health. Mr. John Young, for a number of years at the head of this department, has made it a model of efficiency. To use Mr. Young's own language, the work of the department "embraces (1) the scavenging of all courts and back yards forming a common access to lands and heritages separately occupied; (2) the scavenging and watering of all the streets and roads within the city; and (3) the collection, removal, and disposal of all night-soil, general domestic refuse, and detritus."

The work of public cleansing.

Must satisfy the health officer.

Three branches of the service.

The propriety of cleansing private courts and passageways at public expense is better considered in the practical than in the theoretical aspects. Glasgow has a population of which more than 90 per cent. live in closely built tenement-structures, and of which 70 per cent. live in houses of one or two rooms. Health demands that the common courts and stairs be kept clean. Experience shows that if done properly the owners would pay their private employees more than

Cleansing private passages and stairs.

the small tax — one penny in the pound sterling of rental value — which is collected of them as a special rating for this purpose. There are 11,000 of these courts, etc., to be kept clean, some of which have to be cleansed two or even three times in a day, and all at The system. least once a day. For this work the main cleansing districts are subdivided into sections, which are laid off into about 200 beats, each of which is cleansed by one man under the supervision of a section foreman.

The streets (181 miles) are swept nightly, most of the work being done by twenty-three horse-machines, Street-cleaning. which are followed by the department's removal-carts. A good feature of this work are the iron boxes or bins, with hinged lids, sunk in the sidewalks next the curbing along the principal streets at intervals of forty yards. Men and boys are kept busy brushing up the day litter and depositing it in the boxes, the contents of which are removed by night with the sweepings.

Sprinkling the streets. The summer street-sprinkling is also done by the Cleansing Department; and it is done with great economy, for the simple reason that the amount of the street-cleansing work varies inversely to the amount of street-sprinkling required; and so the regular force of men and horses employed to keep the streets clean during the rest of the year is sufficient to do that work and the watering besides in the summer months. The sidewalks of Glasgow are left to be swept by owners and occupants, who are, of course, required to keep them clean. The system as a whole results in well-cleansed thoroughfares.

Garbage removal. The third distinct portion of the work of the Cleansing Department is the collection and disposal of domestic refuse and night-soil; and this is more difficult and expensive than the other two portions combined. For this service the city is divided into several main

districts, regard being had in this division to the
points of outlet. The central or business part of the
city is served by daily morning dust-carts, each house
being provided with a special form of covered bucket
which facilitates collection. As regards the great
bulk of the population, living in tenement-houses, it
has been found best to collect refuse, including such
excrementitious matter as is not carried down the
sewers, from improved "ash-bins" in the back courts.
Each main district has a force of men engaged in
emptying these bins and wheeling the contents out
to meet the night-carts which ply between the district
and the nearest "despatch station" of the department. It should be explained that each district is
subdivided for this work into six sections, one section
being cleansed every night, and the entire city being
thus served once a week. As the use of the water-
closet system is becoming more general, the amount
of excrementitious matter to be collected by the department decreases. But many large factories, besides the numerous "public conveniences" on the
streets, make use of the "pail-closet" system, the
pails being very frequently exchanged and the removal to the despatch stations being in covered vans.
This system of scavenging is as thorough in execution as it is methodical and complete in its plan.

There are three principal and several minor despatch stations. The most approved in their appointments are the one known as the "Crawford Street
Works," opened in 1884, and that at Kelvinhaugh,
which dates from 1891. Stated briefly, it is the policy
of the department to send out as manure to the farms
just as large a proportion, in bulk and weight, of the
street-sweepings and general refuse as can be made a
marketable article. At Crawford street the carts drive
across a weighing platform to a great dumping and

sorting floor. Street-sweepings, after a little raking to remove newspapers and large articles, are shoveled through hatchways, without further treatment, into railway wagons standing on the lowest floor. The contents of the ash-bins are passed through great revolving double riddles or separating-machines. The larger cinders are sorted out and furnish fuel for the establishment's boilers. The finer ashes and cinders pass down to the floor below into the mixing-machines, where they are met by the discharges from the tanks holding excrementa. The newspapers, old baskets, boots, bricks, broken furniture, etc., pass from the riddles to a sorting floor and thence down flumes to the crematory furnaces, where they burn furiously without the aid of any other fuel, a chimney two hundred and forty feet high making a strong air-draft. The expense of a much closer cremation and of the drying and condensation of manure, which is necessary in the large English towns from lack of a market for bulky fertilizers, is avoided in Glasgow. The heavy, cold Scotch soil is improved by a coarse and ashy manure that could not be used in the middle counties of England. The sweepings of the macadamized roads, which are not salable, are used by the city, on its own bog-redeemed farm of " Fulwood Moss," for filling, " top-dressing," etc. The total quantity of material carted by the department for the year ending May 31, 1893, was in excess of 361,000 tons, and the amount of manure sold was 276,000 tons — the difference being made up of snow, drainage of water from muddy sweepings, materials cremated, and macadam-sweepings. This is a remarkable record. The manure is sold in fifteen counties, much of it going sixty or seventy miles. The city owns its railway wagons (seven hundred of them), and has an arrangement with all the roads by which the manure is carried for

The sorting process.

Crematory furnaces.

Road-sweepings used on a municipal farm.

Sale of fertilizers.

one halfpenny (one cent) per ton per mile, cars returned free. It would be for the obvious advantage
of the city to send out the largest possible quantity
even if nothing more than freight charges were received. The net proceeds are, however, from twenty-
five to fifty cents a ton.

The operations of this department are a charge upon
the general police rate, excepting the cleansing of private courts and tenement stairs, which is paid for by
the proprietors benefited by means of a special levy
of one penny per pound of rental value. There were
employed, on the average, throughout the year 1894,
1053 men — 537 in domestic scavenging, 232 in private
street and court cleaning, and 284 in public street scavenging and sprinkling. The city has invested more
than a million dollars in works and plant, much of this
amount having been lately expended to provide for
the enlarged area and population secured by incorporation of suburbs. Noteworthy is the acquisition of
the so-called Ryding estate of nearly six hundred acres,
which, like "Fulwood Moss," will be conducted as a
municipal farm and a place for the advantageous disposition of a great city's refuse. The total ordinary
expenditure of the department in 1888, including interest, was $370,000. Sales of manure brought in a
revenue of $130,000, and after deducting the cost of
the private-court scavenging met by special assessment, there remained only $190,000 of general charge
to be paid out of the rates for an admirable and complete service of street cleansing and watering and of
domestic scavenging for a population of nearly 600,000
—a net cost *per capita* of only about thirty-five cents.
And this economy is the more noteworthy from the
fact that the ruling motive of the department is that
of the health officer and sanitary engineer rather than
that of the contractor. Since 1890 the tendency has

I.—7

Chap. IV.

Railway
service.

Number of
scavengers
employed.

A second
municipal
farm.

Finances of
Cleansing
Department.

CHAP. IV. been toward an increased relative expenditure. Nevertheless, the cost to the ratepayers is trifling in comparison with the magnificent service that the Cleansing Department renders. I am tempted to go into some details of the method used by Superintendent Young

Purchase of
supplies. in buying supplies (horse-feed, etc.) for his large operations. His department has reduced these matters to so economical and businesslike a basis that it has become purveyor to the Fire Department, the Police Department, the Sanitary Department, the Markets Department, and the Parks and Gardens Department, all of which to a less extent are horse-keeping branches of the municipal administration.

Shortly after the extension of Glasgow's boundaries in 1846, and the consequent reorganization of the municipal government, public attention was forcibly

The development of
slums. drawn to the frightfully crowded and insanitary condition of the central parts of the city. The success which had followed the city's brave efforts to enlarge and deepen the tiny Clyde into a great ocean highway had been attended with a most extraordinary development of industries in the Clyde valley, and growth of urban population. The more fortunate classes moved out of their old homes in the central district of the town to the handsome West End suburbs. The business core shifted somewhat also, and the old buildings were packed with an operative class which Glasgow's new prosperity had drawn by scores of thousands from the Highlands and from Ireland. Most of these people lived there in single-room apartments, and in unwholesome conditions which will not be readily comprehended by future generations. Epidemics, originating in these filthy and overcrowded quarters, invaded the homes of the better classes, and self-protection made some measures of reform a ne-

cessity. It was resolved by the town council to set aside $150,000 for the acquisition of property in some of the worst neighborhoods; but while a considerable investment was made in condemned tenement-structures, the work of building others on the same bad models was going on apace. At length a committee was appointed to make inquiry and report to the council upon the sanitary laws and arrangements of the large cities and towns of the kingdom. Mr. John Carrick, who was a member of that committee, and who at the time of his death in 1890 was the efficient city architect and master of public works, after nearly half a century of inestimably valuable service in the municipal government of Glasgow, is the principal source of my information upon this subject. The report was made in 1859. It observes:

Chap. IV.

Beginnings of reform.

Housing conditions in 1859.

> Originally the "closes" and lanes of the city were not all objectionable. The houses were of moderate height, and unbuilt spaces were attached to many of the dwellings, and promoted ventilation. Now, however, in those localities almost every spare inch of ground has been built upon, until room cannot be found to lay down an ash-pit. Houses, too, which were only intended to accommodate single families have been increased in height, and are found tenanted by separate families in every apartment, until they appear to teem with inhabitants. . . . A worse state was disclosed by an inspection of some of the more recently erected houses for the working-classes. Tenements of great height are ranged on either side of narrow lanes with no backyard space, and are divided from top to bottom into numberless small dwellings all crowded with occupants. Occupation of cellars and sunk flats as dwelling-houses is largely on the increase.

These quotations will show the nature of the evil. As remedial measures the committee advised that new police powers be obtained from Parliament to deal with the height of buildings, the size of apartments, the area and backyard spaces, the lighting and venti-

Remedies proposed.

lation, the provision of water-closet and ash-pit accommodations, ample water-supply, and so on. It
was further advised that the new legislation for Glasgow should increase the powers conferred on local authorities by the General Nuisance Removal Act (Scotland) of 1856, and that specific authority should be
obtained for the appointment of a competent medical
officer and staff of nuisance inspectors; for the prevention of overcrowding apartments by regulating
the maximum number of inmates on the basis of their
air-space; for the prevention of the use of sunk floors
as dwellings; for compelling owners to cleanse and
whitewash house property ; and to prevent the discharge of refuse from certain factories and works into
the common drains. It was still further recommended
that all ashes and night-soil be made the property of
the city, and that all proceedings under the new police
act be taken summarily before the city magistrates.
Special suggestions were added, to the effect that
powers be obtained from Parliament to acquire property for the sake of sanitary improvement, upon payment to the proprietors of sums to be fixed in the last
resort by competent tribunals, and that public baths
and wash-houses be built and opened for the benefit
of the working-classes.

I have enumerated these propositions at some length
because at that time they were so novel and so far in
advance of prevailing notions. With great difficulty
the desired legislation was secured, in 1862, for the
brief and experimental term of five years. To short-
en the story, let it be said that in 1866 the Glasgow
police act was renewed, with amendments, and made
permanent; and under its wise provisions have been
developed those admirable sanitary and cleansing services which I have already described. But in 1866
those parts of the earlier act which related to the pur-

Powers
granted.

chase and improvement of property were made parts of another famous enactment of the same year, by which the town council was constituted an improvement trust for the carrying out of certain definite objects specified in the act. It had become constantly more apparent that drastic measures must be taken with the old part of the city. Nothing short of very extensive demolitions could remedy the evil. There were practically no streets at all; but only a system of " wynds, vennels, and closes," permeating an almost solid mass of tenement-houses.

Other large British towns have followed the example set by Glasgow; and demolition, street-widening, and improved construction under public auspices are no longer a novelty. But Glasgow, it should be remembered, had the courage to lead the way; and the Glasgow City Improvements Act furnished Lord Cross with the model upon which his Improved Dwellings Act was constructed. Glasgow's action was hastened by the fact that several railway companies were seeking access to the heart of the city for great terminal grounds and buildings, and the time seemed especially opportune for a rearrangement and improvement of streets. As laid before Parliament in 1865, the scheme covered an area of 88 acres, which then contained a population of 51,294; the average mortality of the area for some years past being 38.64 per thousand, with epidemic diseases the cause of 36 per cent. of the deaths. The average density was nearly 600 to the acre, and in various parts of the district it exceeded 1000—the total inhabitancy of the city then being 423,723, covering an area of 5063 acres, and showing therefore an average density of 83 as contrasted with 583 in the area to be dealt with. The financial side of the scheme looked plausible. The initial outlay was estimated at about $7,250,000, and it was expected that the re-sale

I.—7*

CHAP. IV.

"Improvement trust" of 1866.

Glasgow as a pioneer in housing reforms.

Statistics of the improvement scheme.

of building-sites would pay back all but $750,000. A new park was to be made at a cost of $200,000, and the paving and sewering of three or four miles of new-made streets was estimated at $325,000. For all the advantages of improved streets, improved health, and improved general appearance of the town, the rate-payers were not to be charged at all dearly.

Its enlarged scope. The council committee which carried out the improvements acquired some further powers and did more than was originally contemplated. Besides purchasing the 88 acres and some other small areas in the crowded parts of the city, they acquired and laid out in streets and squares for working-men's residences two estates known as "Overnewton" and "Oatlands." They also formed an important open space, the "Cathedral Square," in a densely populated neighborhood, and carried out other large enterprises not at first in the list. Their operations were very vigorous from 1869 to 1876, and were coincident with, if not directly the cause of, much house-building and real-estate speculation in Glasgow. A considerable amount of the property acquired by the trustees was disposed of on good terms; but there came a general reaction,— due in part to idle shipyards,— a marked decline in the price of land, and a cessation of sales. For some years the improvement trust was obliged to hold a large amount of property at a reduced valuation. The total cost of all its purchases and improvements, not including interest charges, has been about $10,000,000.

Financial status. For lands sold there has been received approximately $5,000,000. The property still held by the trust is valued, at present reduced prices, at less than its cost. The margin of shrinkage has, however, been practically covered by current taxation, so that the account now stands about even; *i.e.*, the assets and liabilities of the trust are at a balance. The act authorized an

annual assessment of sixpence in the pound of rental
valuation, but the trustees have steadily reduced the
levy until it is now only a halfpenny.

The principal improvement made is a system of The new street system.
modern streets in the center of the city that will be
of advantage for centuries, and will repay the cost
hundreds of times over.   Twenty-nine new streets
have been formed and twenty-five old ones greatly wi-
dened and improved.   The old insanitary tenement Dealing with the tenements.
property has not all been demolished.   The plan was
adopted of tearing out intermediate buildings, opening back courts where none existed, and otherwise
ameliorating such property as the new streets and
the wide swaths cut by the elevated tracks of the invading railways left still inhabited.   In fact the business depression which checked operations, and dis-
couraged and alarmed all Glasgow for the time being,
made the city improvement trust unpopular, and The city as landlord.
obliged the council to proceed cautiously.   The city
is, therefore, to-day a landlord on a large scale, and is
holding really insanitary property for the sake of the
rents, waiting for an opportunity to sell the sites before demolishing the buildings.   Its rents now bring
in annually about $100,000, which sum goes far to-
ward offsetting the interest charge on the property
held for sale.   The improvement trust has given the
city, among other things, the handsome new Alexan-
dra Park.   Since 1892 the trust has, in various ways, Renewed activities.
assumed a fresh activity.   The enlargement of the
city has made necessary new tasks of reform, and it
is expected that Parliament will give renewed and
greatly extended powers, under which various other
areas of Glasgow will be subject to compulsory purchase and reconstruction of streets and houses.

It remains for me to speak of the model tenements,
and of the important series of model lodging-houses,

which this department has ventured to erect and maintain as a part of its reform work.

It was the original understanding that the city's work was to be that of demolition, and that private enterprise, regulated by the new sanitary rules and requirements, would suffice for proper reconstruction and would make due provision for the displaced population. Rather early in their operations, however, the committee found it advantageous to build one or two tenement-houses as a model and example of proper arrangements and construction; and it may be assumed that a good influence was thus exerted upon the character of the large amount of new house-room that builders were at that time providing. These were, however, only incidental undertakings. More recently the council committee has gone into improved-tenement building on a larger scale, and, as it seems to me, with more doubtful propriety. On Saltmarket street, in a very central locality and on the site of old tenement-houses which had been removed, the improvements committee in 1888 expended $50,-000 in building a row of solid tenement-houses, with a dozen shop-rooms on the ground floor; and subsequently there were additional houses of like character built on the same street. The twofold object was avowed of bringing back population to a neighborhood comparatively empty, and of getting some return for valuable property that had been lying unproductive, vainly awaiting purchasers. But it would seem a mistake to attempt to draw population back to the heart of the city. It is the peculiarity of Glasgow that the laboring people live on the inner circle of their work; and this has been so frequently deplored that it would seem decidedly a reactionary move for the authorities themselves to build tenements with the view to bring back the very people

Model municipal tenements.

A doubtful policy.

Counteracting the suburban tendency.

whose dispersion to the suburbs has always been regarded as so important a desideratum. It was, however, the best class of working people for whom the
city provided these new houses, and the real motive
seemed to be the promotion of a market for the adjacent property. Whether wise or unwise, the experiment was not upon a sufficiently large scale to have
very significant results. But now the committee has
entered in a larger way upon this policy of building
municipal tenement-houses. In 1893 a new row of
thirteen tenements in the same neighborhood was begun, containing twelve shops and 127 houses for working people; and two or three other like projects have
been resolved upon. Thus the municipality becomes
the landlord of several hundred families, for whom it
has provided what it deems to be a model type of tenement-house.

Chap. IV.

Municipal house-building on a larger scale.

Much more important and interesting is the experience of Glasgow in providing common lodging-houses.
Every large city has a transient and shifting element
that finds accommodation in the cheap lodging-houses,
and these places are too frequently the haunts of vice
and crime. They had been particularly bad in Glasgow until brought under strict regulation by the new
police acts. There was also an almost irresistible tendency to overcrowd the smallest and most wretched
tenement apartments with nightly lodgers of the ab-
jectly poor class. Partly to relieve this pressure, and
to assist somewhat in the readjustments of population
necessitated by the improvements scheme, and partly
to institute a competition that would compel the
private keepers of such houses to improve their establishments, the council committee in charge of the improvement works opened two model lodging-houses in
1870. So decidedly successful in every way were these
institutions that another one, in temporary quarters,

The munici-pal lodging-houses.

was opened in 1874, to be replaced by a large and permanent one in 1876.   Three more large houses on

Seven such establish- ments. the same plan were opened in 1878, and a seventh and last in 1879.   They have continued to be an unqualified success.   Their incidental advantages as a police measure, in promoting the good order of the city, can hardly be overestimated.   The common lodging-house inspector had 101 houses on his list in 1888, although the city's seven establishments provided about one third of the total accommodation, having nearly 2000 beds out of a total 6273 reported by the inspector. It is a pleasure to visit these municipal hostelries, and see for one's self how cleanly, comfortable, and decent

Arrange- ments and charges. they are.   Every lodger is given a separate apartment, or stall, in one of the high and well-ventilated flats, and has the use of a large common sitting-room, of a locker for provisions, and of the long kitchen-range for cooking his own food.   The charge per night is 3½d. or 4½d. (7 or 9 cents), according to the lodger's choice of a bed with one sheet or with two.   In any case he rests on a woven-wire mattress.   Six of these

A house for women. houses are for men, and one is for women, the charge in the latter being only 3d.   The regulations require of all the common lodging-houses of Glasgow that they shall be exclusively for one sex or the other.

Effect on pri- vate enter- prise. The success of the corporation's houses has had the good effect of leading private enterprise to open similarly improved establishments, with the same scale of prices and conducted on the same strict rules as regards good order and cleanliness.   Thus in 1893, although the total capacity of the Glasgow lodging-houses had increased by 25 per cent. in five years, the number had fallen from 101 to 71, the municipal policy having succeeded in wiping out many of the smallest and worst.   I find that the city's six houses for men, during the year ending May 31, 1888, enter-

tained 647,681 nightly lodgers, and that the house for
women, which is smaller than the others, entertained
33,986. The returns for the preceding year are about
the same. Since then, the number of guests has been
increasing. The cost of the houses, which are substantially built, was about $450,000. After paying all
running expenses and a due amount for deterioration
of property, they yield a net return of from four to
five per cent. on the investment. It costs about $6000
a year to "run" one of the houses, and the receipts
are from $8000 to $9000. They are, therefore, a
source of actual profit to the city, although of course
designed primarily to promote good order and the
welfare of the unfortunate classes. So far as I am
aware, no other city has established lodging-houses
of this kind upon so large a scale, and Glasgow's experience has peculiar interest. Several of the houses
were enlarged in 1894, and it has now become a part
of the regular order to provide every winter a series
of social entertainments in each of these seven model
lodging-houses, with the result, as Lord Provost Bell
assures us, of "not only brightening the lot of the inmates of the houses, but helping materially to remove
temptation from their path."

As a further development of this general policy,
the improvement trustees—*i. e.*, the city council—have
in 1894 entered upon the construction of a "Family
Home," which is designed to supplement the lodging-
houses, and to meet a peculiar need that they cannot
supply. It is to contain 176 separate dormitories,
each of which will be capable of accommodating a
small family and will be designed particularly for the
use of a widow or a widower with small children, who
may be under the necessity of going out to work, thus
leaving the children behind during the day. The establishment will contain dining-rooms and kitchen,

Margin notes:

Self-sup-
porting and
revenue-
yielding.

Centers for
kindly social
service.

The new mu-
nicipal
"Family
Home."

CHAP. IV.

A remarkable innovation.

The public baths.

Five large institutions.

day sitting-rooms and play-rooms and a *crèche,* and a playground will adjoin.   Practical experience in conducting the lodging-houses has shown the need of this family home as a temporary refuge.   It can be made self-supporting on the principle of the lodging-houses, and it will be the first public institution of the kind in the United Kingdom, if not in the world.

As a part of that large scheme of sanitary and social amelioration that I have thus far been describing, are to be regarded the great public baths and wash-houses of Glasgow.   Power to establish such places was obtained in the police acts of 1862–66; but it was not until 1878 that the first one was opened.   Glasgow was not at that time at all well provided with baths; and if private capital had been disposed to embark extensively in the business, the common council would hardly have ventured to add this to its undertakings.   But there was manifest need, and the authorities courageously proceeded to supply the facilities *pro bono publico.*   They have now five large establishments in different parts of the city, the first of which was opened in 1878 and the last in 1884.   Each includes under the same roof very capacious swimming-baths for men and for women and numerous small bath-rooms, every modern facility being provided; and also, as a distinct feature, an elaborate and extensive wash-house for the use of poor families that lack home conveniences for laundry-work.   The substantial character of these institutions will appear when I state the fact that, although honestly and economically built, they have cost more than $600,000.

The swimming-baths are kept open through the entire year, at a uniform temperature, and the pure and soft Loch Katrine water makes them particularly inviting.   Their establishment was an inestimable boon to the working-classes, who needed them as a com-

mon decency of life, and who enjoy them as a luxury.
They are in charge of competent swimming-masters,
and there are swimming-clubs and frequent contests   Popularity
of the swim-
in connection with each of them. Glasgow affords   ming-baths.
the masses so little healthful recreation comparatively
that this feature of the baths is the more appreciated.
The number of bathers exceeds 450,000 a year, and
there is reason to believe that it will increase; although the present average of 1500 per day the entire
year through would seem to justify the city's outlay.
The charges are of course small — twopence for use
of swimming-bath, and a little more for the private
baths, with special rates for school children.

Hardly less useful in the cause of public cleanliness   The public
and decency are the wash-houses. For the trifling sum   wash-houses.
of twopence an hour a woman is allowed the use of a
stall containing an improved steam-boiling arrangement and fixed tubs with hot and cold water faucets.
The washing being quickly done, the clothes are de-
posited for two or three minutes in one of a row of
centrifugal machine driers, after which they are hung
on one of a series of sliding frames which retreat into
a hot-air apartment. If she wishes, the housewife
may then use a large roller-mangle, operated, like all
the rest of the machinery, by steam-power; and she
may at the end of the hour go home with her basket   A boon to
tenement
of clothes washed, dried, and ironed. To appreciate   housewives.
the convenience of all this, it must be remembered
that the woman probably lives with her family in one
small room of an upper tenement flat. The number
of washings done in these houses increased from 76,-
718 in the year 1885–86 to 96,832 in the year 1887–88,
and to 155,221 in the year 1890–91; and unquestionably this patronage is destined to have a very large
future growth.

It would be a decided oversight not to mention the

fact, in passing, for the sake of those interested in noting the advancing socialism of the day, that in each of these establishments the city also separately conducts a general laundry business, drawing its patronage from all classes of society. I observe by reference to one of the printed municipal wash-lists that its charges for shirts, skirts, etc., are at about the current Glasgow rates. This line of enterprise has doubtless been assumed because the baths and wash-houses, while paying running expenses, do not as yet, at their low rates of charge, pay interest upon the investment. The rather undignified entrance of the municipal corporation into competition with the private laundries of the city can hardly find permanent favor; but this is merely incidental, and it detracts nothing from the praiseworthiness of the public services rendered by the baths and wash-houses.

The city in the laundry business.

The municipal functions of "Watching and Lighting" are associated together in Glasgow under the supervision of the same council committee; and the Fire Department is also intimately related to that of "watching," or ordinary police. These three services pertain to the general police government of the city, and their cost is defrayed from the fund provided by the general police rate, as is that of the Sanitary and Cleansing departments, the public baths, and the streets, sewers, and bridges.

"Watching and Lighting," and fire service.

The Glasgow police force is a fine and well-disciplined body of nearly 1400 men. Size and strength have been counted prime qualifications in their selection, and their average height is just under six feet. Their average age is 34, and their average length of service is ten years. They are organized under a chief constable, 10 superintendents, and 28 lieutenants, with a number of inspectors and sergeants in imme-

The police force.

diate command of the patrolmen, or ordinary constables.   A majority of the men are Highlanders.
They are of excellent personal character as a rule, and
very faithful in the performance of routine duties.
The force is universally praised by the citizens, and
those complaints and expressions of criticism and distrust that one hears in any American city are unknown
in Glasgow.   The chief seems to use his own discretion very largely in the selection of new men, and
there is no ordeal of competitive examination to be
passed.   The selection of the chief is made by the
council on recommendation of the committee, and
vacancies in the other offices are usually filled by promotion.   From top to bottom, the police service commands admiration and confidence.

The police courts belong to this department.   Justice
is dispensed by the Lord Provost, and by those members of the council, ten in number, who have been
set aside by their fellows as Bailies or Magistrates.
They arrange a scheme of rotation, and are assisted
by assessors, these being practising lawyers who are
paid for advising the citizen-magistrates on points
of law.   The magistrates themselves are, of course,
not paid; but in order somewhat to lighten their
labors, a stipendiary magistrate, or salaried police
judge, is employed at $5000 a year, who sits constantly
in the central district and disposes of a large share of
the business.   The general police government of the
city also employs a law officer or attorney known as
the "procurator fiscal," who conducts prosecutions,
when necessary, in the enforcement of the sanitary
and other statutes and regulations administered by
the council in its capacity as a police board.

Half the expense of police-force salaries and clothing is met by a government grant, as for all other
municipal corporations in the kingdom, the mainte-

nance of order being in theory and origin a general rather than a local function. The net charge of the police force upon the local rates is only about $250,-000. Glasgow has adopted the plan of building very commodious police-station establishments, in which are sleeping-rooms, kitchens, and mess-rooms for the unmarried members of the force. Retiring pensions are allowed, and everything possible is done by the municipality to promote a high standard of personal character and a strong sense of fidelity among the men charged with keeping the city's peace and order.

Treatment of the force.

The advantage of abundant illumination at night as a police measure seems to me to be appreciated in Glasgow as in few other cities. There is nothing very noteworthy about the gas-lights along all the public streets, unless the commendable clearness with which street names are painted upon the four sides of the corner lamps as well as upon the corner buildings should merit a passing compliment; but very notable and unusual is the illumination by the authorities not only of all private streets and courts, but also of all common stairs. The cost of gas and wages of lighters for illuminating the common stairs alone are greater than the same items of expense for lighting all the public streets of the city.

Public lighting.

A part of the extra outlay is recovered by special assessments; but a considerable margin is a charge upon the general rates. Thus it cost for the year 1887–88 to light private streets and courts about $21,200, of which $12,300 was collected by a special assessment of $3.75 per lamp, leaving about $9000 to be paid from the treasury. The expense of lighting common stairs was $95,500, of which $56,800 was recovered from owners by an assessment of $2.50 per light, leaving the city nearly $40,000 to pay. The net cost to the city of the Street-lighting Department

Lighting courts and stairs.

proper, excluding the two services just mentioned, but including cost of superintendence and central offices that pertain to the three services, was less than $100,000.

The sums that owners pay the city for lighting courts and stairs are perhaps more than they would pay for insufficient illumination if the matter were left in their hands. The excess paid by the city in order to secure proper lighting should be regarded, like the police force and the street lamps, as a legitimate outlay for public protection, convenience, and order. As the Chief of Police has remarked to me, each lamp is as good as an additional constable. The statistics of apprehensions and convictions for crimes show a remarkable increase in proportion to the number of crimes reported, since the improvement trust and the stair-lighting have opened up the many once dark and almost inaccessible rendezvous of thieves and criminals, while the total amount of serious crime has steadily diminished in proportion to the population.

Illumination as a police measure.

The Fire Department of Glasgow is interesting to an American chiefly on account of its modest proportions and trifling cost. The population of Glasgow is greater than that of Boston; but while the fire-extinguishing service of the latter city costs annually about $800,000, I find that the net expense of the Glasgow department for the year 1891 was less than $60,000 — about one thirteenth that of Boston. Glasgow's great saving in this item is due partly to the compactness of the city, partly to its construction of fire-proof materials, and partly to the great pressure in the water-mains. The storage reservoirs being more than 300 feet above the city, there is a pressure in the pipes that varies from 50 to 100 pounds per square inch, being greatest of course at night, when

Small cost of Fire Department.

Various safeguards against conflagration.

I.—8

fires are most likely to occur; and in the large majority of cases the firemen have only to connect their hose with the hydrants and turn on the water. Thus I find that while the department possessed six steam and nine manual fire-engines, and while engines were taken out on occasion of 237 of the 344 fires which were extinguished by the firemen in 1887, yet the engines were actually worked at only fourteen fires. Flames spread slowly in the stone buildings, with their universal stone staircases and flagged hallways. Buckets and hand-pumps, in two thirds of the cases, are sufficient apparatus; and a single line of hose attached to the nearest hydrant answers for nearly all the rest. Glasgow was in earlier times built largely of wood, and its historians record some great conflagrations. But the present city is remarkably solid and non-combustible. The total permanent fire-force numbered 86 men in 1887; 51 policemen being also drilled as an auxiliary fire-force. The number in 1894 is perhaps 100 men as against 800 for Boston. The Glasgow firemen all have houses provided rent free, in flats above the engine and hose rooms, and each man lives apart with his family, being summoned to duty by an electric call-bell from the watch-room below. This plan of course delays the response to an alarm. The service, as a whole, is by no means primitive, however, and, indeed, the accomplished and learned City Chamberlain, Mr. James Nicol, declares that "of all Glasgow's municipal organizations, the Fire Brigade is the most interesting and popular."

Provision for the fire-men.

Until 1860 Glasgow was supplied by a private corporation with water pumped from the river Clyde. The Clyde is but a small stream; and as the development of industries and a great population in the Clyde valley made the quality of the water wholly unsuit-

The water-supply.

able for domestic uses, the volume of supply became inadequate also. A rehearsal of the various schemes proposed from 1834 to 1854 would be out of place here, and it is enough to say that courageous and far-sighted views at length prevailed, and in 1855 the corporation of Glasgow obtained parliamentary authority to purchase the works and interests of the existing water-company, and those of a smaller company which supplied the district south of the Clyde, and to bring in a supply of 50,000,000 gallons a day   Tapping Loch from Loch Katrine, 34 miles distant in the Highlands.   Katrine.

This was a great project forty years ago, when large engineering enterprises were less common than to-day; and its success has been of inestimable advantage to Glasgow. The old supply was abandoned and the new works were opened in 1860. The supply is practically inexhaustible, the average yearly rainfall of the drainage area of Loch Katrine being about 100 inches, and two other lakes in the same neighborhood being utilized as compensation reservoirs. Although the demand has not yet seriously overtaxed the capa-   The system recently city of the existing aqueduct, the entire system has   doubled. been gradually duplicated; and in the course of a year or two the works will have a capacity of 100,-000,000 gallons per day, and suffice for the needs of a population of from 1,500,000 to 2,000,000. At present, a population of more than 800,000 is supplied, and the average daily quantity is 40,000,000 gallons. A few years ago a smaller population used nearly 2,000,000 more gallons; but much attention has recently been given to the stoppage of waste by the use of improved fittings and by vigilant inspection. It is interesting to note the fact that Glasgow uses more   Per capita than twice as much water per capita as Manches-   use of water. ter or Liverpool, and about three times as much as Birmingham. The present daily supply is about 50 gallons to each person, of which about one fourth may be called the trade and manufacturing supply, the rest being the domestic and municipal supply.

It is further worth while to note that Glasgow is able to provide its much more bountiful supply at less expense to the users than is incurred in the large English towns. It is the almost universal plan in the towns of the United Kingdom to levy a domestic water-charge upon the rental value of the premises supplied. The old charge made by the Glasgow water-company was 14*d.* in the £. The corporation reduced it in 1865 to 12*d.*, in 1871 to 8*d.*, and in 1886 to 7*d.* (the large outlying population, however, being charged 11*d.*). It has since been reduced to 6*d.* In addition to this, a public water-rate of 1*d.* in the £ of rental valuation is levied, to defray the expense of water used for various municipal purposes. The water used in manufacturing, etc., is supplied specially at a meter charge of 4*d.* per thousand gallons. For purposes of general comparison with other cities it may be well to state that Glasgow furnishes 40,000,000 gallons of water per day at an average remuneration for all branches of the service of about one American cent for every 200 gallons.

The income of the works in a recent year was more than $800,000, of which, in round sums, $160,000 was derived from the domestic rate inside the municipal limits, $160,000 from the larger domestic rate charged outside the boundaries, $420,000 from the trade supply, and $60,000 from the public rate levied to pay for municipal consumption. The large revenue from the trade supply is noteworthy, as far exceeding that of any other British town. The total expenditure of the department was $600,000, and a net revenue of $200,000 was therefore earned, all of which was applied to the sinking-fund.

Reduction of water-rates.

Revenues and expenditures.

The total capital expenditure up to date is approximately $14,000,000, about one fourth of which represents the debts of the old water-companies assumed by the corporation, and three fourths represents the cost of the new system as finally completed. As against this great outlay, a sinking-fund begun in 1871 has now grown to $3,000,000. Thus, with steadily declining water-taxes, it has been found possible to meet current expenses, including interest, and to pay off about two per cent. of the capital outlay every year. The duplication of the works — *i. e.*, the construction of a second aqueduct and an additional great storage reservoir near the city, with embankments at Loch Katrine which will nearly double its storage capacity — will have cost from $5,000,000 to $6,000,000; but this outlay can be met without increasing charges or taxes by a single penny. The corporation will have nearly a month's supply in its reservoirs, which are 300 feet above the general level of the town and seven miles distant.

CHAP. IV.

Cost of works and debt-payment.

In remarks upon the fire service I have mentioned the great saving of expense due to the immense gravity pressure in the water-pipes. This saving is estimated as equal to more than a fair interest charge upon the entire cost of the Loch Katrine works, or perhaps $250,000 a year. Competent authorities also estimate the yearly saving to the people of Glasgow in the two items of tea and soap as equal to an amount at least quite as large. The Loch Katrine water is almost wholly free from solutions of mineral ingredients, and doubtless its softness results indirectly in very large economic gains. On the other hand, its lack of bone-making material is said to have resulted in much deformity among the children of the poor — a charge that I have not investigated, but regard with skepticism. One of the latest of the

Economic advantages of Loch Katrine water.

I.— 8*

CHAP. IV.

Municipal
hydraulic-
power works.

innovations of the Water Department has been the construction of a great establishment, at a cost of several hundred thousand dollars, known as the "Hydraulic Power Works," for the purpose of supplying water under high pressure as a motive power for elevators, hoists, light machinery, etc. These works, of course, distribute power through a distinct set of pipes. With electric power for distribution also, from its new electrical works, Glasgow will in the early future derive a considerable revenue from this function.

Organization
of Water
Department.

The entire council is constituted a Board of Water Commissioners by Parliament, and a large committee, divided into subcommittees on works and finance, has active supervision. The executive organization separates the financial from the engineering administration, an engineer and his staff having full charge of the works, while a treasurer and his staff have the entire management of the money affairs of the department. This separation of works and finance, quite universal in British municipal government, acts as an excellent check.

Municipal
assumption
of gas-sup-
ply.

Having made the waterworks a grand success, having next begun a corporation park system, and then a consolidated market system (to both of which I shall subsequently refer), and having entered vigorously and hopefully upon the sanitary and city improvement schemes already described, Glasgow was prepared in 1869 to undertake another large municipal enterprise. In that year, after much difficulty in adjusting the details of the arrangement, the gas-supply of the city was transferred from private hands to the corporation, to be managed by the council as an ordinary department. The original cost exceeded $2,600,000. Twenty-five years of management by the authorities has

given unmitigated satisfaction to all the citizens of
Glasgow. The quantity of gas sold had increased
from 1,026,000,000 feet in 1869–70, the corporation's
first year, to 3,126,000,000 in 1890–91, an increase of
170 per cent., while the population supplied had grown
only perhaps 25 or 30 per cent. In 1869–70 the amount
manufactured was 20 per cent. greater than the amount
sold or accounted for. Careful management has reduced this amount of leakage to about 10 per cent.
More than 140,000 meters are in use ; and as it is not
the policy of the corporation to charge its customers
for more than they actually receive, it is inevitable.
that there should be a considerable percentage of loss
in delivery. From $1.14 per thousand feet, which was
charged consumers in 1869–70, the corporation has
been able to make reductions year by year until for
several recent years the price has been fixed at 60
cents. No one will claim that a private company
would have made these reductions while continuing
to supply a satisfactory quality of gas, especially in
view of the fact that the price of gas-making coal has
greatly increased.

Yet the department has been able to construct new
works (it now owns four immense establishments),
pay its interest charges and running expenses, write
off large sums every year for depreciation of works,
pipes, and meters, and accumulate a sinking-fund
easily capable of paying off capital indebtedness as it
matures. The total indebtedness was at the highest
point in 1875, when it reached $5,300,000. The net
debt is now reduced to about $2,400,000, which is very
much more than covered, of course, by the value of
the plant. Whatever competition gas as an illuminant may have to face in the future, the Glasgow corporation works have reached a point of perfect financial security.

CHAP. IV.

Social policy
in public gas-
supply.

In the rather gloomy winter climate of Glasgow, which necessitates a large use of artificial light, cheap gas in all the tenements however humble, and in every passageway, is an inestimable blessing; and the more than doubling of the per capita use, under the city's management of the works, means a vast increase in comfort and happiness that defies statistical expression. Great wisdom and humanity have been shown, therefore, in the policy of smaller earnings and a less rapid debt-payment for the sake of a more rapid reduction of the charge to consumers, and a more rapid growth of the total consumption. These considerations of the general good which dominate the public control of such services as those of light and water can have only small weight in the counsels of a private money-making corporation; and herein lies perhaps the most fundamental reason for the municipal assumption of such functions. No other city in the world, at least outside of Scotland, can at all compare with Glasgow in the universality of the use of gas in the homes of the working-classes.

It remains to speak of the recent experiment of the Glasgow Gas Department in supplying gas cooking-stoves, either selling them at about cost price, or renting them at a moderate charge by the year, half-year, or quarter. To understand the local application of this experiment, it is necessary to recur to the fact that fully 70 per cent. of the people of Glasgow live in houses of one or two rooms, using the same fire for cooking and heating, but spending as little as possible

Encouraging
use of gas as
a fuel.

for mere heat during eight months of the year. All these houses are fitted with gas for illumination. An immense saving would be effected by the use of gas for cooking, besides the consideration of comfort in the summer months when fires for heating are not an object; and these same considerations apply to a majority of the families living in more than two rooms. The city recovers in rents a fair interest and depreciation charge on its investment in stoves, and is at the same time extending the market for its gas.   Since 1885 this business has gone on briskly, the city having a large sum invested in stoves.   During the year 1887–1888 there were sold 1193 heating and cooking appliances, and 1465 were rented.   In 1892 the department had more than 8000 gas-stoves of its own on hire in the tenement-houses, and had in the preceding seven years sold many thousands.   This is not to be deemed a permanent feature of the Gas Department, but merely a passing bit of semi-commercial, semi-philanthropic enterprise, to stimulate the use of gas as fuel in the abodes of the poor.

A transient propaganda.

The Glasgow authorities evidently look forward to a time when the use of electricity as an illuminant will to some extent supersede the demand for gas.   Accordingly they propose to develop the local practice of using gas as a fuel.   So inevitable is the very general use of gas stoves and furnaces in the early future that no possible extension of the use of electricity for lighting purposes can render gas making and distributing plants superfluous.   Meanwhile, the municipal authorities of Glasgow have determined to monopolize the business of distributing electric light and power from central establishments.   They obtained powers from Parliament in 1890 to undertake electric lighting.   In 1892 they bought out an existing private company, and in 1893 they opened a large municipal plant, in the heart of the city, for supplying arc and incandescent lights to private consumers as well as to streets and public buildings.   The experiment is deemed satisfactory thus far, and this enterprise, which is under the management of the Gas Department, promises to have a great development in the early future.

Establishment of an electric-light plant.

Some remarks upon the sewerage may perhaps be
well introduced at this point.   Glasgow has not until
lately been so far advanced in its drainage system as
in many other respects.   Its streets had been well provided with ordinary sewers, but there were no main
conduits or intercepting sewers.   The street-drains discharged their offensive material at frequent intervals
into the Clyde on both sides.   The dredging operations,
which had given deep water and brought a considerable tidal movement up as far as Glasgow, had made
it possible to continue a system which otherwise would
have become absolutely intolerable long ago.   There
was no clear proof, it is true, that the discharge of
millions of gallons of sewage daily into the river was
seriously detrimental to public health, although the
stream was made horribly filthy, and its banks were
most malodorous.   For forty years the authorities
had been considering the question of the ultimate disposal of sewage; and at length, in 1892, a practical
step was taken.   Glasgow is not so situated as to make
the sewage-farm plan a feasible one for the disposition of liquid filth, and it became evident, as experiments in other British and continental cities were
studied, that some system of separation of the solid
ingredients by the aid of chemicals, and with filtration works, would have to be adopted.   In 1894 Glasgow completed, at a cost of half a million dollars, one
of the most perfectly arranged establishments of this
character that modern ingenuity has yet devised.

The sewer system of the eastern part of the town has
been reconstructed, and the mains which carry off the
refuse from portions of the city occupied by nearly
300,000 people have been made to converge at one
point of outfall, on the river bank, up-stream from the
harbor, where the municipality has acquired about
thirty acres of ground.   The works erected thereon

are too elaborate for description in detail. Something, however, should be said, because this new system at Glasgow is representative of what numerous
European cities are now adopting, in pursuance of
one of the most imperative functions that modern
cities recognize, that of sewer-drainage and a disposition of the sewage. The inflowing sewage is received in great vats, where skilful mechanisms skim
off bits of wood and floating substances, and also appropriate the pebbles and heavy ingredients that sink
readily. The inky fluid then passes on through a
channel in which it is treated with milk of lime and
a solution of sulphate of alumina, to assist in the separation and precipitation of the solid ingredients. It
rests for perhaps half an hour in a series of precipitation-tanks, then flows in shallow sheets across the
floors of a series of aëration-tanks. The sludge that
settles in the precipitation-tanks is dropped through
valves into a passageway underneath, and is carried
to several "sludge rams" worked by compressed air,
which in turn force it into a number of powerful
"sludge presses," which squeeze all the remaining
water out of it, and deliver solid cakes of sludge by
shutes directly into railway freight-wagons, standing
on the tracks below. These manurial sludge-cakes
are carried by rail out to the city's extensive new
farm, where fodder is to be raised for the municipal horseflesh that belongs to the Cleansing Department and to the Street Railway Department.
Meanwhile, the comparatively clean water from the
precipitation and aëration tanks is carried to a series
of filter basins. Part of these basins is filled with
gas coke, which, when it has become too foul for further use in that way, is removed and consumed as fuel
for the boilers which make steam to supply the great
engines of the establishment. The other filters are

CHAP. IV.

Chemical treatment.

Compression of "sludge."

Sludge as a fertilizer.

The filter basins.

of stones and sand, on the general pattern that has become approved for purposes of water-purification. From these filters the water passes, clean and innocuous, into the Clyde. Thus the pure water from Loch Katrine, having served its purposes and become foul in use and laden with refuse, and having passed into the sewers, is made to undergo a process that permits its effluence into the Clyde almost as free from foreign ingredients, and quite as odorless, as when it left its cloud-compassed source in the Highlands. This is the modern ideal. Sewage-farms will accomplish that ideal best and least expensively where the situation favors that method. Otherwise such a plan as this which Glasgow has adopted is the satisfactory one. At present it is not a large proportion of the city's total sewage that Glasgow purifies in that manner. But the existing works can readily and at small expense be enlarged to a capacity equal to nearly half the total discharge; and it will doubtless be the council's decision at an early day to provide for the rest by building another precipitation-plant below the city. No very profitable use can be made of the sludge-cakes, but it is calculated that they will at least pay for the cost of their removal to farming land. The purification of the harbor is an object worth the expense that sewage-purification entails on the ratepayers. Indeed, the cost of constantly dredging a fouled harbor is itself equal to a large proportion of the expense of a perfect separation system.

Purifying
the harbor.

Public works
and the con-
tract system.

A city which assumes so many things on its own account might have been expected to undertake the direct construction of its public works. But this would have been foreign to English and Scotch ideas of business propriety. The contract system is universal,— or has been until lately. Every piece of new paving or

sewer-work is let out on contract to the lowest responsible bidder; and while the Glasgow authorities
see no objection to owning and operating common
lodging-houses, tenement-houses, public wash-houses,
markets, slaughter-houses, and assembly-halls, they
would unanimously condemn the suggestion that the
city go into the building business and erect its own
establishments. The English and Scotch working-
men had seemed never to find the contract system
obnoxious, as their American brethren had. Nor until a very recent day have municipal contracts ever
attempted to protect the workmen by clauses pre-
scribing maximum hours and minimum wages. The
master of works and his men have looked out for the
interests of the ratepayers only. They prepare the
plans and specifications, and they carefully inspect the
work as it progresses. It should be added, however,
that since 1890 there has grown up, especially in London, a strong movement for direct municipal employment as against all forms of public contracting.

Streets and paving, sewers, buildings for the fire,
police, sanitation, city-improvement, park, market,
and other departments, and municipal constructions of
various kinds, are designed in the office of the "Master of Public Works and City Architect," and carried
out under the supervision of himself and his staff. In
the English towns this officer would be called "borough surveyor," and in America he would be the
"city engineer," although the Glasgow master of
works has a rather larger scope than corresponding
officials in the United States. The recent incumbent,
Mr. John Carrick, was a very distinguished man among
British architects and civil engineers, and he had held
his office for forty years or more. Probably no man in
the world occupying a like post has planned and carried out a larger amount of solid public work than

Mr. Carrick. He had as his assistants three competent architects, five civil engineers, a large out-of-door
staff of inspectors for buildings, sewers, pavements,
etc., and an indoor staff of draftsmen and clerks.

Street-
paving.   Glasgow paving is nearly all of granite blocks. There
is some wood and some asphalt in use, but neither of
these materials is well suited to the climatic conditions. Granite is cheap in Scotland, and a well-laid
pavement resting on a foundation of concrete is practically indestructible. Mr. Carrick once told me that a
redressing of the surface after ten years' use, with a
shortening of the blocks by 10 per cent, would make
the pavement as good as new for another ten years,
and so on. For current repairs of streets and sewers,
the city of course keeps its own force of workmen.

Absence of
jobbery.   Glasgow has been so fortunate as almost wholly to
escape scandals and imputations of jobbery in the letting of contracts for public works; and the one or
two instances in which vague charges have led to investigation, have only served to vindicate the honesty
and sound business character of the department. The
works as a whole are admirable for suitability of design and solidity of construction.

"Better-
ment" prin-
ciple not in
use.   As regards the financial side of street, sewer, and
bridge making, the whole expense is defrayed from a
public levy on what is known as the "statute labor"
account. In the good old days the statutes of the
realm required every man to turn out and do his share
of work upon the highways. So far as the cities are
concerned, the old requirement has been converted
into a money tax. The special assessment plan for
paving and sewerage is not in use,—although in Glasgow, as all over Great Britain, there has arisen a demand for the adoption in city improvement works of
a familiar American principle known in England as
"betterment,"—i. e., the principle of charging all or

part of a public improvement, such as a sewer, a pavement, a sidewalk, a bridge, or a park, against property directly benefited. "Betterment" will carry the day.

A magnificent municipal building has recently been completed, at a cost of about $2,250,000, with office accommodations for the various departments, which had previously been scattered.

In all of Glasgow's municipal experiences, I find nothing so likely to interest city authorities elsewhere as that which relates to street railways. It is an experience which may well make American cities blush for their own short-sightedness. Street railways, or "tram lines" as they are generally called in Great Britain, were an American invention, and the first ones in London and some other English towns were constructed by American companies. It was none other than that enterprising American citizen George Francis Train who first proposed to build tram lines in Glasgow. Having laid a line in London and another in Birkenhead, Mr. Train undertook in 1861–62 to get parliamentary authority to begin operations in Glasgow. His bill was opposed by the city authorities, who intercepted him by inserting in a bill then pending for the increase of the city's powers in other directions a clause giving the council power to lay tram lines. The new power was not utilized, however, and in 1869–70 two syndicates, one or both being of American origin, again promoted bills in Parliament for power to invade the Glasgow streets with a horse-railway system. Again the authorities were aroused, and the result was a compromise all around. It was agreed that the city should keep the control of its streets, any part of which it was so unwilling to surrender, and that it should construct and own the tram lines, while the two syndicates were to unite in one company and work the lines on a lease. The first lines were opened in 1872, and the lease then made was to terminate in 1894. By its terms the company

Terms of operating lease.

was required to pay to the corporation (1) the annual interest charge on the full amount of the city's investment, (2) a yearly sum for a sinking-fund large enough to clear the entire cost of the lines at the expiration of the lease, (3) a renewal fund of 4 per cent. per annum on the cost of the lines, out of which they were to be kept in proper condition and restored to the city in perfect order and entirely as good as new in 1894, and (4) a yearly rental of $750 per street mile. Such were the money conditions of the lease; and certainly the city's interests were well looked after. But, mean-

Low fares and favorable conditions.

while, the interests of the public as passengers were equally well secured. First, it was provided that in no case should the charges exceed a penny per mile. This, it should be remembered, was at a time when fares were nowhere else less than 2*d*. Further, the parliamentary act described a number of important "runs,"—those most likely to be used by laboring men and large masses of population, several of them considerably exceeding a mile,—and specified that

Working-men's half-penny fares.

one penny should be the charge for these, and that morning and evening cars should be run for working-men at half price, equal to one American cent.

The company which accepted these remarkable terms took advantage of a passing mania for investment in tramways, and sold the lease to a new company of

Experiences of the leasing company.

local capitalists for a premium of about $750,000. This new company experienced hard times for two or three years; for besides running expenses, interest upon the capital invested in the business, and the heavy payments on the four accounts to the corporation, there was the burden of the enormous premium to carry. Not until 1875–76 did it begin to pay its stock-

holders dividends.   After 1880, however, the business
flourished, and dividends averaging 10 per cent. were
paid, after writing off each year a due proportion of
the unfortunate premium charge.

The city was so compact—covering, as I have said,
only 6111 acres of ground before the extension of
1891—that a large mileage of tramways was not to be
expected.   The total of 31 miles at that time served
the public very well, the system providing continuous
lines across the city from north to south and from
east to west, with convenient access from the center
to almost every outlying neighborhood.   In arranging the system originally, just at the time when the
great improvement scheme was fairly begun, the
authorities had in mind a service that would help
them to relieve the central congestion of population
and would aid in the symmetrical development of the
city.   To this end they wished to build certain additional lines that did not seem to the operating company to promise immediate profits.   The system as
scheduled by the act of Parliament embraced about
17 miles of lines, and the city found that it had no
authority under its lease to compel the company to
work additional lines on the same conditions.   A
compromise was made by which the company agreed
to pay the interest and the renewal-cost upon the new
lines, and was relieved from rental and sinking-fund
charges.   This was perfectly fair under the circumstances.

The total capital investment of the city had been
a little more than $1,700,000, interest charges upon
which were paid by the company.   On the 1st of July,
1894, the sinking-fund, provided by the company, had
reached somewhat more than $1,000,000, paying the
full cost of the original system.   There remained the
cost of the newer lines, some 14 miles in extent.   The

I.—9

CHAP. IV.

Failure of negotiations for a new lease.

Municipal operation decided upon.

Unsuccessful negotiations for old plant.

renewal fund had left the system in perfect repair. The city had received in rental money a sum amounting to about $225,000. As for the company, it had paid off its premium incubus, had earned good dividends, and had made due allowance for depreciation in the value of its working plant.

It was expected that when the time came for making a new arrangement, the old company would be granted a further lease, on terms still more favorable to the city treasury and to the general public, and that after 1894 the tramways of Glasgow would yield a large municipal income. But tedious negotiations resulted in a total failure to reach any agreement with the company; and during the progress of these negotiations there began to be heard among the citizens a very distinct demand for the experiment of direct municipal operation of the lines. This demand grew to the point of practical unanimity on the part of the community, and the council, having obtained due authority from Parliament, voted to obey the popular will. It was then expected that the stables, cars, horses, and total operating plant could be purchased from the retiring company. But a new difficulty arose. The tramways committee of the council required from the company a promise not to engage in the operation of omnibus lines in competition with the municipal street-cars, in case the city should take over the company's existing plant at a fair valuation. The company refused to make this agreement, and negotiations were broken off. It was then determined by the council, with the very general approbation of the citizens, to proceed upon its own methods to create a working plant, and to have everything in readiness to begin operations on July 1, 1894.

The first and most important step was the selection of a general manager. Mr. John Young, who had

since 1875 rendered such rare service as the head of
the Cleansing Department, was appointed to the new
post. With an energetic and able committee of the
council behind him, Mr. Young proceeded rapidly to
assemble the elements of the most complete and well-
devised horse-railway system in the United Kingdom.
Nine large stations, at a total cost of $500,000, were
constructed in different parts of the city as car barns,
stables, etc., all of them being built with particular
reference to the early abandonment of horses and
the use of cable and electric systems. Mr. Young
invented an improved type of cars, and several hundred of them were built on short notice. He purchased three thousand fine horses and trained them
for their work, and engaged thirteen hundred men of
unusual intelligence and fitness. In connection with
the stations Mr. Young established car-building and
repair shops, harness-making shops, and other ad-
juncts to a complete and economical organization.
There was much disappointment expressed in Glasgow because it was not found expedient to mark the
municipalization of the street passenger service by
the introduction of improved mechanical motive
power, in place of horses. But there had been too
little time in which to determine upon the best mechanical system, and it was therefore deemed safest
to begin with " horse haulage" and to transform the
lines gradually. There was much discussion of the
question what rates of fare should be fixed. A uniform penny fare had many strong advocates. But it
was finally decided to divide the lines into half-mile
stages and to charge a halfpenny (equal to one
American cent) for each stage. It should be remembered that Glasgow is exceedingly compact, and that
the bulk of the patronage of the tramways comes
from passengers riding less than a mile. It is be-

Chap. IV.

Creation of a
new munici-
pal plant.

Question of
motive
power.

Question of
fares.

lieved that the halfpenny fare for short rides will add a large element of patronage that the uniform penny rate would have missed.   Experience alone can settle the question whether the new rates will be as advantageous as was expected.   After a few weeks of trial it was found advisable, without altering the basis of the system of halfpenny fares, to fix certain long penny "runs" especially for working-men.

Shorter hours for employees.

The lessee company had kept its drivers and conductors at their posts for long hours — often not less than fourteen, twelve being the minimum.   The new municipal management makes a ten-hour day, and fixes a satisfactory schedule of wages.

Success of this new municipal department.

The service was begun on July 1, 1894, with success and high prestige, and with every prospect of proving beneficial to the community and lucrative to the public treasury.   Some extensions of the lines were at once begun, and preparations were also set on foot for the early use of cables on several routes.   Provision was made for the electric lighting of the cars, and in every detail it was determined to give Glasgow, under direct municipal operation, the best surface-transit system in Great Britain.   The experiment can but be observed with the greatest attention and interest by municipal authorities everywhere.

Competition of other transit systems.

Municipal tramways in Glasgow will have to meet the competition of a very elaborate system of omnibuses established by the retiring tramway company, which was left with a great plant on its hands and with plenty of experience and ability.   At the time of the assumption of transit as a municipal function, moreover, there were approaching completion certain lines of underground road to connect with the great railway stations and to provide quick transit across the city ; and it was inevitable that the operation of the underground system should affect somewhat the future of the surface lines. But these considerations had full weight with the council, whose members were broad enough in their views to perceive that the provision of varied and ample means of cheap transit for the people was a far greater desideratum than the making of large profits out of the working of a municipal monopoly.

Of market arrangements in ancient Glasgow I shall have nothing to say, but shall begin with 1865, when by act of Parliament the market management was consolidated and vested in the city council as a "market trust." At present the city owns and controls (1) a great central fruit and produce market in which practically all of the commission and wholesale business of Glasgow in these lines of trade is carried on, and above which is a very large public hall, let by the authorities for concerts and various gatherings. This market is a time-honored institution, and has always been called the "Bazaar." It should, perhaps, be explained that there are no "truck" or retail markets in Glasgow, the small business all being done in the shops. (2) The fish-market is an important establishment, through which several hundred thousands of boxes and barrels of white fish, haddocks, and herrings pass every year. (3) An interesting novelty is the "old clothes market," a great building full of stalls occupied by dealers in second-hand clothing for men, women, and children, in old hats, old shoes, and all sorts of cast-off articles. Undoubtedly its bargains are a blessing to the poor. But far more important than these are (4) the cattle-market, (5) the dead-meat market, (6) the public slaughter-houses, and (7) the great yards and abattoirs at the docks for foreign cattle. In a central and convenient locality the authorities have a tract of twenty acres or more, occu-

I.— 9*

pied with a great roofed live-stock market, having accommodations for many thousands of animals. Adjoining on one side is a separate market for dressed beef, etc., and on the other side are very extensive slaughter-houses. All the trading in live animals in Glasgow — *i.e.*, in native British animals — is done in this cattle-market, and from 400,000 to 500,000 cattle, sheep, etc., pass through it annually. The dead-meat market was established in 1876, when American dressed beef began to arrive in large quantities, as a center of supply for the retail meat-shops. The importation of dressed meat has expanded remarkably since 1888, and the meat-shops have learned to buy dressed meat rather than live animals. So this great market for

"carcasses" maintains an increasing activity. All slaughtering in Glasgow is done in the public municipal slaughter-houses, there being two large establishments in other quarters of the city, besides the one adjoining the cattle-market. Of necessity these places are extensive and well appointed, and it is sufficient here to say that an exceedingly low charge is made for each animal slaughtered. More than a quarter of a million animals are slaughtered in them annually. In addition to these, there is at the docks an extensive establishment exclusively for the reception and slaughter of beeves from the United States, provision existing for the treatment of two thousand at a time. The annual importation of these cattle is about 40,000 head, all of which must be slaughtered at the docks as a precaution against contagious disease. For Canadian cattle, a similar number of which are imported, there is ample provision made by the city authorities on the opposite side of the harbor. The Canadian animals are presumed to be healthy, and many of them go to the farms to be fattened.

The Sanitary Department and the Markets Depart-

ment coöperate in measures for the protection of the
public health against unsuitable food; and the control of slaughter-houses and of flesh, fish, and produce
marts by the municipal authorities is deemed a point
of great advantage.

The city has market property valued at about $1,200,-
000, not including the dock cattle-yards and abattoirs;
and the indebtedness of the market account is perhaps
$700,000.   The income of the market trust from ren-
tals, slaughter-house fees, etc., is $100,000 per annum,
and the total expenditure, including both interest and
sinking-fund, comes well within that amount.   So
that the markets undertaking is, incidentally, a source
of net revenue.

Until 1860 the people of Glasgow had never been
taxed for the purchase or maintenance of public parks.
The " Glasgow Green " on the river bank, a fine tract
of 136 acres, which had been the town commons from
time immemorial, sufficed until that date.   But the
demand for a park in newer Glasgow at the west end,
and the acquisition by legacy of the beginnings of a
public art-gallery, led to the securing of legislation
which constituted the city council a "parks and galleries trust."   The West-end or Kelvinside Park was
thereupon acquired; and some years later, as a sort
of offset, the Queen's Park south of the Clyde was
opened, and the Alexandra Park at the east end,
created by the improvement trust, was given over
for management to the parks administration.   Kel-
vingrove has 80 acres, twenty of the 100 acres originally purchased having been platted and sold on
advantageous terms.   The Queen's Park, of 141 acres,
is an excellent instance of financiering.   The original
purchase was 245 acres, and the sales for residence-
sites have more than paid for the park.   Lands sold

in like manner adjoining Alexandra Park (which contains 85 acres), or lands still held for sale, will more
than repay the cost of this public pleasure-ground.
More recently the parks trust has acquired Cathkin
Braes, a 50-acre tract four miles from the city, and
the years 1890–94 have been remarkable for the development of the park system in many ways. A number
of squares and several old churchyards have also recently become park property; so that Glasgow has,
although tardily, accomplished a good deal in the
important direction of providing small open spaces.
But a great deal more ought to be done for a population of 800,000 which sorely needs playgrounds for

children and recreation space for adults. The policy
of providing playgrounds has now been entered upon
in a practical manner, and will have much to show by
1900. Lands held by the parks trust for sale or
"feuing" will ultimately more than pay the outstanding total indebtedness of about $1,250,000. At
present a rate of twopence in the £ is levied for maintenance of parks, museums, and galleries.

Bequests of two very important private collections
of paintings by old masters, to which additions have
been made by numerous minor bequests and by moderate purchases, have given the corporation of Glas-

gow a picture-gallery which, though somewhat lacking
in the elements of popularity, has educational and historical value of a high order, and which, when properly
displayed in a suitable building and reinforced by
purchases of modern works, will be recognized as one
of the notable art museums of Europe. In Kelvin-
grove Park the corporation has also a museum building containing various collections of antiquities and
of objects illustrating industrial processes and the
natural sciences. Municipal encouragement is aiding
a rapid growth of popular interest in art and science.

Glasgow is now the only important town in Great Britain that has refused to avail itself of the advantages offered by the Free Libraries Act. That act, it may be well to explain, gave town councils the authority to establish public libraries and support them by a tax limited to one penny in the £ of assessed rental valuation, provided the act were adopted by a majority vote of the ratepayers. The matter has been submitted to the voters of Glasgow at three different times — the last plebiscite being in April, 1888, when of 89,000 persons entitled to vote, 13,500 cast their ballots in favor of the act, 23,000 voted against it, and 52,500 did not take enough interest to vote at all. Glasgow has led the other English and Scotch towns in most matters of municipal enterprise, but it lags behind quite unaccountably in respect to libraries. Fortunately, public-spirited citizens have done something to supply the lack. The Stirling Library, founded by a small bequest in 1792, and governed by trustees composed of the lord provost, a committee of the council, and representatives of several other permanent Glasgow bodies, is free to the public as a reference collection and contains about 50,000 volumes. Managed in connection with it is the Baillie Library, recently opened, supported by a fund of nearly $100,000 bequeathed by a Glasgow lawyer. Still larger and more catholic in its character and objects is the Mitchell Free Library, founded by a merchant and town-councilor, who bequeathed $350,000 for that purpose. It has been open since 1878, and has received other important gifts of books and money, so that it has already accumulated 100,000 volumes, having made a progress in its first decade that has hardly been paralleled by any other library in the world. Without large funds, and hampered by most inadequate temporary quarters, the zeal of the coun-

Chap. IV.

Refusal to adopt Free Libraries Act.

The Stirling Library.

The Mitchell Library.

cil committee on libraries, and the indefatigable efforts of the wise and accomplished librarian, Mr. Barrett, who has held that post from the outset, performed great things. In 1891 a removal to adequate quarters began a new era for this excellent institution. The Mitchell Library's periodical room, containing 300 or more current publications, is the completest in Great Britain for practical use, and is crowded with readers. In this and the Stirling collections, Glasgow possesses the nucleus of a magnificent public library. Mr. Barrett is in hearty accord with the best American ideas of library administration, and he would make the library a true people's university. His ideal for Glasgow is a central library with ten branches, each having reference, loan, news-room, and lecture-room departments; and he assures me that with the coöperation of the existing foundations, the penny rate allowed by the Free Libraries Act would accomplish it all. It is certainly to be hoped that some means can be found to placate the hostile shop-keeping element which has hitherto defeated the act because it means more rates to pay.

A proposed municipal library system.

Poor relief and education.

Poor-relief and public education are not in the United Kingdom made functions of municipal corporations, but are intrusted to distinct elective local bodies. None the less it may fairly fall within the scope of this résumé to state briefly how the people of Glasgow provide for these two extremely important objects. In a word, let me say that Scotland, urban as well as rural, is divided into parishes, each of which has an elective board that levies poor-rates, dispenses relief, and has entire charge of the indigent; while elementary education in Scotland is now universal and compulsory under the management of elective school-boards, school taxes being collected

by the several parish authorities, although the jurisdiction of the Glasgow School Board extends over the
entire city. A magnificent array of public-school
buildings has appeared in Glasgow since 1873. Indeed it would not be easy to name any other city in
the English-speaking world that has within a period of
twenty years created so complete a "plant" for the
work of elementary education. In the old times, parish schools and private schools were the rule in Glasgow as well as throughout Scotland. How the facilities provided by the Glasgow School Board have
gained in favor may be shown through a few summary figures. In 1881 the enrolment in public
schools was 37,263, in Roman Catholic schools 13,-
864, and in all other schools 19,680. In 1890 the
numbers were 65,306 in the public schools, 15,354 in
the Catholic schools, and 5739 in all others. The
non-Catholic private and church schools are rapidly
giving way before the superiority of the schools provided by the public board. As I have explained in a
previous chapter, the Glasgow School Board is composed of fifteen members, elected on general ticket
by the whole city every three years, the voters having
the privilege of cumulating their votes; that is to
say, the elector may give one vote apiece to fifteen
candidates, may give fifteen votes to one candidate,
or may distribute his fifteen votes in any way he likes
among any number of candidates between one and
fifteen. The result in Glasgow has been satisfactory.
The board is widely representative, has the public
confidence, and has been able to proceed boldly and
brilliantly with its work.

Pupils' fees are the rule in British public schools;
but inasmuch as school attendance is compulsory, it is
obvious that there can be no enforcement of fees as
against the very poor. There is a close relationship

Growth of
the Glas-
gow public
schools.

Election of
School
Board.

between the School Board of Glasgow and the Boards of Guardians of the Poor; and it is a part of the duty of these guardians to pay the school fees of all children whose parents are indigent.   With Glasgow's great density, and its close commingling in the same neighborhoods of all classes of people, it would not be practically feasible to attempt to instruct all children, rich and poor, in the same rooms.   An ingenious provision in the fixing of tuition fees affords a practical classification of pupils.   Accessible in every district are schools having the same quality of instruction, and the same advantages in all particulars, but having three very different scales of tuition charge.   The wealthier classes, as a rule, patronize the higher priced schools, and thus keep their children from contact with the children of poverty.   There is nothing in the system to prevent a poor man from sending his child to the school that exacts high fees if he chooses to pay the difference, and *vice versa*. The system would not be approved in America, nor would it be feasible in rural communities.   But it is a practical success in Glasgow, and it has given the public-school system a leverage against the private schools that could never have been gained by any other means.   The higher fees that the richer children pay go toward the maintenance of the system as a whole, and do not procure any superior facilities. Pupils' fees do not raise a large proportion of the sum needed to support the schools, and since 1889 they have been greatly reduced.   Thus in 1890 the levy of school-rates by the board procured a revenue of £77,-000, and from the annual grants made by the general government £70,000 was received, while from pupils' fees there accrued only £27,000.   In the period from 1881 to 1891 the board expended £500,000 ($2,500,000) of borrowed money for new buildings.

Classification by means of fees.

School finances.

The public authorities of Glasgow realize the modern necessity of technical education that shall at once help to sustain the great industries that are the mainstay of the community, and help young men to enter upon the means of a livelihood without abandoning their native city.   A number of older institutions have been amalgamated under the name of "The Glasgow and West of Scotland Technical College," governed by a board of thirty trustees, of whom the town council names several, while others are appointed by the school-board, the Glasgow University, the engineers and ship-builders, the Trades' House, the Merchants' House, and other permanent and representative bodies. The scientific and technical evening classes of this great institution have a total attendance of some three thousand young men, most of whom are apprentices or working artisans.   The day classes have also a considerable attendance.   The institution is made directly promotive of the ship-building, chemical, and textile industries of the Clyde valley.

I am tempted to devote some consideration to the work of poor-relief in Glasgow,— to the methods and results of that branch of local administration which taxes most heavily the resources of the community. But I have elsewhere explained the mode of creation of the boards that administer the poor-law in three separate Glasgow districts or parishes; and there is, perhaps, nothing sufficiently distinctive in their management of poor-houses and infirmaries, their conduct of insane asylums, and their dispensation of outdoor relief to require a detailed account.   It is enough to say that the practical success attained by the competent and faithful administrators of the poor-law is more worthy of praise than the system itself, and that it will be a distinct gain when the care of the poor becomes a direct municipal function.   It should

Chap. IV.

Provision
for technical
education.

The care of
the poor.

be added that Scotland will undoubtedly have extended to it, with the least possible delay, the popularization of the poor-law system that was embodied in the Local Government Act of 1894 for England and Wales. That act abolishes plural voting and makes any citizen, male or female, eligible for membership on the poor-law boards. It will in due time, doubtless, be followed by legislation that will wholly or in part assimilate the administration of poor-relief with other tasks of local government.

I have only to add to this exposition of the development of the Glasgow municipality some brief remarks upon the work of a special municipal agency to which, more than to anything else, the greatness of Glasgow is due, and which promises by its untiring energy and great resources to bring Glasgow at the end of the nineteenth century to the position of a commercial and manufacturing community of a million inhabitants. It is to the department known as the "Navigation," or more precisely as the "Clyde Navigation Trust," that I have reference. The beginnings of Clyde improvement under the auspices of the town council date back to 1750. The greatest shipyards of the world now line the banks of a stream that was readily fordable in those days; and indeed it is said that there are residents of Glasgow who still remember the stream in that condition. The original management of the deepening projects by the council was subsequently altered in such a way as to admit to the board of Clyde-navigation trustees certain representatives elected directly by the shipping interests and by the larger taxpayers of Glasgow. The provost and council are, however, *ex officio* the dominating element, and the management of the harbor must be regarded as a municipal enterprise, credit for its magnificent success being accorded to the munici-

pality. The revenues of the trust are derived chiefly
from certain harbor charges known as tonnage dues,
goods dues, and crane dues. Everything pertaining
to the harbor is a part of the monopoly of this municipal board. The supply of ships with water; the
service of harbor tramways; the use of graving-docks;
the rentals of weighing-scales, of cranes, and of various yards and offices,— all contribute to the revenues.
A remarkable and interesting service of ferries and
harbor steamers, operated directly by the trust, has
been found both convenient for the public and finan-
cially profitable. The number of passengers trans-
ported is about 15,000,000 annually. Possibly it was
the city's success as a common carrier on the harbor
that had much to do with the readiness of the Glasgow public to entrust the general tramway system to
direct municipal management. From all sources, the
annual revenue of the Clyde trustees is from $1,750,-
000 to $2,000,000. Much of this sum goes to pay in-
terest on the large indebtedness of the trust; but the
revenue is ample enough to justify the constant development of great projects. Thus within the past few
years millions have been spent in the construction of
new docks; and a further general deepening of the
entire river, to keep pace with the increasing draft
and size of steamships, is now in progress. At the
present rate of improvement, it will not be long before
the accounts of the trust will show that $100,000,000
has been expended, since the beginning, in its improvement works. So courageous an investment has
deserved the great results that have accrued from it.
Without it, Glasgow would have remained a small
inland town. It must always stand as the most striking example in the history of municipalities of a
greatness achieved by deliberate purpose in the face
of extraordinary difficulties. The Clyde improvement

project was the initial one in a series of brave municipal undertakings that in my opinion render Glasgow the most praiseworthy of all modern cities.

All municipal taxation in British cities takes the form of rates levied upon the rental value of occupied lands and buildings. In Glasgow the rates are divided between owners and occupiers in a manner which

could not be described without entering into much detail. The general financial position of the municipality is excellent. Its debt is not formidably large, and most of it is potentially covered by the growing sinking-funds of prosperous and productive departments. The numerous undertakings of the municipality, far from imposing heavier burdens upon the ratepayers, promise in the years to come to yield an aggregate net income of augmenting proportions, to the relief of direct taxation. Glasgow has shown that a broad, bold, and enlightened policy as regards all things pertaining to the health, comfort, and advancement of the masses of the citizens may be compatible with sound economy and perfect solvency.

CHAPTER V

MANCHESTER'S MUNICIPAL ACTIVITIES

SIR J. R. SOMERS VINE, a high authority upon the municipalities of England, has said of Manchester that " by the excellence of its local *régime* it has come to be regarded, and not without good reason, as the foremost example of English modern municipal government." Certainly the symmetrical and virile character of its municipal institutions entitles it to a place of leading importance in any account of the well-governed cities of the world. Manchester's progress as a manufacturing and commercial center has been a long series of triumphs. In none of our great American cities have the municipal organization and its appurtenances compared at all favorably with the achievements of industry, commerce, and private enterprise. Manchester presents the picture of a populous community created almost wholly by the developments of modern industrialism, magnifying its municipal interests and concerns, and bringing as much wisdom, energy, and farsightedness to the management of the affairs of the municipal corporation as its most experienced citizens were bestowing upon their large private undertakings.

Manchester has been fortunate in the possession of a strong municipal consciousness. The corporation seems to occupy as large a place in the minds of Manchester citizens as in those of any German city. Its

Manchester's
municipal
spirit.

activity is not hampered by any distrust of its character and ability, or by any narrow theories as to the proper limitation of its functions. It is intrusted with the care of general local interests, and its organs are so devised and arranged that it can adapt its operations readily to changing needs and conditions.

Population and area.

This Lancashire metropolis is the center of a great and dense population. Within a radius of twenty miles from the Manchester town hall there are dwelling more than three million souls. But Manchester itself is a compact municipality, with 505,000 people by the census of 1891, and 520,000 as estimated in 1894. In 1890 Manchester annexed suburbs, as had also been done in 1885. With these considerable enlargements of territory, the municipality includes 12,911 acres, or

Compared with Chicago.

about 20 square miles. As a matter of comparison, it may be remarked that Chicago in 1890 had twice the population of Manchester with an area of 160 square miles. But it is to be remembered that the borough of Salford, though a distinct municipality, is as essentially a part of the great industrial community of Manchester as is any ward inside of Manchester's corporate limits. Salford has a population exceeding

Salford as a part of the " Greater Manchester."

200,000, and an area of 5171 acres. If the plans for the union of Salford with Manchester should be carried out, there would be a community of nearly or quite 750,000 people occupying somewhat more than 18,000 acres, or 28 square miles. Here we have an average density four times as great as that of Chicago. But if Manchester's bounds were extended more generously, so as to include a population as large as that of Chicago, the average density of the two cities would

Compared with Brooklyn.

not perhaps be very different. ⸢Brooklyn in 1890 had a population greater than that of Manchester and Salford, housed in an area somewhat more restricted. The character of the housing accommodation of Man-

chester and Salford is somewhat similar to that of
Brooklyn, the small, "self-contained" house prevailing as against the Glasgow, New York, or Paris type
of tenement-house.

Previous to the enlargement of the corporate limits
in 1890, Manchester was governed by a council of 76
members, and was divided into seventeen single and
one double ward. The double ward was a central
and very populous one, not convenient to subdivide,
and therefore accorded six instead of three councilors.
At present there are twenty-four single and one double
ward — equivalent to twenty-six regular wards. There
are twenty-six aldermen and three times as many ordinary councilors, making a representation of four
from each ward — a total governing body of 104 men.
It is the Manchester plan, in selecting aldermen, to
assign one to each ward.   That is to say, the council
itself promotes the senior councilor from a given
ward to the rank of alderman, and the ward elects another councilor to fill the vacancy.   This method
amounts, virtually, to giving the wards four instead
of three members and makes the aldermanic distinction as merely nominal as it could well be.   One hundred and four men form a rather large administrative
body; but there is no reason to consider it too large
for an advantageous management of the various corporate affairs of so great a city.   These men well
represent the responsible citizenship of Manchester,
and they find strength and resources rather than confusion and weakness in their numbers.

*Number of
wards.*

*Council of
104 men.*

The working organization of the Manchester council is so excellent and methodical that it may well
claim some of our attention. The full body ordinarily holds two meetings a month. The mayor presides, and in his absence the deputy mayor takes the
chair. The mayor is almost invariably an alderman,

*Organiza-
tion of the
council.*

CHAP. V.

Mayor and deputy mayor.

Standing committees.

Frequency of meetings.

A hundred subcommit- tees.

and it is not uncommon to pay him the compliment of a reëlection for a second year. The deputy mayor this year is the alderman who served last year as mayor. There are some sixteen grand standing committees of the council, with an average membership of perhaps twenty, some being larger and some being smaller. Each alderman and councilor is assigned to duty on three different committees. Such at least is the rule, though there are a few exceptions. The mayor is a member *ex officio* of every standing committee, besides being chairman of a so-called " general purposes" committee that meets at his call. Each committee has its chairman and deputy chairman, and it apportions its work to a number of subcommittees, to each of which the chairman and deputy chairman belong. The committees meet more or less frequently according to the nature of their duties. Thus the finance committee and the watch (police) committee hold weekly meetings, while the cleansing committee, the gas committee, the waterworks committee, and several others meet once in two weeks, and the art-gallery committee, the baths and wash-houses committee, and others find it sufficient to assemble once a month. The subcommittees meet as frequently as occasion requires. Careful synopsized reports of the committee meetings are brought to the full council. The system combines high specialization of oversight with complete harmony and centrality. The mayor as a member of all committees is in touch with all departments. Each councilor by virtue of membership in several committees has a varied range, and each great committee with twenty or more men includes some representative of all or nearly all the other great committees.

The subcommittees, of which there are nearly a hundred, give every councilor some particular work to do. The more carefully this Manchester system of committees and subcommittees is studied, both in theory and in practice, the more worthy of admiration it seems. The following list of standing committees, arranged alphabetically, will indicate the chief departments of municipal activity in Manchester, and the mode of partition that has been found advantageous: (1) art-gallery committee, with subcommittees on the audit of accounts, on the art building and care of the galleries, and on art, *i. e.*, purchase of pictures, etc.; (2) baths and wash-houses committee, with subcommittees on the audit of accounts and on each one of eight important establishments in different quarters of the city; (3) cleansing committee, with subcommittees on audit, on estates, on works and stores, on horses and provender, on new districts, and on the garbage works at Water street and Holt Town; (4) finance committee, with subcommittees on audit and charitable trusts, and on stock and bonds; (5) gas committee, with subcommittees on audit, on each of three great gas-works, on street mains and lighting, and on electric lighting; (6) general purposes committee, with subcommittees on amalgamation and on parliamentary matters; (7) improvement and buildings committee, with subcommittees on audit, on central district, on northern district, on southern district, on purchasing and widening of streets, on building-by-laws, and on the Victoria Arcade; (8) markets committee, with subcommittees on audit, on cattle plague, on central markets, abattoirs and slaughter-houses, on Smithfield Market, and a special one on matters regarding provision for dealing with foreign cattle; (9) parks and cemeteries committee, with subcommittees on audit, on Alexandra Park, on Ardwick Green, on Birch Fields, on Cheetham Park, on open spaces, open-air baths and nurseries, on Philips Park and

Marginal notes:

CHAP. V.

Committee on art-gallery.

On baths and wash-houses.

On cleansing.

On finance.

On gas-works.

On buildings and improvements.

On markets.

On parks and cemeteries.

I.—10*

On paving
and street
work.

On free
libraries.

On sewage
disposal.

On sanitary
administra-
tion.

On town
hall.

On police.

On water-
supply.

On ship
canal.

On technical
instruction.

A permanent
but flexible
system.

Cemetery and open-air bath, on Queen's Park, on Queen's Park Art Museum, on Southern Cemetery, and on music in the parks; (10) paving, sewering, and highways committee, with subcommittees on audit and offices, on yards, and on each of the southern, northern, and central districts; (11) public free-libraries committee, with subcommittees on audit, on reference library and general purposes, on reference-library extension and on the selection of books, and five subcommittees on specified groups of the fifteen neighborhood branch libraries; (12) rivers committee, with subcommittees on audit and on the sewage-disposal scheme; (13) sanitary committee, with subcommittees on audit, office and clothing, on nuisances, on unhealthy dwellings, on hospitals and analyst's laboratory, and on the Shop Hours Act, etc.; (14) town hall committee, with subcommittees on officers and audit, on decorations and furnishing, on stationery, organ, bells, and clocks; (15) watch committee, with subcommittees on audit, on clothing for the police, firemen, etc., on weights and measures and petroleum, on lock-ups, etc., on fire-brigade and theaters, and on hackney-coaches; (16) waterworks committee, with subcommittees on sale, supply, street mains and appeals, on audit, on the new Thirlmere aqueduct, and on hydraulic power. Besides these sixteen, there is a large committee on the Manchester Ship Canal, under the mayor's chairmanship, which includes, besides others, the chairmen of all the standing committees, and there is one on technical instruction, with subcommittees on the municipal technical school, on the municipal school of art, on audit and grants, and on new buildings.

This arrangement of committees is by no means an unalterable one, and it can be made as flexible as the changing and expanding character of municipal business could possibly require. But while its details are changeable on demand, its principles are fixed and lasting. Our larger American cities have yielded so habitually to the temptation to create a separate board or commission for every new or important undertaking, that they seem to have lost all sense of the importance of a unified, central administration that can be held directly accountable. It is for their benefit primarily that I have thus recapitulated the specific committees of the Manchester council, to which is intrusted the oversight of all the branches of administration, and which perform their duties far more efficiently and responsibly than do the detached commissions that control the several departments in such a system as New York's, for example.

The supervisory services of council committees do not, be it said, make any the less needful the employ- ment of a highly skilled and well-salaried chief as the executive head of each working department. Under the town clerk there is an elaborate organization of solicitors and staff employees. Similar things may be said of the City Treasurer's Department; and also of the City Surveyor's Department, with its architects and civil engineers. The Police Department is organized under a chief constable who has great authority, and the Fire Brigade, the Sanitary Department, the Gas Department, the Markets Department, the Public Parks, etc., are each under a chief superintendent. The city's large staff of officials is appointed by the council on grounds of fitness and with expectation of permanence on good behavior.

Manchester has brought an enviable degree of ability and energy to the provision for its citizens of those common services that are admittedly the function of modern municipal corporations. Besides the maintenance of a suitable system of streets and high-

ways, it is everywhere agreed that the supply of water and the disposition of sewage and waste material pertain to the business of a municipal government. Manchester is disadvantageously situated as respects an easy and natural solution either of the water prob-
Water-supply of a million people. lem or of the drainage problem. But splendid resources have risen superior to all difficulties. A private company formerly supplied Manchester with water, from works in the adjacent hilly country, at Longdendale, some eighteen miles distant. In the year 1847 the city purchased the plant, and it has been greatly developed since that time. There are now thirty square miles (19,300 acres) of drainage ground, supplying sixteen reservoirs at Longdendale which have an aggregate area of 854 acres and a storage capacity of nearly 6,000,000,000 gallons. This system has been delivering about 25,000,000 gallons per day and supplying a million people in Manchester, in Salford, and in several adjacent districts which buy water from the Manchester corporation.

It was long ago perceived that the Longdendale supply could not suffice for the future Manchester, and much thought and inquiry was bestowed upon the question whence to derive a large additional quantity of pure water. Finally it was decided that the
Lake Thirlmere acquired. famous "Lake Country" in Cumberland afforded the best available supply, and by parliamentary action in 1879 Lake Thirlmere became the property of the Manchester corporation. This sheet is very small, but its drainage basin is of considerable area, and the rainfall of the district is extraordinary, varying from 52 to 137 inches per annum. It was decided to raise the lake fifty feet above its natural level, and thus to double its area and to increase its capacity to more than 8,000,000,000 gallons, making possible a discharge of fully 50,000,000 gallons per day. The aque-

duct from Manchester to Thirlmere will exceed nine-
ty-five miles in length, and the new works were begun
in 1890.   They have been pushed rapidly, and will
soon be ready for use.   The corporation has invested
$16,000,000 or more in the Longdendale works, which
it has not ceased to develop, and the estimated cost
of the Thirlmere works and aqueduct is $17,000,000.
Water rates are so adjusted as to make the depart-
ment self-sustaining, besides providing for all sink-
ing-fund requirements.   Manchester rates are much
higher than those of Glasgow, the Scotch city being
by far the most satisfactorily supplied with water of
all the large British towns.   But its rates are practi-
cally the same as Birmingham's, and less than those
of Liverpool.   Under seriously difficult conditions, the
Manchester authorities have found an admirable set-
tlement of the water question.

The drainage question has been an equally difficult
one.   Manchester is so surrounded by populous towns
that its drainage into the small river Irwell had long
been extremely objectionable, while sewage-farms in
that particular district were thought to be out of the
question.   At length, when the work on the ship
canal made the further use of the river as a trunk
sewer an impossibility, science had gone so far in suc-
cessful experiments with sewage purification as to
point out a prompt remedy for conditions that were
growing intolerable.   Authority to borrow $2,500,000
was secured, and in 1891 a large beginning was made
toward a system of precipitation and filtration works,
similar in some respects to the still more recent Glas-
gow works that I have already described.

Manchester had long before this met the problem
of garbage disposal more successfully than any other
city in the world.   The lack of proper means for the
disposal of sewage had necessitated a very general

Chap. V.

An aque-
duct ninety-
five miles
long.

What to do
with sewage.

Collection
of garbage
and waste.

use of a system of "pail-closets" for night-soil, of which there were recently not far from 70,000 in use in Manchester. The contents of these closets have for years been collected by the covered vans of the Sanitary Department once, twice, or even oftener every week, at the same time that they collect garbage, ashes, and kitchen refuse in general, from the domestic ash-bins. The city owns several hundred thousand great sheet-iron pails, which the teamsters of the Sanitary Department cover with rubber-rimmed lids when they are removed and replaced by empty pails. The contents of these pails go into enormous closed evaporators at the "Works," and come out as a dry powder which, mixed with a percentage of burned bones and perhaps with a portion of the ashes and street-sweepings that are brought to the same establishment, is sold as a fertilizer and brings a good price. The garbage is consumed in furnaces. From some of the collected refuse the city makes a commercial quality of mortar, and from slaughter-house refuse it makes carbolic soap. It has for some time also employed the plan of buying low ground near the city and gradually filling it with the non-combustible refuse for which some dumping-place must be found, thus making good building-land which it subsequently sells. The adoption of a sewage-purification system will naturally lead to the general use of water-closets in place of pail-closets; but the great "Sanitary Works" of Manchester will not become obsolete, and they will remain a credit to the city, and an example to other places that would learn how to dispose of the garbage and miscellaneous refuse of a populous community.

Utilization of refuse.

The oldest of all municipal gas-supplies.

Perhaps no other city can point to so long an experience as Manchester's in the public operation of gas-works. This business has never been in private hands, but was begun by the local authorities in 1807, in the very early days of the introduction of gas as an illuminant. The municipal gas manufacture and sale has grown to enormous proportions, many neighboring townships being Manchester's customers for gas as well as for water. An area more than twice as great as the city itself is supplied with gas from the municipal retorts. The daily consumption in 1894 varied from 5,000,000 cubic feet a day in summer to 22,500,000 in winter. The ordinary price is 2s. 6d. (60 cents) per thousand feet. More than 81,000 private consumers and more than 15,000 public lamps are supplied. For the last year's operation of which accounts are at hand, the gas-works, besides furnishing public illumination at actual cost and the private supply at a moderate price, earned above all expenses (renewal funds being reckoned as current expenditures) a clear sum of more than $500,000, of which nearly $200,000 was applied to interest and sinking-fund payments on account of the capital investment, and more than $300,000 was paid over to the general city treasury as net profits. In 1893 Manchester entered upon a plan of great enlargement and improvement of its gas-plants, and in the course of a few years it is expected that several million dollars will be thus expended.

Success of the enterprise.

The Manchester gas committee, like that of Glasgow and some other British cities, is doing all that it can to encourage the use of gas as a fuel, and to that end it rents many thousands of heating and cooking appliances. Like Glasgow also, the municipal corporation of Manchester has (in 1893) constructed a great central electric-lighting plant, and has entered definitely upon the policy of supplying electricity for public and private illumination and eventually also for power. It should be remarked that one of the latest achievements of the waterworks committee has

Gas as a fuel.

Municipal electrical works.

Hydraulic and electric power.

been the construction at an expense of about half a million dollars of a station for the distribution of hydraulic power.   Thus the Manchester municipality, having better facilities than any private company could have for the economical operation of power plants and the distribution of power through water-mains or wires, has assumed that function both for the benefit of the industrial community and also for the sake of profits to the public treasury.

Municipal market system.

Some fifty years ago Manchester purchased the manorial rights under which the local markets had been private property, and the system has been developed in many directions, to the great convenience and advantage of the citizens considered both as consumers of food-products and also as ratepayers.

Abattoirs.

There are extensive municipal abattoirs connected with the market system, and the cleansing and food-inspection departments are the better able to serve and protect the community by reason of the concentration of the general food-supplies in public markets.   The rents and tolls of the various market-places yield a large revenue, out of which maintenance charges are paid, and full provision for interest and for yearly instalments of capital investment is deducted, after which nearly a hundred thousand dollars a year is paid into the city income fund for the relief of the tax rate.

Net revenues.

Municipal street railways.

In 1875 Manchester began the construction of street railways — a policy that has been continuously pursued.   More than forty miles of tram-lines are the property of the corporation, there being also about ten miles of private lines within the municipal bounds.   The municipal lines are rented to an operating company on terms that pay the city more than ten per cent. upon its investment.   Nearly a million dollars has been expended in laying the rails, and yearly

rentals of more than a hundred thousand dollars are
received.   Repairs and renewals are made by the city
authorities and charged to the operating companies.
After sinking-funds and interest charges have been
duly considered, there remains a handsome net profit
for the city.   Salford's corporation tramways are
leased to the same company.   Both cities have found
their tramways policy amply successful already, and
the prospect for increased revenues in the future is
very bright.   The code of rules to which the leasing
companies are subject is very minute and stringent,
dealing with every detail of operation, in the interest
of the public.   One clause in the Manchester leases
declares that "every lease of the tramways shall imply
a condition of re-entry if the lessees do not run carriages
each way every morning of the week and every evening of the week (Sundays, Christmas Day, and Good
Friday always excepted), at such hours as the Corporation think most convenient for artisans, mechanics,
and daily laborers, at fares not exceeding $\frac{1}{2}d.$ per mile
(the lessees, nevertheless, not being required to take
any fare less than $1d.$), provided always that in case
of any complaint to the Board of Trade of the hours
so appointed, the said Board may have power to fix
and regulate the same from time to time."   This provision, made as long ago as twenty years (1875), when
tramways were first begun in Manchester, illustrates
well the spirit in which the whole matter has always
been regulated.   A workman's morning and evening
ride for a penny is a municipal service worth ac-
complishing.

It is the unanimous sentiment among the citizens
of Manchester that no private company should be
allowed on any pretext to occupy with its wires, pipes,
or rails any portion of the public thoroughfares.   For
this reason, Manchester has made determined efforts

CHAP. V.

Salford's
tram lines.

Provision of
workmen's
cars.

to obtain the right to operate a municipal telephone
system.   But the intention of the national post-office
at an early day to make the telephone service a part
of the postal administration, has stood in the way of
Manchester's preferences.

In the many branches of its health administration
Manchester is alert and energetic.   Its housing arrangements are so different from those of tenement-
built Glasgow, that sanitary inspection and the removal of cases of infectious disease do not occupy so
imperative and so large a place in the municipal administration.   But these services are duly provided
for and efficiently carried out.   Under parliamentary

acts relating to unhealthy dwellings the Manchester
authorities are acting with much vigor, condemning
and demolishing houses that are beyond redemption,
and requiring the approved reconstruction of those
that are not too bad to be spared.   As in Glasgow,
very eminent medical and sanitary engineering talent
is employed on behalf of the municipality, and the
average conditions under which the people of Manchester live and work are growing constantly more
wholesome.   The " Manchester Dwellings Reconstruction Scheme of 1891," based upon provisions of
the great public act of 1890 relating to the "Housing
of the Working Classes," is destined to accomplish a
wide-spread reform, aided by the new thoroughfares
that have been required in order to reach the ship
canal and docks, the opening of which is clearing
away many insanitary dwellings.

Manchester has imitated the continental cities in
making comprehensive municipal arrangements for
the burial of the dead.   The arguments in favor of
municipal cemeteries are, it seems to me, well-nigh
conclusive, and with the rapid growth of our cities
they become stronger every year.   All cities have

found it necessary to exercise strict oversight in the Chap. V. interest of the general health over the disposal of human bodies, and the maintenance of public cemeteries greatly facilitates such supervision. The Manchester cemeteries committee has adapted the service of its burial-grounds to the needs of the public at every point. The two great cemeteries are so subdivided as to furnish separate grounds for the Church Cemetery arrangements. of England, the dissenting Protestants, the Roman Catholics, and the Jews. Prices are arranged upon scales that make possible a decent burial, with inscription on stone over grave, at about four dollars for adults and three dollars for children, this charge including all cemetery fees and expenses. The purchase prices of "freehold graves" vary from ten to thirty dollars — prices that are very low, under the circumstances. The committee furnishes monuments and stone or iron work at reasonable prices, and for small annual fees or moderate commutation sums will agree to maintain any specified condition of turf, plants, or shrubs, either by the year or in perpetuity.   The value of this public cemetery service to the people of a great community like Manchester — although it saves them great sums Value as a moral and social service. of money — is far beyond any computation in money terms.   It is a moral and social service that the municipality owes to its citizens, and that it is in position to perform incomparably better than any other agency. There are, of course, numerous private cemeteries in and about Manchester; but the inevitable tendency will be toward their gradual disuse.   The municipal authorities find it easy to administer the cemeteries in such a way as to make them entirely self-sustaining, as regards both original cost and current expenditure.

It is obvious that there are advantages of practical administration in the Manchester plan of bringing the management of public parks and cemeteries under

CHAP. V.

Public parks.

one head. Manchester has no very large parks, the Alexandra of sixty acres being the most extensive, while Queen's, Philips, and Birch Fields have each about thirty acres. Besides these there are nearly twenty small parks and recreation grounds. The total area of 214 acres of parks, though not large, has the advantage of being well distributed, easily accessible, and solicitously managed for the best results to the community.

There are several other social services that the Manchester corporation provides, with marked benefit to the public. One of these is the maintenance of assembly-rooms in all parts of the city which are rented for any proper purpose at very reasonable prices. The chief architectural pride of the city is its great town hall, recently built at a cost of $5,000,000 — regarded as the finest municipal building in the British Empire, and admirably arranged for the purposes of the council and the municipal departments. Its large hall is always for rent for public meetings, concerts, and balls, and small rooms are available for committees or societies of limited membership. There are several older town halls in other parts of the city which are rented for social uses of all kinds, and various other buildings of municipal ownership similarly available. This function of the government is one that has been assumed gradually because the city owned buildings, rather than entered upon *de novo* as a comprehensive scheme. But its benefits are so great that it will in the future be extended rather than reduced; and it is being carried out as symmetrically, with regard to the different quarters of the town, as the system of markets, or parks, or as any other general service.

It was in or about the year 1880 that the Manchester authorities resolved to establish a system of public

Municipal assembly-rooms.

A permanent policy.

baths throughout the city, and in the course of a decade they had opened eight very ambitious and capacious establishments at a cost of nearly a hundred
thousand dollars apiece. Connected with each bath   Public baths
is a public gymnasium, and some of the establish-   and gymna-
                                                              sia.
ments also have assembly-rooms. The fees paid by
bathers are very small, the policy of this department
being to encourage the largest possible use of the
institutions rather than to earn profits. As yet, the
baths fall considerably short of self-support, the cost   Not yet self-
of maintenance being heavy, especially in winter. But   supporting.
like the parks and recreation grounds, and like the
public libraries and reading-rooms, the baths are
deemed an agency of civilization that the authorities
ought to provide. Ultimately, it is very probable that
this department will be developed to the point of full
or approximate self-maintenance without advancing
the low fees that are collected from school-children
and the general public.

Hardly any other social service performed by the
Manchester corporation is so widely appreciated by
the community as the maintenance of free public
libraries. Manchester early adopted the Free Libraries   The free
Act,—*i. e.*, decided by popular vote to open public   libraries.
libraries and maintain them by a yearly rate of one
penny in the £ sterling of assessed valuation, in
accordance with a general act of Parliament. Since
1865 Manchester has pursued this policy, with great
satisfaction. The libraries now contain about 250,-
000 volumes, of which 100,000 or more are kept in
a central reference-library building where they are   Fifteen
accessible to everybody from early in the morning   branches
                                                              and reading-
until 10 o'clock at night. There are also some fifteen   rooms.
branch libraries and reading-rooms, of which nine are
extensive, with perhaps 15,000 or 20,000 books each,
while half a dozen are principally newspaper and

I.—11

periodical reading-rooms, with a few hundred books to be read on the premises. These branches are much frequented in the evening by working-men, being kept open until 10 o'clock. Connected with each one there is a separate boys' room open from 6 to 9 P. M. The total number of books issued each year approaches 2,000,000. The municipal investment on account of libraries has been a million dollars; but the sinking-fund accumulations are now equal to three quarters of that amount, so that annual charges for interest and liquidation are light. Eighty thousand dollars a year suffices for all such charges, as well as for purchase of new books and running expenses of the entire system. Thus for about fifteen cents per capita per annum, the people of Manchester are supplied with what is perhaps the most efficient and popular system of free libraries and reading-rooms to be found in any city of the world. In the single item of the access to "want" advertisements that the supply of British newspapers in the numerous reading-rooms gives to working-men, the cost of the whole system is saved to the wage-earning classes, the reading-rooms thus serving the purpose of intelligence and employment bureaus, and helping in the prompt distribution of labor to the points where it is demanded through a region thick-studded with manufacturing towns.

Large results at small expense.

Useful to working-men.

Manchester has fallen into line with all the leading industrial centers of Europe in recognizing the advantage of promoting under municipal auspices those branches of special and technical education that have bearing upon the principal local trades. The general provision of elementary instruction is left with the school-board. But the municipal council concerns itself seriously with the task of helping working-men's sons to attain special skill in the crafts and industries to which the town owes its prosperity.

Technical education.

Formerly the chief technical schools were under private auspices; but they have been made over to the city authorities, and about $100,000 a year is expended in their conduct, while the city's capital property of this character is worth nearly $1,000,000. The Manchester Municipal Technical Schools include a great spinning and weaving school in which everything pertaining to those industries is taught in such a manner as to abet at all points the maintenance of Manchester's supremacy in textile industries; a school of art and design; and several important schools of mechanical arts, engineering, and practical trades. The fees are low, and there are many free scholarships which are awarded on merit. The attendance is large, and the system supplements in a highly satisfactory manner the well-administered elementary schools, which do not retain the average lad beyond his thirteenth or fourteenth year. The technical evening classes are well attended by apprentices whose day hours are occupied. The technical schools provide instruction in literary and commercial subjects, elementary science, drawing and designing, bookkeeping, type-writing, shorthand, and modern languages, as well as in engineering subjects, mathematics, physics and practical electricity, applied chemistry, woodworking, metallurgy, all building trades, sanitary engineering and plumbing, bleaching and dyeing as well as spinning and weaving, and numerous other subjects and trades. Dressmaking, millinery, and domestic pursuits are also taught to young women.

The municipal council has (in 1894) constructed the finest technical school building in Great Britain. In 1891 a committee of the council visited German and Swiss technical schools, and reported the dangerous inferiority of Manchester's facilities. A revolution has been accomplished since the committee raised its note

CHAP. V.

Adapted to textile and other local industries.

New building.

of alarm.   What English manufacturing centers have learned from the Continent, those of America must learn from England.   This technical-instruction committee, which proceeded to reorganize the municipal work of Manchester in their department, made the following declaration:

Objects of the school.   The principal object of the municipal technical school is to provide instruction in the principles of those sciences which bear directly or indirectly upon our trades and industries; and to show, by experimental work, how these principles may be applied to their advancement.

The aim of the school is distinct from that of the University colleges, inasmuch as it is designed to teach science solely with a view to its industrial and commercial applications, and not for the purpose of educating professional scientific men.   It, however, offers to students of the university colleges the opportunity of technical instruction in the industrial application of certain branches of science.

The technical school requires that all its day students must possess on entrance a sound general education, and it must therefore look for its supply of suitably prepared students to the grammar schools and other secondary schools, and to the higher grade elementary schools.

The school also provides evening lectures and laboratory and workshop practice for apprentices, journeymen, and foremen, in the scientific principles underlying their respective trades and industries, and especially aims to bring to their knowledge newly-discovered processes and methods for the purpose of improving any special trade, or of introducing new branches of industry.

But municipal encouragement of practical instruction does not stop in Manchester with the maintenance of this system of advanced technical and art schools.   From the Technical Instruction Exchequer Subsidies for technical instruction.   Account the municipal council makes various annual grants, aggregating perhaps $30,000, as subsidies and tokens of interest and good will, to other local schools that are carrying on some work in technical science,

manual training, or practical trades instruction. At CHAP. V.
least half of this amount goes to the Manchester
School Board, and $5000 is contributed to Owens College in promotion of its scientific work. Small grants
also are made to special schools and societies: as, for
example, $600 to the Manchester and Salford Practical and Recreative Evening Classes Committee, $750
to the School of Domestic Economy, $250 to the Christian Arts and Crafts School, $1250 to the Manchester
Grammar School, $1500 to the Lower Mosley Street
School's Evening Classes, $500 to the Union of Lancashire and Cheshire Institute, and $250 to the Catholic Collegiate School. The subsidies are allowed upon
the quality and extent of the work these and other
aided institutions are doing in the field for whose
cultivation the Municipal Technical Instruction Exchequer Account was opened. The policy may be
explained to be that of securing the largest possible
amount of technical teaching for the money expended, this end being furthered by subsidies to private
schools, and by free scholarships, as well as by maintenance of municipal institutions.

The municipal art-gallery is eminently creditable The art-gallery.
to the people of Manchester, and is highly appreciated
as an educational adjunct. The art committee of the
council holds semi-annual exhibitions, with the very
active coöperation of the best British artists. The
permanent collection is rapidly increasing in extent
and value. Moreover, the Manchester corporation in Municipal music.
various ways encourages musical culture. It provides
good music in the parks, employs an organist who
gives frequent concerts in the great hall of the municipal building, and lends official patronage to a very
excellent local college of music.

Manchester's crowning project has been the great
ship canal, opened in 1894 after ten years of coura-

I.—11*

CHAP. V.

The ship-
canal pro-
ject.

geous struggle against huge obstacles. For many decades the idea of an artificial connection with the sea
had been in the minds of the men of Manchester, but
it was not until 1877 that it was taken up with a
purpose to carry it into execution. It began as a
movement among public-spirited men of the general
Manchester district, who formed themselves into a
company. Their plans were heartily supported by
all the communities of the Lancashire region that the
proposed canal would serve. Several years were required to obtain the necessary parliamentary authority, inasmuch as the Liverpool interests and those of
several railway companies were strenuously opposed
to any plan that would make Manchester a seaport.

Its cost.

At first $25,000,000 was estimated as the inclusive cost
of the entire project; but as the work proceeded it was
found that $50,000,000 must be provided, and finally
the figures were raised to $75,000,000. The company's
resources were exhausted, and the municipal corporation of Manchester came to its relief, furnishing the last
$25,000,000, and securing control of the enterprise by

Municipal
aid and con-
trol.

a majority representation on the canal board. Eleven
of the twenty-one directors of the canal are appointed
by the Manchester town council from its own membership. The Manchester municipal corporation can
point to numerous examples of town governments that
have made dockage, wharves, harbor-deepening, and
the general appurtenances of a seaport one of their
chief corporate functions. Glasgow has long pur-

Other ex-
amples.

sued this policy, with results of the most gratifying
character. Liverpool's vast unified system of docks
is vested in a public board intimately related to the
municipal corporation; and other seaport towns, British and Continental, have assumed financial responsibilities on account of their trade by water that are
relatively greater than those of Manchester's new un-

dertaking. As a direct investment, it may be many
years before the ship canal will justify itself. But
Manchester and the surrounding district are finding
the indirect results to be of enormous value. Not a large
number of first-class vessels patronized the canal in
1894, although its depth, width, spacious locks, and
vast terminal docks and wharves at Salford and Manchester are upon a scale that invites the greatest ocean
freighters. But if the ships are not at first crowding
the canal's accommodations, it is because of great
changes, in Manchester's favor, in the rates of competing transportation routes. Formerly it cost as
much, or more, to transfer a cargo of cotton at Liverpool and deliver it by rail in Manchester — a distance of
some 35 miles — as to bring it from America to Liverpool. The fact that these charges have been greatly
reduced to meet the canal's competition militates
against the revenues of the canal company ; but none
the less it benefits the industrial community to serve
which the canal was constructed. Several years,
doubtless, will have elapsed before the wisdom of the
municipality's investment in the canal will have ceased
to be a controverted question. But while far-sighted-
ness is not a universal faculty, it happens that the
short-sighted view has not prevailed in Manchester.
This magnificent public work will remain a monument
of civic faith and energy for centuries after the inef-
fectual opposition that delayed its construction has
been forgotten. The canal, together with the new
water-supply and other vigorous new projects, is preparing Manchester for a twentieth-century career of
vast prosperity.

Chap. V.

Indirect ad-
vantages.

Reduced
charges of
competing
routes.

CHAPTER VI

BIRMINGHAM: ITS CIVIC LIFE AND EXPANSION

SO similar in general scope are the municipal activities of Manchester and Birmingham that with some omissions and suppressions it is quite conceivable that an account of the one corporation could be made to do service with readers outside of England for an account of the other. An intimate acquaintance with the history and the present undertakings of the two municipalities of course reveals abundant individuality in the life and career of each; but for purposes of international comparison either would suffice entirely as an English type. A recent English writer has expressed a common opinion when, remarking that "municipal reformers look to Birmingham as the eyes of the faithful are turned to Mecca," he further declares that "Birmingham was the first to initiate, in a broad and comprehensive spirit, the new régime of municipal socialism on which our hopes of improvement in the condition of large towns are now so greatly dependent," and that "there, some twenty years ago, municipal statesmanship arose with the brain to conceive and the hand to execute enterprises which were really commensurate with the difficulties and the problems of a rapidly growing city." The facts would hardly sustain this claim of priority and preëminence. It is true that in the decade following 1873 the Birmingham corporation evinced a

Birmingham as a "municipal Mecca"

constructive and a reconstructive energy that has led to the transformation of the town. But Glasgow had already set the example on a larger scale for nearly every one of the series of municipal enterprises that Birmingham inaugurated, and Manchester had also led the way in several. The outblossoming of the municipal spirit in Birmingham has been magnificent, and the array of tangible results is indeed brilliant. But the conscientious investigator cannot well admit that Birmingham has contributed more than Glasgow to the solution of the problem how to apply municipal remedies to the relief of sanitary and social evils in crowded industrial towns, or that it has accomplished as much as Manchester or Glasgow in the municipal management of productive public services. It has, however, accomplished enough to give it place and rank with these two; and that should be sufficient honor.

Chap. VI.

Compared with Glasgow and Manchester.

There has always been a Birmingham, but the town was not incorporated until after the reform acts, when, like Manchester, it obtained its charter in 1838. There were local commissions and authorities of one character or another, however, whose powers were not at first made over to the new municipal council; and not before 1851 did the corporation acquire full authority over public works and complete municipal jurisdiction throughout its entire area. Even then the municipal authorities were passive rather than active, and content to administer corporate affairs honestly and economically without entering upon any very bold or innovating policies.

Corporation fully established in 1851.

It is not easy to believe that a city which has attained such splendor of development and such perfection of administration could have accomplished it all within the working lifetime of one man. For the light they throw upon the whole course of municipal

Results in one man's lifetime.

evolution in England since 1835, some remarks made at the jubilee celebration of the Birmingham corporation on the last day of October, 1888, may well be quoted. At a special meeting of the town council the honorary freedom of the borough was bestowed upon Mr. P. H. Muntz, M. P., who had been active, fifty years before, in the task of procuring the charter. I quote from the Birmingham " Daily Post" of November 1, 1888 :

> The minutes of the previous meeting of the council having been confirmed, the town clerk read the resolution conferring on Mr. Muntz the honorary freedom of the borough, a copy of which had been engrossed and illuminated upon a silk and vellum scroll.
>
> The mayor, addressing Mr. Muntz, said it was a matter of congratulation to the members of the town council that they were able to welcome his presence on an occasion which would form an epoch in the annals of Birmingham. Mr. Muntz was one of the founders of their municipal liberty. It was to him and those who were associated with him that Birmingham owed its municipal self-government ; and now, when fifty years had elapsed since the royal charter creating Birmingham a borough was signed, it was their privilege to be able to offer him personally their thanks for heroic struggles in years gone by, for achievements which would fill a conspicuous page in the history of Birmingham, and for benefits which had been the foundation of the prosperity of Birmingham. Fifty years ago Birmingham had 180,000 inhabitants, with property rated at £475,000, and a burgess-roll of 6000, qualified by the £10 rental; but to-day it had 450,000 inhabitants, with property assessed at £1,772,000, and a constituency composed of 77,000 burgesses, who voted under the qualification of household suffrage. Fifty years ago meadows and fields surrounded Birmingham; to-day a chain of houses linked the town with what were once small outside villages, and formed with them practically, though not administratively, the greater Birmingham — perhaps the Birmingham of the future. There were fifty years ago numerous independent governing bodies, who derived their power from the unwelcome source of self-election. To-day they had a municipality freely elected by the widest suffrage, which transacted business of

Contrasts of
fifty years.

great magnitude and of the most responsible and varied character. The streets and footpaths were then, as a celebrated author
said, "painfully paved," imperfectly watched and lighted, and
the cleanliness of the town, the culture of the artisan classes,
the health of the town, were comparatively neglected; and the
disposal of the sewage was an unsolved problem. Now they had
streets, public buildings, sewage works, works connected with
the health department, baths and parks, free libraries, a mu- Municipal
improve-
ments.
seum, and a host of other matters which challenged compari-
son with any town in the United Kingdom. Their progress during the fifty years had been on the whole gradual and steady.
Occasionally it slackened and almost retrograded. On the other
hand, it progressed with giant strides under the influence of
men inspired by a high standard of public duty, whose ability,
integrity, and devotion enhanced the value of their municipal
work, and aroused the council to great enterprise. So important
had been the work of the council that the council became a
training-school for Parliament; for he found that, including Mr.
Muntz, there were eleven gentlemen who had passed the mayoral
chair, and, in addition, two or three other distinguished members of the council, who had occupied, and some of them still
occupied, a seat in Parliament, and he might say with great distinction too. It was fitting, therefore, that they should signalise
the fiftieth anniversary of the municipal life and progress of the
town; and they could not better mark it than by connecting it
with Mr. Muntz, who had passed some of the best years of his
life in the service of the corporation, who had fought and won
for them municipal emancipation. The name of Muntz had been
closely allied with the industry and prosperity of the town;
indeed, they allied it with half a century of municipal existence.
What was the freedom of the borough? That question was once
asked of Mr. Muntz's former colleague, Mr. Bright, whom they
were still proud to call their representative. He answered it as Freedom of
the city.
follows: "Last week one of my acquaintances asked me what
was intended by the freedom of the city—whether there was in
it that was useful or valuable, any privilege or right that the
man could care for. I told him that, as I understood, there was
nothing in it which could be put into the scales and weighed,
nothing that could be measured by the rule; but there was
something in it much more precious, if rightly considered, than
silver or gold." Thus, by conferring the freedom of the borough
on Mr. Muntz they expressed their thanks to him for services
rendered in days gone by—for his active participation in the

administration of the town during its infancy, and also for his having supported their administration later, when they were able to march more progressively than they had done at the beginning. The freedom also expressed the gratitude of his fellow-citizens, their deep respect, their reverence, and their wishes that many more years were in store for him, gladdened by the knowledge that the good seed which he had sown was multiplied and increased a hundred-fold. In conclusion, his worship handed the roll conferring the freedom of the borough to Mr. Muntz, with the remark that an appropriate casket was in preparation for it; and he then offered him the right hand of fellowship as the second honorary freeman of the borough of Birmingham.

Mr. Muntz, having signed the roll, was loudly applauded on rising to acknowledge the presentation. He said he accepted the privilege of the freedom of the borough in the same manner and in the same tone in which it was given by the mayor. He scarcely knew how to find words to thank them for the honor they had done him. It was an honor largely enhanced by the fact that the council, as the representatives of the ratepayers and burgesses of Birmingham, had unanimously agreed to con-

Mr. Muntz's retrospections. done his offenses — at all events to approve his conduct, for the nearly sixty years he had worked in the midst of them in every capacity. Only those who had gone through the ordeal of applying for the charter which was the foundation of their liberties and the foundation of the present meeting could have any idea of the enormous labor that was requisite to carry it through. He remembered when he first came to reside in Birmingham — then a very young man — it seemed to him a very strange fact that in that large and prosperous town the people had nothing to say in their own government, that they were a mere village with two or three county magistrates to govern them, and with the addition of three or four local bodies — he forgot the exact number — who did little bits of work on their own account. He made enquiries of several people, and found that at that time it could not be altered; but a year or two afterwards the government passed the municipal corporations bill, which included a clause giving the crown power, on application from the ratepayers or burgesses of any town, to extend the powers of a corporation to them. On the passing of the act he applied to several friends to take the matter up and make an application, but he found no one would listen to him. It seemed as if there was a sort of apathy which was to him incomprehensible. He went

round to one after another, and at last persuaded his friend
William Scholefield, who was afterwards their member, and
Clarence Scholefield and some other gentlemen to sign a requisition to about a hundred of the principal people in Birmingham to meet at the public office and to decide whether they
would apply for a corporation or not. At that meeting it was
decided that they should apply. He need not go into the details
of all the troubles they had to get the charter of incorporation
which was signed that very day fifty years ago, for it was then
that their difficulties really began. They had to encounter an
opposition the virulence of which was extraordinary. There
was a very large and influential body who decided that they
would not have the incorporation of Birmingham. He remembered that a very comical matter occurred about that time.
Lord John Russell, who afterwards was the greatest enemy the
corporation had, pronounced a decree that the Whig government would never allow any further extension of liberty. Upon
that the men of Birmingham declared that Lord John and his
colleagues had lost the confidence of the people of Birmingham
— at which Lord John was very much incensed — and that nothing short of household suffrage and vote by ballot would satisfy
them.   When they applied for the corporation, there came out a
celebrated placard, written in large letters, from an association
well known in those days — "Quack, quack, quack! Household
suffrage, vote by ballot, and corporation for Birmingham!
Quack, quack, quack!" That placard sounded very pretty, but
in spite of it, and of all the opposition, they had got household
suffrage, vote by ballot, and a corporation for Birmingham. All
that was now consolidated, but before they obtained that consolidation they were opposed by every species of litigation, and
the government were assured that if they got the control of the
police into their hands it would be the police of the political
union, and would only be let loose to disturb the town.   However, with a great deal of difficulty they got the right to control
the police, and after that various improvements ; and ultimately,
in 1851, they got a consolidation act agreed to by all parties, which
placed the powers of the various local bodies in the hands of the
council. That was the end of their long labor, which he thought
had lasted from 1836 to 1851. That was a long time, and there
certainly was no end of trouble, but he always said to his friends,
"Remember the old Chinese proverb 'Patience and persever-
ance make mulberry leaves into satin,'" and they worked pa-
tiently and determined not to rest until they got all they claimed.

Popular self-government in Birmingham by means of municipal institutions had indeed a difficult and tedious ordeal to endure before the opposition to it melted away. But the ground was cleared in the period that ended with the act of consolidation in 1851, which removed the independent boards and commissions, vesting all their powers in the town council, and which gave large new powers in the direction of sanitary and general improvements to the municipal authorities. The following twenty years witnessed a gradual development, and was a period of respectable administration. The Birmingham of 1871 was not a town that could have attracted the stranger, or that could have been pointed out as a remarkable illustration of modern municipal enterprise. But conditions were all ripening for the outburst of civic patriotism and energy that was soon to effect so notable a metamorphosis.

Concentration of power in the council.

The Birmingham of 1871.

Fortunately, Birmingham had from the outset secured good men as councilors and mayors, and the time came when a growing local pride, an increased number of wealthy men who were able to retire from active control of great industries and manufactories, and a revival of interest throughout the kingdom in the sanitary conditions of the towns, gave Birmingham an exceptionally influential body of councilors. Foremost among these municipal statesmen was Mr. Joseph Chamberlain, then in early middle life, but already possessed of a great fortune accumulated in successful manufacture. In November, 1873, Mr. Chamberlain was elected mayor. He had served for several years in the council, and had gained a great influence. He brought to the mayor's chair an intimate knowledge of Birmingham's affairs, a strong ambition to accomplish great things, and a political and administrative ability that have since commanded the world's recognition.

Advent of Mr. Chamberlain.

Birmingham at this time was supplied with water and gas by private companies.   Several unsuccessful attempts to municipalize the water-supply had been made in the years previous to Mr. Chamberlain's mayoralty.   He was determined to bring both these agencies under the direct management of the council, and circumstances made it the better diplomacy to begin with the gas-works.   Two competing companies were supplying the citizens of Birmingham and lighting the streets.   Mr. Chamberlain undertook private negotiations, and found that it would be possible to induce these companies to sell out their works and business on terms that seemed to him reasonable.   He then presented the subject to the council, making an elaborate argument in favor of his proposed policy, particularly from the financial point of view.   He pointed out the growing need of municipal revenues for objects not directly remunerative, and held that the municipal management of the gas-supply would yield large net profits with which sanitary and educational expenses could be met.   He expressed confidence in the business ability of the council, and enumerated reasons why the municipality could manufacture and sell gas more economically than the private companies.   No phase of the subject was neglected in Mr. Chamberlain's comprehensive presentation.   The council was so completely convinced that a resolution favoring the purchase was adopted by a vote of fifty-four to two. When a few months later it was voted to ratify the purchase, there was only one opposing vote.   A large price was paid,— some $10,000,000,— but the bargain has proved very profitable.   The first year's profits were about $170,000, and they have steadily advanced until they are twice that amount.   Yet it has been found possible since 1875 to reduce the price to consumers from about seventy-five cents per thousand feet

Municipalizing the gas-supply.

Mr. Chamberlain's arguments.

The council convinced.

Success of the policy.

CHAP. VI. to about fifty cents. This reduction and other favorable arrangements have promoted the diffusion of gas among the poorer classes. The municipality in 1889 conceded the eight-hours day to its employees (nearly 2000) in the Gas Department, and in other respects there have accrued social as well as financial benefits from the policy of municipal operation.

Next, the water-supply. Success in his gas policy made it the easier for Mr. Chamberlain in the same year, 1874, to gain assent to the proposition of a municipal water-supply. The arguments for public water are obviously more irresistible than those for public lighting works. The mayor's plans were approved unanimously. Mr. Chamberlain's high personal position in the business community aided in the negotiations with the water company as in those with the gas-companies. The price paid for the existing waterworks was about $6,750,000. The company's supply had been inadequate, and a large part of the population had depended upon wells, many of which were dangerously contaminated. Mr. Chamberlain laid down the principle that a municipal water-department ought to be self-sustaining, but ought not to earn surplus profits. He advocated the policy of increasing and improving Doubling the per capita supply. the supply and of reducing the water rentals, rather than that of earning profits for the relief of the general ratepayers. Under municipal operation the works were extended, and the actual daily supply was doubled, while the cost per gallon to consumers was much reduced.

The great supply of the future Birmingham has now outgrown the old sources, and municipal enterprise has gone far afield for the great and inexhaustible supply of the future. What the municipality bought twenty years ago was a composite system of supply from neighboring streams and deep wells. As the demands upon the storage reservoirs had increased, new wells were sunk, or some additional stream was brought into requisition. And this mode of increase from time to time has been pursued by the corporation until now. But it has reached a natural limit; and it became evident several years ago that some bold project for the acquisition of a large, new source would have to be adopted. The uniformly brilliant results that had followed all the large experiments of the so-called "Chamberlain era" sufficed to give the council and the community the courage to face a still more costly undertaking. It was found that the most desirable of all possible sources of supply was the Elan river and its drainage basin, eighty miles distant in Wales. Powers were obtained from Parliament to acquire control of a great expanse of uninhabited Welsh moorland, lying at a height of from 800 to 2000 or more feet. Dams and reservoirs in that district, and eighty miles of aqueducts, would give Birmingham a supply good for a hundred years, and for a future population of several millions, and the ultimate cost of the undertaking would approximate $35,000,000. The present system necessitates a large annual outlay for pumping, while the "Welsh supply" will distribute itself by gravity. This saving will go far to pay the interest on the cost of the new undertaking; and if the water rentals are for a period of years restored to the schedule that existed in 1875, the entire stupendous project can be executed and made to bear its own financial burdens, including a sufficient sinking-fund, without drawing anything from the general municipal treasury. As in Glasgow, so in Birmingham, it is argued that a supply of soft, pure mountain water will save the citizens a vast amount in their soap bills and tea bills, besides conducing greatly to the development of numerous lines of manufacture.

Eighty miles to the Elan.

Advantages of the "Welsh undertaking."

For example, they contend that the soft water in steam-boilers will effect a saving of thousands of pounds sterling every year to the Birmingham factories.   The new system is to be constructed gradually, and Birmingham can easily sustain the financial charge.

But to return to Mr. Chamberlain's eventful years in the mayor's chair,— for he was twice reëlected, and therefore served continuously for three years,— there remains to be described his crowning achievement as a municipal statesman.   It was the boast of the third Napoleon that he found a Paris of brick and made it a Paris of marble.   Mr. Chamberlain's improvement scheme, which has resulted in the transformation of the central district of Birmingham, was not so showy or ambitious as the Paris reconstructions, but in its way it was not less noteworthy, and it may claim marked superiority in its freedom from financial scandals, and in the soundness and economy of its business methods.   Glasgow had made progress with its courageous renovation of the slums, as described in a previous chapter; and, guided largely by Glasgow's experience, Parliament had enacted the Artisans' Dwellings Act of 1875.   Under this act it was permissible for the local authorities of any large town to mark out an insanitary area for reconstruction and improvement; and upon approval of the scheme by the Local Government Board, and final parliamentary ratification, the municipal council could proceed to buy under compulsory powers at fair prices all the lands and buildings included in the area of the scheme, and could then rearrange streets, clear away condemned houses, and dispose of sites for the construction of sanitary dwellings on approved plans. Mr. Chamberlain had taken a great interest in the passage of this bill through Parliament, and at once proposed its application to Birmingham.

Some street improvements in the heart of the town had been effected from year to year, and the ingress of railroads, particularly, had broken through the huddled masses of old houses crowded together in narrow streets, lanes, and courts. But nothing radical had been accomplished, and the great town of Birmingham, having by that time nearly 400,000 people, had grown up around a nucleus surviving from old village days, unwholesome, mean, and altogether disgraceful. Mr. Chamberlain was not the less mindful of the public health, if he was equally zealous for the appearance of the town, and appreciative of the opportunity to secure a handsome business street or two, with modern public buildings and mercantile edifices. In his admirable history of the corporation of Birmingham, Mr. Bunce gives the following report of a part of Mr. Chamberlain's speech on July 27, 1875, when he presented the "Improvement Scheme" to the council:

It might run a great street, as broad as a Parisian boulevard, from New street to the Ashton road; it might open up a street such as Birmingham had not got, and was almost stifling for the want of—for all the best streets were too narrow. The council might demolish the houses on each side of the street, and let or sell the frontage land, and arrange for rebuilding workmen's houses behind, taking the best advantage of the sites, and building them in accordance with the latest sanitary knowledge, and the requirements of the medical officer of health. Having made such a scheme as that, the council would have to go to the Local Government Board, and they would institute an enquiry, and should they approve of the scheme, they would carry through Parliament a provisional order which would have the force of law, so that the council would get the advantage of a private improvement act, without the responsibility and cost, which were thrown upon the government. This act having been obtained, the council would have the power of compulsory purchase of the whole of the property, without paying one penny for the compulsory sale. This was an important provision, for the British Parliament had, for the first time, recognized something higher than property. They should not have to pay the landlords what was termed *solatium;* they would be able to acquire the property at a fair market price, without anything added for compulsory purchase. Having got possession of the property, the council would proceed gradually to lay out the streets and open up the approaches. The council were not, except as a last resort, to undertake any building speculation, but were to employ others to carry out this work. Another important facility was given to the council which they had not hitherto enjoyed. Having obtained the freehold of the land, they were no longer bound to sell what they did not want for their improvement. They might lease it for years, and consequently secure for future generations of ratepayers the advantages hitherto secured by a few large land-owners in the town. They had a power, also, under the act, to raise loans, and the Treasury had power to lend them the money at $3\frac{1}{2}$ per cent., and those loans were to be repayable in a period of fifty years, and any deficiency, if there was any, as the result of such changes, would be thrown upon the borough rate, to which the ratepayers proportionately contributed. He did not suppose that such a scheme as he had suggested could be carried out without some expense to the ratepayers, but it would not involve nearly so much expense as the bit-by-bit improvements which they were making in the town, and which never repaid in proportion to their cost.

Financial aspects.

Several years were required for the preliminaries, but Mr. Chamberlain's project was adopted with spirit and energy, and with results that have thus far vindicated most strikingly the sagacity of his predictions. The chief monument of the undertaking is " Corporation street," Birmingham's finest public thoroughfare and business avenue, splendidly built up with new and solid structures that will become the property of the municipality when the seventy-five-year ground leases expire. The area included in the improvement scheme was about 90 acres in extent, and was covered with about 4000 houses, in which from 15,000 to 20,000 people were living. The mortality rate of this district was very high, in some streets

The project as carried out.

being several times as great as that of the more favored parts of the city. The condemnation proceedings
were tedious and delayed, but the city's estimates of
value were generally sustained by the courts, and the
gross outlay amounted, as Mr. Chamberlain had predicted, to about $8,000,000. It was not expected that,
after creating new streets and rearranging the district,
the city could wholly recoup itself by sales or leases   Financial
of building sites. It was anticipated that about one   results.
third of the expenditure would have to be met out of
the municipal treasury. As revenue accounts now
stand, the improvement scheme costs annually for interest, sinking-fund, and various charges about $400,-
000, and receives in rentals about $300,000. But the
rent-roll will grow considerably, and the interest and
sinking-fund charges will diminish; so that within a
very few years the turning point will have been reached,
and this department of the municipal administration
will yield a surplus revenue. In fifty years from the
time of the investment, the debt will all have been
paid off, and then the ground rents for twenty-five
years, or thereabouts, will accrue to the municipal
treasury as clear income. And at the end of that
period the leases will fall in, and the improvements —
chief of which are the palatial business houses that   Eventual
line both sides of Corporation street — will become   corporate
                                                          revenues.
municipal property without cost to the city or compensation to the retiring lessees. Then, as Mr. Chamberlain has said, Birmingham will be the richest
municipal corporation in the kingdom, and it will bless
the memory of the council of 1875 that had the fore-
sight to make such plans.

In so far as a working-class population remains in
the area dealt with, there has been a vast improvement in the average health. The municipal authorities
have tried the experiment of building and renting a

I.—12*

CHAP. VI.

Municipal
model cot-
tages.

Brilliant
success of
improve-
ment
scheme.

considerable number of model five-room cottages. As a health measure, the improvement scheme of 1875 has repaid all that it cost, while as a project for the modernization and adornment of a commercial city that possesses a due measure of local pride, it has also been justified. But in the end, perhaps, it will have attracted still greater attention as a brilliant financial stroke, and as a demonstration of the rate-saving possibilities that lie in land municipalization.

It was during Mr. Chamberlain's period of municipal leadership that a fourth great project, the existing drainage system, was given its determining character. The small river Tame is the natural outlet for the drainage of Birmingham and the surrounding country. But its further pollution with sewage had long since become intolerable. The sewage committee of the council had made exhaustive inquiries, and had reached the conclusion that for Birmingham the sewage-farm system would offer the true solution.

Sewage-
farms.

Drainage
Board of the
Tame and
Rea valleys.

In a limited way the system was begun, but practical difficulties prevented its large development until after Parliament had passed the Public Health Act of 1875. This act authorized the union of contiguous municipalities and districts for the formation of a Drainage Board with comprehensive authority to deal with the sewage of a region whose parts belonged naturally to the same drainage basin. Mr. Chamberlain, as mayor of Birmingham, presided in 1875 over a joint meeting of representatives of the towns and rural districts pertaining to the valleys of the Tame and Rea. Birmingham comprised most of the population, but only about one fourth of the area. Not to dwell upon details, let it be said that the union was duly formed, under a managing board of twenty-two members, to which the mayors of Birmingham and Aston Manor belonged *ex officio,* while the other twenty included eleven from the Birmingham council and one each from nine outside districts. It was a work of great difficulty that lay before the commission, but its chairman, Alderman Avery of Birmingham, gave years to its consummation. By successive purchases a farm of some 1500 acres, possessing all the requisites of location, slope, and subsoil, was acquired. Great sewer tunnels, intercepting the street mains, carry the foul liquid out to the subsidence-tanks at Saltley, where treatment with lime assists the precipitation of solids, and the liquid, by irrigation and soil filtration, is at length carried off through underground tiles, pure enough to pass into the adjacent streams, and eventually into the river Tame, without doing the slightest violence to the spirit or the letter of those stringent acts that now forbid the pollution of English rivers. At first, the disposition of the "sludge" in the subsidence-tanks was a hard problem. When spread out over the soil, it was so offensive that it rendered the very name of "sewage-farms" odious in all the vicinage. But after a time it was learned that the sludge could be spaded into shallow trenches, covered with fresh soil, and thus gradually absorbed as a fertilizer without causing any annoyance whatsoever to the neighboring farmers. In fact, the Birmingham sewage-farm is altogether a wholesome and agreeable tract of land, under high cultivation, and exceedingly rich in crops. The subsoil is pure gravel, and constitutes a natural filter-bed. The farm can be gradually extended as the quantity of sewage increases, and the system is fully equal to any test to which it can ever be subjected.

Irrigation system established.

Solving practical difficulties.

The system of intercepting sewage-tunnels and filtration-farms was only one half of the great scheme for the proper disposal of refuse that was adopted by Birmingham in the seventies. Until that system were fully developed, it was obvious that the sewers should be kept as free as possible from solid waste. In 1871, with more than 73,000 houses in the town, there were less than 4000 water-closets. For the most part there Collection of garbage and refuse. was in use a most objectionable system of "middens." The water-closet as a substitute not being immediately feasible for lack of sewage-disposal works, the so-called Rochdale system of closet-pans and ash-tubs was introduced on a large scale. This system has been continued, with a high degree of local approbation. Although there are now more than 20,000 water-closets in use in Birmingham, the pan-closets are nearly twice as numerous. The "pans" are heavy galvanized iron cylinders, 18 inches in diameter and 15 inches deep, and the city owns a vast supply of them. They are easily removable, and once every week, in the night, the closed vans of the Health Department remove them, substituting cleansed cylinders. Each house is also supplied with a specially designed ash-tub, for kitchen garbage and other solid refuse as well as ashes; and the contents of these are emptied into a box attached to the van that removes the "pans." The whole work is organized by districts with perfect system. There are several receiving-stations, all located on canal wharves. The coarser garbage is consumed in furnaces, of which there are Cremation system. about fifty in operation. The fine contents of the ash-pits are mixed with a portion of the contents of the closet-pans, forming a fertilizer that is removed by canal-boats and sold to farmers. But most of the Making fertilizers. material from the pans is made into a dry, powdered fertilizer by evaporation in special machines. The heat derived from the burning garbage suffices to work the evaporating machines. The "poudrette" fertilizer is sold at $30 a ton. The residuum of the incinerated garbage is a mass of "clinkers," useful for concrete or mortar, for road-making, or for filling low ground.   The Health Department makes large use of the canals that radiate from Birmingham, and owns thirty or forty capacious canal-boats, which are in constant use for the removal of fertilizers and other final products of the sanitary works which deal with the cleansings and refuse of a great city.   All in all, Birmingham has evolved a most complete and satisfactory system for the public management of every form of waste material — a system adapted in all its parts to the actual conditions of the place.

Chap. VI.

A municipal canal-boat service.

The elaborate reorganization of the Health Department of Birmingham dates from 1875.   Besides the disposal of sewage and refuse, the health committee of the council was charged with the inspection of houses and removal of nuisances, with maintenance of epidemic hospitals and disinfection facilities, and with milk and food inspection.   Dr. Alfred Hill, who still serves in that capacity, was appointed Medical Officer of Health, and a great increase in the staff of inspectors at once wrought a marvelous change.   From 20,000 to 30,000 nuisances a year were reported and abated. Within seven or eight years, more than 3000 wells, used by 60,000 people, were condemned on the ground of serious sewage contamination, and permanently closed.   Domestic cleanliness was enforced, zymotic diseases which had prevailed were successfully attacked, and within a few short years an average yearly death-rate of about twenty-six per 1000 was reduced to twenty or less.   This signified the saving of from 2000 to 2500 lives each year, the prevention of scores of thousands of cases of illness, a marked increase in the average longevity, and particularly a revolution in the survival and health of infants in the poorer streets.   The average for the whole city does not express the measure of benefit reaped by the streets and

Reorganized Health Department.

Closing contaminated wells.

Great reduction of death-rate.

CHAP. VI.

districts most seriously concerned. There were local-ities where the death-rate had averaged year by year from sixty to eighty per 1000 inhabitants, and where a few years of the new sanitary administration reduced the rate to from twenty to twenty-five. Birmingham is a naturally healthy place, and the high death-rate had been due to remediable conditions. Twenty years of reformed health arrangements have wrought a com-plete transformation, and amount in their aggregate results to one of the chief triumphs of city govern-ment in this generation.

Marvelous results in special dis-tricts.

Birmingham illustrates well the recentness of the general movement among commercial towns, elsewhere as well as in England, for parks and recreation grounds. Until 1856 the town did not possess a square foot of land devoted to such purposes. In that year a ten-acre park was presented to the corporation, and in the next year one of thirty-one acres was given by another local benefactor. Agitation for more such grounds became rife, and Aston Park of fifty acres was acquired in 1864. It was in 1873 that Miss Ryland gave Can-non Hill Park of nearly sixty acres, and within the next ten years four or five other smaller parks and gardens were added to the list. More recently there have been several other acquisitions, so that the parks committee has in keeping some fourteen parks and grounds, with a total extent of 350 acres. If this area is nothing very impressive, it should be understood that Birmingham's parks are easily accessible, well distributed, and handsomely maintained as true plea-sure gardens for the people.

Parks and open spaces.

In charge of the same committee of the council (the parks and baths committee, which also maintains cemeteries somewhat upon the plan of those described in the foregoing account of Manchester) are the Bir-mingham public baths. For some reason, the idea

Cemeteries as in Man-chester.

of municipal baths obtained favor in England many
years earlier than the period of the public health acts
and the more thorough sanitary reforms.   It was in
1844 that the "Association for Promoting Cleanliness
among the People" was formed in London, and in
1846 Parliament passed the Baths and Wash-houses
Act, under which municipal and other local authorities
were permitted to establish public baths and laundries, at low prices, in the interest of health and decency.   Birmingham people were ardent in the movement, and voluntary association was superseded by
municipal action in 1848, when the council adopted
the baths act.   It was in 1851 that the first establishment was completed and opened at a cost of about
$120,000.   Its popularity was immediate, and it was
patronized by a hundred thousand bathers a year.
In 1860 a second establishment was opened, followed
by a third one in 1862.   The bathers soon averaged
two hundred thousand a year, and gradually increased
to three hundred thousand.   In 1863 a fourth great
establishment was opened, and the bathers at once
increased to four hundred thousand.   These are, of
course, in perennial use, and artificially warmed in
winter.   But the committee also provides open-air
summer baths in two or three of the parks.   The
school-children of Birmingham have the pleasure and
benefit of splendid swimming-baths, the year around,
at the price of a halfpenny for each bath.   Citizens
who wish to pay for Turkish baths find them provided at a shilling.   It is not attempted to make these
establishments fully self-sustaining.   The running expenses of the system are more than $35,000 a year,
and the receipts from bathers are less than $30,000.
The city, moreover, has interest to pay on an investment of $350,000.   But when the benefits to school-
children alone — not to mention the hosts of young

Beginnings
of public
baths.

Birming-
ham's muni-
cipal estab-
lishments.

Open-air
summer
baths.

Charges, and
financial
status.

working men and women — are considered, the net charge against the rates is a trifling matter for a rich city of half a million people.

The laundry feature of the Birmingham baths was abandoned some years ago, because its limited patronage proved that it was not a public necessity. In Glasgow this auxiliary has been growingly successful. But the housing accommodation of the two cities is totally unlike. The Glasgow family lives in a flatted tenement-house, often with only one or two rooms at its command, and with no separate facilities for washing. There are no such buildings in Birmingham. Each family lives in a small but separate house, and provision is made for washing. The public wash-houses of Birmingham were the result of a theory rather than the outcome of a pressing local condition, and they had to be abandoned. The experiment was not, however, a costly one, inasmuch as the abandoned laundry quarters were needed for the extension of bathing facilities.

Municipal
wash-houses
not wanted
by Birming-
ham house-
wives.

Perhaps in no other municipal undertaking has Birmingham ever shown a finer enthusiasm than in the establishment and development of the free-library system. It was in 1850 that Parliament passed the first Free Libraries Act, and in 1855 that important amendments made it better available for local adoption. The Birmingham voters confirmed the action of the council, and adopted the libraries act early in 1860. The act, in brief, authorized the levy of a penny rate for the creation and support of free libraries and museums. At that time, such a rate was productive of an income of about $17,500. The libraries committee reported that "the scheme, as a whole, should comprise a central reference-library, with reading- and news-rooms, a museum and gallery of art, and four district lending-libraries, with news-rooms attached." Within seven or eight years this whole system had been created, and the number of volumes in all the libraries had reached fifty thousand. The patronage was enormous from the very beginning. In 1872 the innovation of Sunday opening was made, in the face of an opposition at first strong and bitter, but afterward altogether withdrawn. A fire in 1879 that destroyed the central reference collection only served to demonstrate the popularity of the institution. The citizens contributed large gifts of money, and the restored library soon exceeded in all respects that which was destroyed. The branch libraries have now been increased in number, the aggregated volumes exceed 200,000, and the yearly issue of books reaches 1,000,-000 or more, while the patronage of the newspaper and periodical reading-rooms has grown to a remarkable total. The devotion of the best citizens has been shown in generous gifts of special collections; and the central library has many rare and distinctive features that add to its charm and its value. The library rate has been increased somewhat from the original penny, and the department has an income of about $65,000 a year for all purposes, including the art museum and gallery.

The municipal art-gallery began modestly as an annex to the central library. But so many gifts have been made to it by the public-spirited citizens of the town that it has come to assume both proportions and importance. It is now well housed, adequately maintained, and highly popular. As an outgrowth of this art museum, Birmingham maintains a central school of art, with several branches, chiefly for night pupils from the working-classes; and the desirability of the undertaking has been proven by the fact that three thousand or more pupils avail themselves of the opportunity to study; nearly all of these pupils being instructed in various applications of art to the local industries in which they are employed.

Like Manchester and other progressive towns, Bir- New policy mingham availed itself promptly of the opportunities in technical education. afforded by the Technical Instruction Act of 1889, as supplemented by an act of 1890 which makes available for the support of technical education a large part of the excise taxes which formerly went to the national treasury. Thus the so-called Exchequer Contribution Fund now gives Birmingham every year a sum which, after providing for police superannuation, etc., leaves from $30,000 to $40,000 for the maintenance of municipal technical schools. The corporation proceeded at once to open temporary schools, and to make plans for a great central building to cost $300,000 or more, which is to be opened before the end of 1895 as one of the best-equipped technical schools in the kingdom. It need not be added that the school-board of Birmingham, which provides ample facilities for elementary instruction, is in full sympathy with the municipal policy of practical education along lines that shall train boys and girls to places of usefulness and assured self-support in the local industrial community.

I have yet to refer to Birmingham's policy as respects street railways. George Francis Train's famous attempts to introduce tramways in the British towns in 1860 did not neglect Birmingham. Mr. Train was granted an experimental concession which Corpora- he failed to utilize, and in 1861 the corporation itself tion's street- car lines. obtained parliamentary authority to build tramways. But nothing was done until after the General Tramways Act of 1870 was passed. At length in 1873 the council laid the first line, at a cost of $75,000, and leased it for seven years to an operating company.

From time to time other lines have been built and leased; but the corporation's limits included only 8400 acres until November 9, 1891, when they were increased to 12,365 acres by the annexation of suburbs then containing some 50,000 people.   Thus, when the corporation's street-railway system was under construction, the average distance from the center to the circumference of Birmingham was only two miles; and twenty-two miles of tram lines are the total extent of the municipal ownership.   Outside of the city's jurisdiction, the operating companies have extended the lines by a still greater mileage.   In the future, undoubtedly, these extensions will be acquired by the Birmingham corporation at a fair valuation, in accordance with the methods prescribed in the General Tramways Act.   The present municipal lines are operated in part by horse-power and in part by steam, with cable and electricity also introduced on certain routes.   The terms of rental are worthy of mention.   First, the leasing companies agree to pay 4 per cent. on the full municipal investment for the first fourteen years of the lease, and 5 per cent. for the remaining seven years.   Second, the companies also pay an annual sum which at compound interest will accumulate a fund equal to the whole capital outlay at the end of the twenty-one years' lease.   It is calculated and agreed that 4 per cent. for fourteen years and 5 per cent. for the remaining seven years will suffice to raise the full amount of capital.   Meanwhile, also, the companies pay all current charges for repairs and maintenance of the lines, upon receiving bills certified by the city surveyor.   It should be remembered that Birmingham is able to borrow at very low rates; and it is clear that these terms are profitable to the municipality.   At the end of the twenty-one years, the earning value of the franchises will have

CHAP. VI.

Limited by
narrow mu-
nicipal
boundaries.

Terms of the
leases.

Favorable
rules and
regulations.

increased, and new leases can be executed on terms still more advantageous to the city. But while Birmingham has thus protected the ratepayers so handsomely, it has accomplished even more in the guarding of the interests of the traveling public. Every detail as to rates of fare and character of service is prescribed in the by-laws and regulations that the companies have to accept. The minuteness of the requirements touching duties and conduct of drivers and conductors, furnishing and lighting of cars, and so on, would amaze an American community.

Extension
of boundaries desirable.

It is readily apparent that it would have been advantageous for Birmingham to have secured many years ago a large increase of territory. The municipal gas-works, the drainage system, the water-supply and the transit system already serve an area much greater than that which is included within the boundaries as now extended. The city should have had direct control over the streets and house-building of this suburban area, and should have been in position to lay down for itself the tram-line extensions.

Municipal
market system.

Birmingham at an early day (1824) acquired from the manorial lord the market rights which had long been held as private sources of emolument, and there has been developed a series of important public markets, which aid in the cheap "*approvisionment*" of the city, and make more feasible and certain the thorough health inspection of food-supplies. The markets yield a considerable net revenue.

Growth of
the debt.

In 1872, just before Mr. Chamberlain became mayor, Birmingham's municipal indebtedness was somewhat more than $2,500,000. Since then, it has raised in loans for what may be called investments of capital about $45,000,000. A portion of this sum has been repaid, but the debt still stands at approximately $40,000,000. This would be a formidable sum if there

were little or nothing to show for it, or if it had for
the most part been sunk in unproductive expenditures.
But the support of this huge outlay has not added
anything to the rates, which remain almost exactly
what they were in 1873. Birmingham's finances are Not a public burden.
consolidated and admirably managed, and the average
interest rate on its debt is a little over three per cent.
Mr. Chamberlain had foreseen the necessary growth
of unproductive expenditures, and had favored the
municipal control of productive monopolies of supply
as an offset. His forecasts have been justified. Municipal water, gas, tramways, markets, etc., have, from
the financial point of view, been completely success-
ful. In all the municipal financiering, the accounts Successful financiering.
of the several departments are kept distinct; and it
is the laudable ambition of each council committee to
make the revenues of its particular department go as
far as possible toward meeting the current expenses.
Each specific investment is provided with a sinking-
fund that must extinguish the debt within a prescribed
period; and thus the great volume of indebtedness is
as easily and precisely managed as if it were only one
tenth as large. Viewing the expenditure as a whole,
it has been made more advantageously by far than The commu-nity en-riched.
any private firms or companies could have effected it,
and the community, as individuals and as a corporate
body, is the richer at least by two or three dollars for
every dollar of the forty or fifty millions that the corporation has dared to borrow and invest.

CHAPTER VII

SOCIAL ACTIVITIES OF BRITISH TOWNS

BEFORE passing on to a survey of the government of the great English metropolis, there may be some advantage in a rapid review of the growing municipal activity of the provincial towns. The accounts that I have given of the social progress under municipal auspices in Glasgow, Manchester, and Birmingham will suffice as representative sketches of individual towns, although Liverpool, Leeds, Nottingham, Sheffield, Edinburgh, and several other large centers would furnish instructive pictures of recent municipal development. It will be enough if a remarkable period of awakening and improvement in the British towns can be made the more clearly comprehensible by a summary grouping of facts and statistics.

A period of municipal progress.

The chief motive in all this work of town improvement has been the promotion of the health and civilization of the community. Commercial considerations and the sentiments of local pride have played their part. A wholesome spirit of emulation in good works has come to the aid of the local leaders whose own motives were of a higher order. One town's enterprise in the matter of a noble water-supply has powerfully stimulated action in other towns. An attractive system of libraries and reading-rooms in A or B, has had a decisive effect upon C, D, E, and F. In a review of

Dominant motives.

some of the departments of municipal activity that
are now most characteristic of the English towns,
there is no need of any attempt at a classification of
functions.   There is a limited usefulness, sometimes,
in distinguishing between monopolistic services of
local supply, and other services not regarded by economists as naturally tending to monopoly.   And for
financial purposes there are obvious advantages in
distinguishing between the revenue-earning or productive services, and those that are supported wholly
or chiefly out of rates or taxes.   But no such classification can ever serve a permanent end.   At least it
must yield to frequent revision.   As to many departments, the classification would only register a prevailing policy.   Thus, water-supply is commonly managed
as a self-sustaining and moderately productive department, while drainage with sewage-disposal is considered unproductive.   But in point of theory it would
be perfectly feasible to reverse the management of
these two equally necessary and complementary services, and to distribute water freely, charging the
expense against the general treasury, while making
the disposal of sewage and other waste a productive
municipal monopoly.

The large British towns have had the wisdom to
perceive of late that a good water-supply is the most
imperative of all local considerations.   They have
learned that a public supply is desirable because no
private company can find it profitable to make account of the motives that should govern the fixing of
a permanent system.   I have mentioned in detail the
great water undertakings of Glasgow, Manchester,
and Birmingham.   These costly supplies of pure water will result in a wonderful variety of indirect com-
pensating advantages to their respective communities,

CHAP. VII.

Classifica-
tion of
functions.

Question of
water-sup-
ply.

and, considered as public investments, are unimpeach-
ably sound; but as private investments they would
have been ruinous, for the simple reason that a private company could not have turned indirect benefits
into cash dividends. In general, it is the approved
plan of British towns to obtain soft and pure water
from high sources, so that it may be introduced and
distributed by gravity. Pumping expenses are thus
saved; and this saving — as against the cost of a system which pumps up and artificially filters a contam-

inated river water — is enough to pay a large part of
the interest on the initial cost of a mountain supply
brought a long distance by aqueduct. Moreover, the
advantage of the gravity system for the Fire Department and for hydraulic-power works represents another large annual saving. It is, therefore, the policy
of the British towns to secure control, each for itself,
of some elevated and uninhabited area whose water-
shed it can preëmpt, and whose extent gives assur-
ance of a quantity of water large enough for future
needs.

I have mentioned Glasgow's Loch Katrine supply,
Manchester's acquisition of Lake Thirlmere, and Birmingham's bold project of a supply from the Elan in

the mountains of Wales. Liverpool has also gone to
Wales for its supply, which it derives from Lake
Vyrnwy, and conveys a distance of 68 miles through
aqueducts. This splendid public work was completed
in the summer of 1892, some $10,000,000 having been

expended upon it. Bradford, one of England's most
progressive municipalities,— a town of some 225,000
inhabitants,— has also gone far afield for a safe and
permanent supply of water. It had protected its existing nearer sources by the purchase of large areas
of land to guard against possible contamination; but
now it has secured as a heritage for future genera-

tions (by terms of the Bradford Water Act of 1890)
" the almost uninhabited and uncultivated moorlands
at the sources of the river Nidd on the slopes of
Great Whernside, distant 40 miles from the town,"
whence an unfailing supply of pure water will be
brought by aqueducts. Cardiff, the Severn seaport   Cardiff's
and South Wales metropolis, purchased the works of a   mountain
private water-company in 1879 at a cost of $1,500,000,   supply.
and since then has spent $3,000,000 more upon a
scheme which brings the purest of water from the
Taff Fawr valley, distant 32 miles in the hills. Bolton, an excellent type of the best manufacturing
towns, with a population approaching 125,000, brings   The case of
its admirable water-supply from the Entwisle moors,   Bolton.
which fortunately are only a few miles distant, although the works have cost about $4,000,000. Shef-
field has since 1887 purchased the waterworks from
a private company at a cost of $7,500,000, and is im-   Sheffield,
proving them. The sources are some miles distant   Leeds, Hull,
and are of a fortunate character. Leeds, the great   Nottingham,
Yorkshire manufacturing town, has an elaborate sys-   Leicester.
tem of storage and filtering reservoirs and pumping-
works through which it distributes the water of the
river Washburn; and Hull, Yorkshire's seaport, has a
good public supply. Nottingham and Leicester, also
representative manufacturing towns of approximately
200,000 inhabitants each, municipalized both water
and gas some twenty years ago, with good results.

The magnitude of municipal investments in waterworks may be illustrated by the statement that the
outstanding indebtedness of English and Welsh local   Huge invest-
authorities on account of this one item has reached   ments in
$200,000,000 and is nearly one fifth of the aggregate   waterworks.
of local debts. Most of this vast outlay has been incurred since 1870. Sinking-funds are accruing to
meet maturing obligations; and the completion of
I.—13*

water systems for the larger towns makes it almost
certain that after the year 1900 the annual cost of new
works will be less than the annual growth of sinking-
funds, and thus the net volume of waterworks indebtedness will decrease.

It is interesting to note the fact that English local
authorities are taking up the question of sewerage
and sewage-disposal with such vigor that they are now
spending more every year in that direction than upon
water-supplies, although the aggregate indebtedness
for sewer-works in 1892 was only half as great as the
water debt, having reached just $100,000,000. In a
recent year, $4,000,000 of borrowed capital was spent
upon new public waterworks, and $5,000,000 upon
main drainage-works and sewage treatment. Such is
the energy with which English municipalities take up
great questions and deal with them in the order of
their importance. It will not be necessary to cite
many instances, in addition to those presented in the
three foregoing chapters. Sheffield is spending a
great sum upon its Blackburn Meadows sewage-pre-
cipitation works. Salford, which obtains its water-
supply from Manchester, has carried into operation a
very elaborate scheme for the collection and artificial purification of sewage—an exceedingly creditable
system for this public-spirited town of 200,000 people.
Oldham, also in the Manchester district, a fine town
of 150,000 people, famous for its weaving industries,
is now spending a million dollars upon works for the
interception and treatment of sewage. Chorley, in
the same neighborhood, has a good system of sewage-
farms. Leicester has developed a sewage-farm of
about 1400 acres, and is a model corporation in its
sanitary engineering system. Leamington, in War-
wickshire, furnishes an illustration of excellent sani-

Side notes:

Question of sewers and sewage.

Drainage-works investment.

Sheffield.

Salford.

Oldham and Chorley.

Leicester.

Leamington.

tary arrangements in a smaller town. It has fewer
than 30,000 inhabitants, but its water-supply is derived
from lofty hills, and its sewage is successfully treated
by land irrigation. Shakespeare's town of Stratford,
in the same lovely Avon valley, is also a model of
cleanliness, with a good public water-supply and a
sewage-farm of the most modern character. The large
towns of Wolverhampton and West Bromwich are
among the English municipalities that have adopted
the sewage-farm as the true solution of a difficult
problem. The same thing is true of ancient Canter-
bury, of Tunbridge Wells, and of Darlington. Practically all the large British towns have now executed
main drainage-works of a permanent character, and
it only remains for those that are still draining into
rivers or the sea either to divert the intercepted sewage to irrigation farms, or else to establish works on
the Manchester model for artificial precipitation and
cleansing.

Municipal gas-works were undertaken by many of
the English towns, at the same time that the water-
supply was municipalized. The arguments in favor
of the public control of gas-supplies are certainly not
so strong as those that can be urged in the case of
water. The gas business rests upon a more strictly
commercial basis, and furthermore it does not involve
any of those far-reaching questions as to the source
and nature of the supply that, in most cases, make it
wise for towns to manage their own water. But if a
city wants excuses for assuming the manufacture and
sale of gas, they are numerous enough. It is itself
a large consumer, in street-illumination and public
buildings. The distribution of gas requires the use
of the public streets for pipes; and a private company's occupation of any part of the streets is con-

CHAP. VII.

sidered highly objectionable in England and in Germany. Gas is necessarily a monopoly product; and its sale at somewhere near cost can only be expected of the public authorities. In many incidental ways, the authorities are at an advantage in the business. Some of the arguments that would apply even in America have a greatly added force in England.

General use of gas in British towns.

Vastly more use must be made there, for climatic reasons, of artificial light. Gas is almost universally used by all classes in England and Scotland, while in America refined petroleum is largely used. An abundant supply of a cheap illuminant is a social desideratum of the highest consequence in a country where during the winter the daylight does not suffice for indoor occupations a longer time on the average than from five to six hours in the twenty-four.

A boon to the poor.

The boon of cheap gas to the poor in tenement-houses, for instance, is inestimable. It is one of the foremost agencies of civilization. Again, an abundant use of artificial light in the gloomy towns of England and Scotland is a potent safeguard against crime. One is constantly told by chiefs of police that "each light counts for a constable."

As a police measure.

Financial considerations.

It was, however, largely from revenue considerations that the English and Scotch towns assumed the gas business. They believed that they could not only cheapen gas to the consumers and provide a more ample street-lighting, but also earn net profits and thus reduce the rates. Not to enter upon a detailed discussion, I can only say that it is almost the universal testimony in Great Britain that the municipal gas enterprises are a brilliant success. They have steadily reduced the selling price, and largely increased the

Efficiency of public management.

consumption. Their management has been as efficient and economical as that of the private companies. They have been able, while selling gas at a low price,

to pay expenses and interest, accumulate sinking-
funds, enlarge the plants and make good all current
depreciations, and still pay net profits into the municipal treasuries. The price in the large towns is generally from 50 cents to 75 cents per 1000 feet. The
net profits are in most places kept low by reductions
of price whenever they tend to become very considerable. But when the initial cost of the works has been
paid off, it will manifestly be feasible to maintain
prices and to pay into the town treasuries the large
sums that now go to sinking-fund and interest accounts; and then the gas-works will be very productive properties.

In 1893 there were in the United Kingdom 185 com-   Number of
munities that maintained public gas-supplies, the   municipal
number having increased from 148 in 1883. Of these,   gas under-takings.
34 were in Scotland and 6 in Ireland. Belfast, Limer-
ick, Tralee, and Newry are the chief Irish towns that
make their own gas. The Scotch list includes all of
the principal places, the Edinburgh corporation having several years ago purchased the plants of two gas-
companies that had supplied Edinburgh and Leith.   Wide popu-
The notable thing about municipal gas in Scotch towns   lar distri-
is its marvelously wide distribution to the homes of   bution of gas
in Scotch
the people, and the extent to which the municipality   towns.
makes itself responsible for public lighting. Thus,
according to returns for 1893, the number of consumers (that is, of separate accounts) in the town of
Paisley was 14,346; in Aberdeen there were 24,475;
in Dundee, 32,629; in Edinburgh-Leith, 61,397, and in
Glasgow, 156,980. In these Scotch towns the munici-   Lighting
common
pal authorities light the common stairs of tenement-   stairs in
houses as well as the regular streets; and it is prob-   Scotland.
ably true of Edinburgh, Dundee, and Aberdeen, as it
certainly is of Glasgow, that the common stairs and
courts of tenement-houses are lighted at a greater cost

for gas and wages than the public streets. Thus the total number of public gas-lights reported from these Scotch towns was as follows: Paisley, 1,682; Aberdeen, 3,824; Dundee, 4,746; Edinburgh, 11,522; and Glasgow, 20,648. Considering population and area, these numbers of public lights are unprecedented.

Another interesting outcome of the assumption of the gas business by the Scotch municipal authorities, and to some extent also by the English, is the attempt to encourage the use of gas as a domestic fuel by supplying stoves and fixtures at a very low rental and by keeping them in order and repair. Edinburgh has adopted Glasgow's policy in this regard, and Aberdeen and Dundee are also leasing and selling gas-stoves. Convenience and economy will undoubtedly make gas the ordinary domestic fuel of the future in these towns, and, as purveyors of gas, the municipal authorities would seem to be justified in providing such facilities as will hasten the innovation. But whether they can wisely attempt in the future to compete with private enterprise in supplying stoves and utensils, either of their own manufacture or under the contract system, must remain for experience to determine, the presumption being wholly in favor of private enterprise. The important point, however, is that in these Scotch, and in some English, towns the fuel-supply, following the water- and the illumination-supply, is fast tending toward the form of a local-service monopoly, and that as such it is already passing into the hands of the municipal authorities for manufacture and distribution. It is further to be observed that as soon as the demand for fuel gas becomes sufficiently large it will be manufactured separately, and at much lower prices than the differently constituted illuminating fluid, and will be distributed in separate pipes. It is to be remarked, also, that if electricity should supersede gas as an illuminant, the existing gas-works would be available for the fuel-supply, and would not, therefore, as some persons have predicted, lose their value.

Comparing the returns of the 185 public gas un-dertakings in the United Kingdom with those of the 429 private companies, it appears that, if London and its adjacent populations (which are still chiefly sup-plied by private companies) were omitted, the public works are supplying considerably more than half of all the consumers, and making rather more than half of all the gas. And the municipal supply is steadily gaining upon the private supply. Although the re-ports of 1893 showed that the receipts of private com-panies were £12,693,000 and those of public gas-works only £5,983,000, it was further shown that the public works supplied 1,203,574 consumers as against 1,213,-322 for the private companies, while the public de-partments also supplied 201,484 public lamps, the private works supplying 288,021. The huge metro-politan consumption, however, swells enormously the volume of gas made and sold by private companies ; and the public gas is only about 60 per cent. as great in amount. Outside of London, the great towns still supplied by private companies are Liverpool, Dublin, Sheffield, Bristol, and Hull. On the side of municipal supply are nearly all of the enterprising commercial centers : Glasgow, Manchester, Birmingham, Belfast, Edinburgh-Leith, Leeds, Bradford, Nottingham, Bol-ton, Leicester, Dundee, Aberdeen, Huddersfield, Old-ham, Salford, Rochdale, and a host besides. The ordinary gross receipts of municipal gas-works in the United Kingdom have now reached an aggregate of more than $30,000,000 a year, and the expenditures are about $24,000,000. The local indebtedness on ac-count of gas undertakings exceeds $75,000,000, and this large investment is both safe and profitable.

Comparative statistics of public and private sup-plies.

Nearly all large towns have public gas-works.

Debt and finance.

CHAP. VII.

Question of
street rail-
ways.

Liverpool's
municipal
lines.

Almost exactly one third of the mileage of street railways in Great Britain has been constructed and is owned by the municipal or local authorities. I have explained in detail the policies of Glasgow, Birmingham, Manchester, and Salford. Liverpool also has preferred to control tram lines as a part of the street surface, and has kept them in municipal hands. The Liverpool system embraces about thirty miles, most of it double-tracked, and has cost $1,500,000. It is operated by a leasing company which pays rents amounting to 10 per cent. on the city's investment. Inasmuch as the corporation pays only about 3 per cent. interest, and the maintenance expenses are not heavy, it is obvious that the rentals are rapidly paying off the original cost, besides leaving a considerable sum for net profits which Liverpool applies to the general cost of such works as street-paving. In the early future Liverpool's tram lines will be far more remunerative than at present; for under renewed leases the city can secure a higher rental.

Terms of
Sheffield's
lease.

Sheffield a few years ago constructed ten miles of tram lines, which are leased on terms that will soon have made them an unencumbered municipal asset, and a source of much profit. Glasgow's experiences must have interest for Sheffield, because the lease to the Sheffield Tramways Company, executed in July, 1875, for twenty-one years, expires in 1896; and the municipal corporation can at its option acquire the working plant, after which it may re-lease the system on terms of increased advantage or, with special parliamentary consent to be had for the asking, it may venture upon direct municipal operation. The form of the existing Sheffield lease is deserving of mention. First, the company pays the city a yearly interest on the full amount of the city's investment and outlay of all kinds connected with the tramway system. Second,

the company pays a minimum yearly rental of £100 Chap. VII.
($500) for each street mile of railway, with the further
proviso that if the company earns a dividend of 10
per cent. an additional £50 of mileage rental is to be
paid, with further similar increases on a sliding scale
for every additional 5 per cent. of dividends. The
principle of the sliding scale is introduced in numerous contracts between English municipalities and
street-railway operating companies. As yet, the companies are too young for maximum pecuniary results.

Newcastle-upon-Tyne, Bradford, Leeds, Oldham,
Huddersfield, Sunderland, Blackpool, Dundee, Green- Other muni-
cipal sys-
tems.
ock, Birkenhead, Preston, Blackburn, Bootle, South
Shields, Plymouth, and Eccles are among the towns
that have entered upon the policy of municipal street
railways. The Bradford lines are leased to two companies which pay respectively £300 and £400 per mile
per annum. The Sunderland lines are leased at 4½
per cent. on cost, together with a sliding scale rental
like Sheffield's. The Newcastle system is profitably
leased at about 10 per cent. on the investment. According to a recent return, there were in Great Brit-
ain 274 miles of publicly owned lines, and 573 miles Mileage of
British
street rail-
ways.
of lines owned by private companies. The mileage
of municipal lines would be much greater than it is,
but for the fact that the suburbs of English cities as
a rule lie beyond the corporate limits; and in many
instances the companies that are lessees of lines inside the limits are owners of suburban extensions.
The private companies were all chartered for twenty-
one years; and inasmuch as the decade from 1872 to
1882 witnessed the initiation of a great majority of
the street railways, the franchises are beginning one Falling in of
franchises.
after another to fall in. Under these circumstances,
the evident sentiment is favorable to the acquisition
of private lines by municipal authorities; and the

CHAP. VII.

Demand for municipal operation.

Advantages of public ownership of tracks.

Huddersfield's direct management of transit.

next few years will add very much relatively to the mileage thus controlled.

To some extent, moreover, there is apparent in Great Britain a demand for municipal operation. There is, of course, no necessary connection between the ownership of the lines as a part of the surface of the highways and the operation of a common-carrier business. One of the chief reasons for municipal ownership of the lines is the better control that it gives over the local transit system as an aid to the wise distribution of population throughout the town's area, on grounds of the public health and general welfare. It also has its great advantages in helping to make more apparent the natural right of the public treasury to the rental values that arise out of the monopoly of tram lines in the streets. It has been found under the system of leases to private operating companies that it is not difficult to secure favorable conditions for the people as to fares, working-men's cars, school-children's privileges, and the like.

The notable instance of direct municipal operation is that of Glasgow, whose new policy I have already described. In England, the case of Huddersfield is conspicuous. This enterprising Yorkshire town of 100,000 inhabitants has entered with much boldness upon the direct management of public works; and having tried corporation water, gas, and electric supplies, and municipal parks, cemeteries, markets, baths, libraries, and technical schools, it was not content until in 1890 it obtained parliamentary authority to operate steam tram lines. The experiment was begun with enthusiasm and is deemed successful. About twenty miles of lines are owned and worked by the council, and a recent report showed nearly 4,000,000 passengers carried in a year. Rates have been made low, and the system is locally popular.

In 1893 two other municipal corporations—namely, Plymouth and Blackpool—entered upon the business of common-carriers. Blackpool is a favorite seaside resort on the west coast, and has rapidly grown to a town of more than 25,000 people. Its municipal authorities are now operating electric street railways as a part of an exceedingly active municipal program. Plymouth is an ancient town with modern proclivities which will soon have reached its full 100,000 of population, and with its immediately adjacent communities is already much larger than that. Its experience in the conduct of street railways is too brief as yet to afford any instruction, but it will be worthy of future note. It is significant that the Liverpool corporation some time ago decided to obtain parliamentary authority to operate street railways, its immediate object, perhaps, being to improve its position for making advantageous terms with leasing companies. The general progress of street railways in the United Kingdom may be illustrated by the fact that a total investment in them of $20,000,000 in 1878 had grown to nearly $70,000,000 in 1893; that a mileage of less than 300 had grown to about 1000; that 146,000,000 passengers in 1878 had increased to nearly 600,000,000 in 1893; and that gross receipts, which were in the former year less than $6,000,000, were $18,000,000 in 1893. These are not formidable figures when brought into comparison with corresponding statistics that show the enormous expansion of street railways in the United States. But the English systems are preparing to give us, within ten years, some extremely interesting experiments in the field of municipal operation.

The perfect unity of British municipal administration makes it possible to consider each department in its bearing upon all the rest. Thus it is evident that the future of municipal tramway operation is inti-

CHAP. VII.

Blackpool as another instance.

And also old Plymouth.

Liverpool's position.

General progress of street railways.

Municipalizing electricity.

CHAP. VII. mately connected with the development of electrical appliances. Some of the most important municipal corporations have as yet declined to construct electrical works, but the more general tendency in Great Britain bids fair to be toward the municipalization of electricity. The towns are beginning with a central lighting-plant, and are proposing also to furnish power for machinery. It is expected that when an approved system of electric transit is devised, the municipal electric works will be prepared to furnish power to the lessee tramway companies, unless the town should prefer to operate the tram lines directly. As yet, there is comparatively little electric street-lighting in England, outside of London. Municipal works have lately been entered upon in Manchester, Cambridge, Oldham, Huddersfield, Brighton, Portsmouth, Burnley, Blackpool, and several other towns.

Light and power plants.

For nothing else except waterworks have British local authorities since 1870 expended so much money as for improvements that may be grouped under the words harbors, docks, piers, and quays. England's shipping interests are of vital importance, and the navigable estuaries are so frequent that a great number of thriving towns have access to the sea. It is deemed in England a sound policy for towns to improve their facilities for commerce even at great expense. The cost for the most part is sustained by harbor-dues and tolls, and is therefore levied upon commerce rather than upon the ratepayers. Liverpool's vast system of docks has been considered one of the marvels of our generation. There are more than thirty of these huge artificial basins, with a quay-frontage of twenty miles. It is justly claimed by Liverpool that it "has doubled its population and its trade every sixteen years during the present century."

Harbors, docks, piers, and quays.

Liverpool's docks.

Its preëminence as a port is not, however, to be so absolute henceforth. Manchester's great canal, with the docks and quays at Manchester-Salford, is intended to bring a large part of Liverpool's former ocean freight traffic directly to the mills of the spinning and weaving district ; and Southampton's notable harbor-improvements are designed to divert much of Liverpool's old-time transatlantic passenger business. But these recent sources of competition are only stimulating Liverpool to greater efforts, and new port facilities and shipping conveniences on a large scale are the order of the day.

Meanwhile, Swansea and Cardiff, on the south shore of Wales and on the north coast of the Bristol Channel, have grown to colossal importance as seaports. Swansea has practically doubled its population since 1881, has fifty acres of docks, and has a great export trade in copper, tin-plate, and various metal products. Cardiff has had a still more remarkable growth, and ranks as the third port in the British empire. Recent enlargements give it a dock area of 150 acres, and its various harbor improvements are on a generous scale. The rise of Cardiff has at length awakened Bristol, which was once a far greater shipping-point than Glasgow or Liverpool, and which has been surpassed by one rival after another for no reason so potent as that of their superior civic and municipal energy. Bristol is now carrying out extensive harbor improvements. Plymouth with the protection of its Sound by a great breakwater, and with its shipbuilding industry and its adjacent navy-yards, has more than regained its old-time importance as a rendezvous of ships and a trading port. I have alluded to Southampton's new harbor undertakings. The Thames improvements and the London docks are matters of common knowledge. On the east coast

I.— 14

CHAP. VII.

Liverpool's activity under new competition.

Swansea as a seaport.

Remarkable rise of Cardiff.

Bristol's awakening.

Modern Plymouth.

Southampton.

one finds a striking array of new harbor improvements. Old Boston has built a new municipal dock at much expense, and is reaping the benefits of a commercial awakening. Hull has accomplished important works that are reviving its shipping interests, and Stockton is another old port that is finding new life. At Sunderland and Newcastle, the great coal-shipping ports, astounding improvements have been carried out within a recent period, millions upon millions having been spent for new docks, deep channels, and all the paraphernalia of the best modern harbors. And I have by no means exhausted the list of seaport towns where important harbor-works have lately been accomplished or begun. In 1891 the outstanding loans of English and Welsh local authorities for harbor and dock improvements amounted to nearly $160,-000,000; and even this vast sum falls short of the total outlay of the past thirty years. British trade and commerce thrive by reason of these great collective undertakings that are so characteristic a part of the modern municipal and governmental policy.

Next after waterworks and harbor improvements, in the list of undertakings for which the English towns and localities have incurred indebtedness, comes the item of street and road improvements, against which there are outstanding loans of perhaps $145,-000,000. In reality, the street and road debt can only suggest the magnitude of the work that has been accomplished, inasmuch as highway construction and paving work are so largely paid for out of current revenues. It is not many years since England was a country of wretched highroads and of abominable town streets. All this has been changed, and the transformation, which has been costly, has seemed to impose a heavy burden by reason of its rapidity. But it

Boston, Hull, and Stockton.

Sunderland and Newcastle.

Aggregate cost of harbor improvements.

Highway reconstruction.

would have been a good investment at almost any
price. Fortunately, the work has been done in a permanent manner. Street pavements, whether of granite blocks, of asphalt, or of wood, have been laid upon
an indestructible foundation of concrete. The macadamized roads are so solidly founded that they will
endure for centuries.

A solicitous regard for the food-supplies of its population is one of the recognized duties of the modern
English town. This concern has manifested itself in
the municipalization of markets; and the town which
has not provided one or several great and elaborately
appointed market-houses, is not considered progressive. Municipal slaughter-houses are becoming numerous, and every detail in the supply of a town with meat
is closely supervised by the public authorities. About
$30,000,000 of outstanding loans for market and abat-
toir improvements gives evidence of a movement that
is at once recent and wide-spread. Moreover, every
town is obliged to have its public analyst, whose laboratory is conducted under the general direction of
the medical officer of health, and who is constantly
engaged in the detection of food adulterations. Food
inspectors, as emissaries of the Sanitary Department,
are aggressively making the rounds of the markets
and milk-shops, and the very existence of so good an
organization acts as a deterrent and protects the consumers against unwholesome food. The crusade in
behalf of pure milk is waged with especial vigor, and
with incalculable benefits to the health of young children. The public markets not only promote the efficiency of the health-inspection of food, but also enable
the masses of the population to supply themselves
more cheaply than would otherwise be possible. In this
way they promote Britain's commercial supremacy.

CHAP. VII.

Public parks
as a new
enterprise.

Extent of the
movement.

Liverpool.

Sheffield's
metamor-
phosis.

Leeds.

Notting-
ham's plea-
sure-
grounds.

Within the memory of men still young, the majority of British industrial towns were practically without any parks, public gardens, or recreation-grounds whatsoever ; and those that had such grounds possessed them through good fortune rather than any act of public policy. Such a thing as a municipal department for the provision and administration of public pleasure-grounds was almost unheard of. Even the old-time village greens and town commons had for the most part been occupied and built up by encroaching landlords. An entire change has come about, and every town has created its system of parks and gardens. Many of these pleasure-grounds have been the gifts of public-spirited citizens. Liverpool's municipal policy in regard to parks has been magnificent. It was entered upon in about the year 1867, and has been steadily continued with brilliant results from every point of view. Sheffield — once so devoid of such attractions, now supplied with a dozen charming parks and recreation-grounds in which are museums, galleries, and baths — is a fair type of the esthetic metamorphosis of the British industrial towns. Leeds is another of the great manufacturing centers whose municipal authorities have recently created a full system of parks and gardens. Let us take the summary record for Nottingham, as another instance : " The town possesses an arboretum, about eighteen acres in extent, in a very picturesque situation ; there are also several broad walks for a total length of about three miles, besides public cricket- and play-grounds containing about 150 acres, the greater part of which were set out under the Local Inclosure Act. Bulwell Forest, a piece of uninclosed land containing about 135 acres, has been acquired by the corporation, and is maintained as an open space for the use of the inhabitants. Nottingham has greater bathing facilities provided for the inhabitants than any other town of its size in the kingdom" (its population being about 225,000). But it would be a much briefer task to enumerate the towns that have neglected parks than to give a list of those that have recently accomplished creditable things in this direction. Municipal councils have recognized the wholesomeness of the athletic tendency that makes young English folk of both sexes so fond of outdoor recreations, and are everywhere providing playgrounds. Old commons are being restored to their rightful public use; churchyards and ancient cemeteries are being made over into small parks; and the private parks of old families are, either by gift or by purchase, falling to the inheritance of the municipalities. So many of these open spaces have been municipalized without the incurrence of public debt that the total achievements of the movement could hardly be inferred from the existence of local loans to the extent of $20,000,000. It is safe to assert that the real value of the park and pleasure-ground acquisitions of the English towns since 1870 is several times that amount.

Simultaneously with the closing of ancient burying-grounds adjacent to churches, and the utilization of many of them for small parks in the very heart of populous towns, there has been recognized a necessity for large cemeteries under public administration; and the municipal authorities have quite generally assumed the duties prescribed by Parliament for public-burial boards. It would be superfluous to recite the social and sanitary benefits that accrue to modern town populations from a comprehensive public treatment of the problem of the interment of the dead. Perhaps $15,000,000 would fail to represent the recent investment of English local authorities in the provision of public cemeteries.

I.— 14*

CHAP. VII.

Municipal
baths and
wash-houses.

Interest in public baths and wash-houses had been aroused throughout the United Kingdom much earlier, as has been shown in the chapter on Birmingham, than the need was felt for parks and open spaces. The condition of the crowded town populations was such that bathing facilities seemed to be more imperatively required than pleasure-grounds or libraries. The demand was recognized by most of the large towns. I have given an account of the experiences of Glasgow, Birmingham, and Manchester in providing splendid systems of public baths; and Liverpool, it should be said, has kept fully abreast of its contemporaries, having established seven well-distributed bathing institutions, under a policy begun before 1850 and extending to the present time, and at a total cost of perhaps $800,000. I have alluded to Nottingham's remarkable bathing facilities. The Oldham corporation has constructed great public baths as a memorial to Sir Robert Peel, and is extending the system. Coventry, an old town throbbing with new industrial life, and fortunate in the possession of a most intelligent and energetic municipal government, has established admirable baths as a part of its long list of municipal enterprises. Salford does not send its young people to Manchester for such luxuries as swimming-baths, but has provided four distinct establishments at a cost of $200,000. Among other towns — not to attempt a full list — that have adopted the baths and wash-houses acts, and provided admirable public establishments of this character, are Sheffield, Huddersfield, Halifax, Birkenhead, Hanley, Bolton, Leicester, Plymouth, and Kidderminster.

Liverpool's
system.

Nottingham
and Oldham.

Coventry's
enterprise.

Salford,
Sheffield,
and other
towns.

The housing
question.

The topic to which I must next allude belongs rather to the future than to the past. The character of the housing of the people has come to occupy almost or quite the chief place in the minds of British sanitary and social reformers and municipal statesmen. I have recounted the great projects of Glasgow and Birmingham, which have led the way; and it is evident that within the coming quarter-century a marvelous transformation will have been wrought throughout the towns of the kingdom. A notable beginning has been made in several other towns besides those whose efforts have been described. Liverpool, with a population that is denser and is less favorably housed than that of any other English town, has approached the problem with energy and persistence. In the ten years from 1881 to 1891, nearly 5000 houses were demolished in Liverpool, about 10,000 new houses having been erected in the same decade. In the next twelve months, to 1892, there were 437 houses taken down and only 371 new ones built. Of the 437, more than half had been bought up by the municipal authorities as a part of the work of the council committee on insanitary property. Liverpool has seen the financial advantage of Mr. Chamberlain's Birmingham plan, and has acquired a great amount of property for the sake of clearing off condemned houses and widening the streets, and then instead of selling the building sites it has leased them for 75 years. The Liverpool corporation has also invested considerable sums in model tenement-houses, and is the direct landlord of hundreds of working people. Millions have been expended in these Liverpool improvement projects, and the policy is to be maintained. It is easy to calculate that strict and wise regulations to prevent the improper construction of new houses, coupled with a steady plan of demolishing old houses as they become unfit for habitation, must in a few decades result in a reconstructed city, with a diminished death-rate and a higher tone of civilized life. The Scotch town of

CHAP. VII.

Good examples followed.

Liverpool's demolition of insanitary houses.

The town as landlord.

Liverpool's model tenements.

Greenock some years ago cleared away several acres
of wretched old cottages, and built as municipal property about two hundred houses with perfect sanitary
arrangements, in which a thousand people are living.
Still earlier, the Huddersfield authorities had carried
out a large scheme of a similar kind, which has proved
a good pecuniary investment. Even Dublin, the Irish
capital, has entered upon the policy of municipal tenements, having completed nearly a hundred small houses
in 1890, which are a great success in every way.

Sheffield, whose civic and municipal regeneration
has been so marvelous, adopted in 1876 a scheme for
the acquisition of property, the tearing down of unfit
houses, and a revision of the central street system.
The work has been steadily prosecuted at a large
cost, and with benefits innumerable. Bradford is
another great town that has been completely re-
modeled, with sanitary results that could hardly
have been anticipated by the most sanguine advocates
of the bold municipal program that was entered upon
in the seventies. The general interest in the question
of housing reforms led to the enactment by Parliament in 1890 of a very elaborate general measure entitled the Housing of the Working Classes Act, which
goes much further than any previous legislation in
confirming to local authorities a wide range of power
both as to the acquisition of property and its clear-
ance of insanitary structures, and also the provision
of new houses whether directly by the authorities or
by private owners in conformity with plans approved
by the municipal governments. Under the favorable
methods provided in this law, there has begun to appear a considerable activity in many quarters.

This care for the decency and wholesomeness of the
working-man's home has been attended by intelligent
effort to provide special accommodations for the classes

of people who ought, temporarily or permanently, to
be removed from residential quarters.   Particular
activity has been shown in the establishment of mu- Hospitals
nicipal hospitals for cases of infectious disease; and diseases.
epidemics not only of cholera, smallpox, and typhus
have thus been brought under control, but those far
more dangerous maladies scarlet fever, diphtheria, and
even measles, have been checked in their ravages.   In
hardly any other direction have the British towns accomplished more than in their triumph over the de-
structiveness of infection, and the result is largely due
to the provision of epidemic hospitals.

Every city has a floating population that finds shelter
either in the so-called common lodging-houses, or else Municipal
as lodgers sleeping on the floors of the already over- houses.
crowded homes of the tenement-house families.   The
well-being of the town requires close supervision over
this class of people, and the other British towns to some
extent are following the example of Glasgow by conducting municipal model lodging-houses.   So-called
industrial schools, which are in fact homes for neglected or misdemeanant children, provide everywhere
for another element of the town population that needs
to be separately sheltered and trained; and for the
seaport towns the industrial schools frequently take Industrial
the form of " training ships."   But these schools, like homes, etc.
the local workhouses, the lunatic asylums, and the
whole mechanism of the relief of the poor, although
closely associated with the municipal life and development, do not ordinarily come under the direct administration of the municipal councils, and may be
regarded as belonging rather to local administration
in general than to the municipalities distinctively.

The adoption of the Free Public Libraries Act by
the greater British towns has been almost unanimous,

and many of the smaller municipalities have also by popular vote instructed their councils to provide reference and lending libraries and free reading-rooms. A list of these municipal libraries would require citation of the names of nearly or quite a hundred towns. Besides Birmingham and Manchester, with about 200,000 volumes each, Leeds is to be mentioned as approximating that number, while Liverpool, Sheffield, Salford, Bristol, Nottingham, Bolton, Bradford, and Newcastle have municipal libraries that will soon have reached the 100,000-volume mark. Among the towns that have from 25,000 to 50,000 volumes or more are Birkenhead, Blackburn, Brighton, Cambridge, Cardiff, Coventry, Derby, Halifax, Oldham, Plymouth, Portsmouth, Rochdale, Tynemouth, and Wolverhampton. A great number of towns, which have somewhat recently begun to levy the rate of a penny in the pound for libraries and reading-rooms, have already accumulated collections of from 10,000 to 25,000 volumes which are rapidly growing. The free reading-rooms, open at night, are everywhere popular with workingmen.

Municipal art-galleries are by no means as common as municipal libraries; but there is a strong awakening, in all the British towns of any considerable size or standing, of the kind of local pride that could never rest satisfied without such agencies as museums of art, of science, and of local history and archæology. A beginning once made, such institutions grow by natural processes of accretion; and their development everywhere in England, within thirty years, would require a long chapter if it were to be recounted with any detail. The dignity of all the provincial towns is enhanced by this joint recognition of history and of esthetics, and the whole life of each community is made the richer and better rounded.

The great Education Act of 1870, under which elementary instruction became a public interest, has resulted in the creation of a new educational "plant" of buildings and furnishings, the magnitude of which is evidenced by an indebtedness on this account of about $100,000,000. But the circumstances under which the national-school system was founded made it appear necessary to intrust its conduct in each town to a separately elected school-board rather than to the existing town councils and local authorities. In my judgment it would have been far better if in the incorporated towns the council had been authorized to administer the Education Act. Just so it would be better, also, in my opinion, if poor-relief within all municipal districts should be in the hands of the municipal government rather than in those of specially elected boards of guardians of the poor. Sooner or later, I am convinced, the British people will perceive the advantage of a complete unification of local government; and then the school-board and the guardians of the poor will become, simply, a couple of standing committees of the town council, as the police-board and the health-board now are.

The new technical education acts have wisely recognized the town councils rather than the school-boards, and there is growing up in every large center of British industry a system of general and special instruction in all the scientific, artistic, and technical principles and processes that pertain to standard lines of manufacture; and this system is under complete municipal control as a department of the work of the town council. It is supported in part by local rates,— the technical education acts having authorized municipalities to levy a penny rate for such schools,— and in still larger part by subsidies out of the royal exchequer. Manchester and Birmingham, as I have

CHAP. VII.

Public education.

A question of administration.

Municipal technical schools.

How supported.

shown, are entering magnificently upon this policy. But so also are many other towns, some of them having begun years ago. Nottingham learned that it was in danger of losing its preëminence in certain special textile lines, and discovered some years ago that its declining trade was due to the rise of Chemnitz in Saxony, and further, that the success of Chemnitz was due to a system of municipal technical schools of weaving, dyeing, designing, and so on. Nottingham has adopted the German policy, with gratifying re-

sults. Oldham, like Manchester, is adapting great technical schools to the needs of its cotton industries.

Huddersfield, the center of the Yorkshire woolen industry, has applied the same policy. Kidderminster,

the great carpet town, maintains its school of design.

Bradford is in line with its contemporaries. Sheffield and Leeds have taken steps in the same direction of

technical instruction. Swansea maintains schools of metallurgy and of mechanical engineering, on account of their benefit to its vast metal-working industries.

Hanley and Burslem, the chief towns of the famous " potteries " district, have one its " Government School of Design " and the other its " Wedgwood Institute," — both of which teach the technical science and the decorative art that bear upon the wonderful special industrial developments of the region. Besides the

pupils who take advanced instruction in the municipal art, science, and technical schools, there are tens of thousands of practical young workers who are attending night classes, and obtaining knowledge and skill that not only help them as artisans to earn good wages in the shops of their own towns, but in turn aid the towns to maintain and to increase their industrial prosperity. These municipal schools are not narrow in their local specialization, and their facilities of instruction as a rule extend over a broad range of scientific and technical knowledge; but they also adapt themselves with a commendable elasticity to the actual trade position of their own districts — whether ship-building or metal-working, pottery, decoration or the brewing of beer, cloth-weaving, the refining of sugar, or the manufacture of chemicals. The elementary schools encourage their pupils to continue their studies in night classes, and the municipal authorities intervene to help the growing lad to adjust himself in the environing industrial society. This new field of municipal activity has, evidently, an important future in the British towns. There are single manufacturing centers where from fifteen to twenty thousand pupils, who are nearly all young artisans and apprentices, are attending the evening technical and applied-art classes under the auspices of the municipal government. This is a new development of the highest significance. England now believes that she has found in technical education the best form of "protection" for her industries.

Adaptation of schools to local industries.

England's new scheme of industrial "protection."

CHAPTER VIII

THE GOVERNMENT OF LONDON

M ETROPOLITAN London, the greatest and most
enlightened city this world has ever seen, has
never had a legal existence, a fixed boundary line, or
a municipal government. For limited purposes the
metropolis became in 1889 an administrative county,
and acquired a representative council; but previous
to the Local Government Act of 1888, which gives all
the counties of England elective councils, the metropolis had no distinct organization or corporate
form. London, the ancient city, had retained its old-
time bounds and its venerable charters; but its area
was only one square mile and its resident population was less than forty thousand, while metropolitan London had attained a population more than a
hundred times as large, spread over an area of at least
a hundred square miles, and Greater London lay in
the three counties of Middlesex, Kent, and Surrey,
with huge suburbs in Essex and encroaching outposts
in Hertfordshire, including, altogether, from five hundred to a thousand square miles, with a population of
six millions or more. It was governed in the most
anomalous manner by Parliament directly as an inter-
posing providence, by the ministers of the Crown, by
the magistrates of the several counties, by special
boards and commissions, and by many scores of parish
vestries and other minor local authorities. The acts

London the
metropolis.

London the
ancient city.

"Greater
London."

of Parliament that affected one feature or another of
the administration in whole or in part of the metropolitan area were legion, and were scattered through
the statute-books of centuries.   Truly this great aggregation of people and interests had a perplexingly
intricate organization.   But still it was somehow governed.   Its vast expanding life as one social, commercial, and industrial entity found its organs.

London's
governing
arrange-
ments.

How London has been governed in the past, how it
is governed at present, how it is meeting the various
social and economic problems of modern metropolitan
life — these are questions eminently worthy of consideration by all who would study municipal matters.
For London is the capital not only of the British empire, but in some sense also of the whole world.   Its
experiences are of universal interest and importance.
In it the new forces of urban life are at work in most
significant ways.   It is slowly but surely evolving central municipal institutions to meet its peculiar needs.
Its population is waking up with a sense of unity, and
with a new perception of great things to be done
through united municipal action for the common welfare.   As I have observed in my introductory chapter,
it is only lately that the people of advanced industrial
nations have learned to accept the fact that life in
cities under artificial conditions must be the lot of the
great majority; that it is the business of society to
adapt the urban environment to the needs of the
population; that such life should not be an evil or a
misfortune for any class; that there should be such
sanitary arrangements and administration as to make
the death-rate of the city smaller than that of the nation as a whole; that there should be such educational
facilities as to insure to all the young people of a city
the most suitable physical, intellectual, and industrial
training.   The masses of the people in London are

Its munici-
pal evolu-
tion.

The new
ideals.

Chap. VIII.

Now ac-
cepted in
London.
rising to some comprehension of these truths, and they are beginning to clamor for social and governmental reforms. The immediate future of London is fraught with magnificent possibilities. From the extreme of chaos, disorganization, and uncontrolled freedom of individual action, it is not impossible that the great metropolis may early in the twentieth century lead all the large cities of the world in the closeness and unity of its organization and in the range of its

The collec-
tivist trend.
municipal activities. Municipal socialism, so called, has a better outlook in London even than in Paris or Berlin, although as yet London has given fewer tangible evidences of this trend than has any other center of civilization. However that may be, the London questions have assumed an extraordinary importance in England, and to understand them reasonably well it is necessary to review and analyze with some care the government of London.

From the benefits of a half-century's reform legisla-

London ex-
cluded from
the reform
acts.
tion, under which town life and government has flourished elsewhere throughout the United Kingdom, London was almost wholly excluded. To review rapidly a movement already described in these pages, the ever-memorable Reform Act of 1832, which gave representation in Parliament a modern and rational basis, was soon followed, as a part of the reform program of the day, by a general municipal government act which abolished the ancient and exclusive privileges of the merchants' and trades' guilds, and enlarged the municipal corporations by the inclusion of the whole body of citizens paying a certain minimum amount of rates. This act of 1835 is the most signally important piece of legislation in all the history of modern city governments. Similar to it, and a part of the same general movement, were the act of 1833 reforming the Scotch municipalities, and that of 1840 which rendered a like service

to those of Ireland. Apart from minor differences in the three acts, this legislation gave a uniform framework of municipal government to practically all the large towns and cities of the United Kingdom. It preserved the old-time government by mayors, aldermen, and councilors, while doing away with close corporations and throwing open the municipal franchise to the new classes of electors who had received the borough parliamentary franchise in the reform of 1832, the councilors becoming the direct representatives of the burgesses or citizens. Half a century witnessed much additional legislation, which was embodied in the great municipal government consolidation act of 1882; but the general plan of 1835 remains unchanged because experience has given it the stamp of thorough approval.

The system re-outlined.

But London was excluded from the operation of this act that gave healthy and popular representation to all the other large communities of England. The situation of London was exceptional, and Lord Russell announced that its reform must be made the subject of a separate act. For more than fifty years that promised reconstruction and modernization of London government has been awaited in vain, except in so far as various special enactments are to be regarded as advance instalments of reform — the new administrative county government being a very substantial instalment.

Neglected London.

The conditions of medieval town life seem to have been fairly well met by a local government that was in the hands of the organized mercantile and trade bodies — the associations of burgesses who secured the old borough charters and revived the local liberties that had languished under feudal tyranny. But when in the later days the organization of industry was revolutionized, and the towns were growing at

The olden guilds.

I.—15

an unprecedented rate under the new forces of modern life, the government by the self-perpetuating guilds became totally obsolete and inadequate. The guilds had remained as close corporations with their old names and old privileges, but they included few, sometimes none, of the actual working members of the trades whose names they bore, and they had no longer any relation to the industrial life, nor were they in any sense representative of the community at large. In short, their pretenses to exclusive governmental authority had become absurd and intolerable. Elsewhere they were disbanded and their accumulated estates were applied to public objects, or else they survived merely as social or mutual-benefit clubs; but in the City of London they held their ground, and they remain to-day, their authority being only slightly diminished.

Survival of the guilds in London.

Let us examine briefly the survival of old-time municipal government as it exists within the narrow bounds of London proper, before passing to the discussion of the great metropolis that has overflown the limits of the old City walls. There are nearly eighty of the so-called City companies, these being the survivors of the medieval guilds. They are commonly known as the Livery Companies, because on occasions of ceremony their members of the higher grade wear distinctive garbs that date from the reign of Edward III. The twelve principal companies, in the order of precedence, are the Mercers, Grocers, Drapers, Fishmongers, Goldsmiths, Skinners, Merchant Taylors, Haberdashers, Salters, Ironmongers, Vintners, and Clothworkers. It might seem superfluous to give the long list of minor companies; but each name contains a picture of the old London life of periods when nearly all the reputable citizens were grouped as members of these quaint callings. Alphabetically arranged, and

The eighty "Livery Companies."

Twelve chief guilds.

omitting the twelve already named, the London companies are: Apothecaries, Armourers and Braziers, Bakers, Barbers, Basket Makers, Blacksmiths, Bowyers, Brewers, Broderers (Embroiderers), Butchers, Carmen, Carpenters, Clockmakers, Coach and Coach-harness Makers, Cooks, Coopers, Cordwainers, Curriers, Cutlers, Distillers, Dyers, Fanmakers, Farriers, Fellowship Porters, Feltmakers, Fletchers, Founders, Framework Knitters, Fruiterers, Girdlers, Glass-sellers, Glaziers, Glovers, Gold and Silver Wire-drawers, Gunmakers, Horners, Inn-holders, Joiners, Leathersellers, Loriners, Makers of Playing Cards, Masons, Musicians, Needlemakers, Painters, Parish Clerks, Pattern Makers, Pewterers, Plasterers, Plumbers, Poulterers, Saddlers, Scriveners, Shipwrights, Spectacle Makers, Stationers, Tallow Chandlers, Tinplate Workers, Turners, Tylers and Bricklayers, Upholders, Watermen and Lightermen, Wax Chandlers, Weavers, Wheelwrights, Woolmen.

The companies were originally designed to regulate the callings whose names they bear, and to benefit the members and their families in various ways. They became incorporated, and at length they assumed joint control of the government of the City. Admission to them was by the four methods of purchase, patrimony, apprenticeship, and honorary vote, all of which remain in vogue, although the apprenticeship is now, of course, a mere matter of form. The guilds are societies of gentlemen. Great endowments have accumulated from the gradual increase of modest estates or charity trust funds that were acquired by the companies for the most part several hundred years ago.

The aggregate annual income of the London guilds is not far from $5,000,000, most of it being derived from the rents of the house property that they own in all quarters of the metropolis. They have estates in many parts of England also, and the capitalized value of all their holdings would probably far exceed $100,-000,000. The Mercers and Drapers are the richest, with incomes of $400,000 or $500,000 each; while the Goldsmiths, Clothworkers, and Fishmongers are reputed to be worth $250,000 or $300,000 a year. A number of other companies are very wealthy, while many of the minor guilds have trifling incomes. Half of the companies have their own halls, some of which are among the notable architectural survivals of the old-time London; and most of those which are without their separate buildings transact their business at the central Guildhall. A large number of the original old halls were destroyed in the great fire of London. About one fourth of the income of the companies is derived from charitable trust property, and is devoted to the support of almshouses, to educational purposes, and to general charity. A large part of the remaining sums is spent in lavish ways, not less than half a million dollars a year going for banquets and entertainments. In many of the companies the members are paid substantial fees for attending ordinary meetings. Membership varies from a mere handful of men in the smallest companies to about 450 in the largest, the average being not far from 100, and the total membership of the entire number being in 1894 about 8800, as against 9500 fifty years ago.

How their incomes are expended.

The resident population of the City of London proper was fifty thousand by the census of 1881, and thirty-seven thousand by that of 1891. The City is a business district, with a day population ten times as great as that which sleeps within its narrow limits; and it is entered every day except Sundays and holidays by more than a million souls, most of whom reside in Greater London. The members of the guilds do not, of course, to any extent live in the City. But

The "City" and its population.

those who reside within a radius of twenty-five miles
are entitled to have a part in the City's government.
They vote, in one or another of the twenty-six City
wards, for aldermen and common councilors. Each
ward elects an alderman for life, and each elects a number of common councilors for a one year's term, the
whole number of common councilors being 206. The
Lord Mayor, aldermen, and common councilors form
a great court, or governing body, that controls all the
affairs of the City. Recent legislation has made it
possible for resident householders to assist in electing
councilors and aldermen ; but the affairs of the municipal corporation remain practically in the hands of
the close and self-perpetuating guilds. The Lord
Mayor — whose jurisdiction, it should be understood,
extends only throughout the limits of the small,
inner City — is chosen annually from the ranks of
the aldermen. The Court of Common Hall — i. e., the
entire body of liverymen of the guilds — selects two
aldermen who have served as sheriff of London, and
from these two the group of aldermen designate one
to fill the office of Lord Mayor. Reëlection to that
office is an honor rarely bestowed. When the year is
ended, the Lord Mayor turns the Mansion House over
to his successor, and continues to serve the City as an
alderman who has " passed the chair." Of the present
aldermen about half have "passed the chair,"— i. e.,
have served their year as Lord Mayor,— and none of
them has served a second time. The Queen almost
invariably bestows knighthood upon the Lord Mayor,
and he emerges from his brief and always exceedingly
expensive months of lavish entertaining in the Mansion House with the handle of " Sir " to his name.

The City corporation, with its headquarters in the
noble old Guildhall, has, like the individual companies,
large estates, chiefly in the form of house property ;
I.— 15*

and it also owns the great markets of London. Its affairs are administered by committees of the council. The City proper has its own separate police system, its street and drainage authorities, its educational work, and its various functions. Its liverymen, besides voting for members of Parliament in the districts where they actually live, assist in electing two members for the City of London. It is not to be disputed that the corporation of London, with its constituent guilds, has become a great privileged monopoly, held together by the powerful but selfish interest of some nine thousand influential men. It was, perhaps, in 1873 that Mr. Gladstone in a speech at Nottingham declared that the London guilds must be reformed, and their great sums of money devoted to public purposes. Previous to that utterance the liverymen were to a considerable extent Liberal in politics, but since then they have become almost unanimously Conservative. In 1880 a parliamentary commission was appointed to inquire into the history, status, and revenues of the London companies; and its voluminous report, published in 1884, is marvelously interesting. This commission, composed of men of the highest weight and authority, advised the reform of the guilds by law, and the application of their properties to public uses.

A privileged monopoly.

On reform of the guilds.

Recent years have witnessed on the part of the working-men and the Liberals of Greater London a series of determined assaults upon the companies; but as yet there has been no result except a marked change in the conduct of these societies. They have begun to make a large use of their funds for the purchase of parks and open spaces in and about the great metropolis, and for the endowment of technical and general education, principally in London, but also in other parts of the British Islands. The "City and Guilds of London Institute," endowed by a number of the com-

Their growth in public spirit.

panies, supports great central institutions for technical education, and it grants subsidies to night classes
in the practical trades throughout the United Kingdom.   Two or three of the companies are contributing
heavily to the maintenance of polytechnic institutes
and "people's palaces" for the young working-folk of
London.

Sooner or later the guilds will be obliged to surrender their political and municipal privileges, and
public opinion will compel them to account openly   Destiny of
for their funds.   Possibly their endowments may be   the City and
construed by Parliament as public trusts, and devoted   guilds.
by law, after the analogy of the old London parochial
charity endowments, to the promotion of the general
welfare of the metropolitan masses.   However that
may be, the county council, as the representative of
the aroused and gradually centralizing municipal life
of the greater London, will eventually undermine the
venerable charters and privileges of the City, and will
reduce the central district to the status of one of a
series of subordinate parts of an inclusive municipal
corporation.   This survival of the unreformed medieval borough will pass away within a few years; and
those who have never seen a Lord Mayor's show on
the ninth of November should not postpone the sight
too long.

But we must turn from this anomaly, this fossilized
relic of medievalism, to the vast modern city in which   The expan-
it is embedded.   What are the bounds of Greater Lon-   sion of
don?   There are a hundred or more diminutive old   London.
parishes within the area of the City — the inner technical London.   Outside this center, parish after parish has been invaded by the steadily extending rows
of brick houses and the metropolitan street system.
At least a hundred thousand people are added every
year to this great aggregation that we popularly call

CHAP. VIII.

London.   One may go east or north or south or west from Charing Cross, and almost despair of ever reaching the rim of the metropolis.   In fact, at the time of the reform acts, the urban district had confessedly grown beyond all knowledge and control.   It covered

The parishes and vestrymen.

scores of parishes, each of which was governed upon ancient rural lines by an elected board of vestrymen, whose business it was to provide for street-making, paving, drainage, public lighting, and other concerns, and to levy the rates wherewith to pay the cost of parochial government.   No two parishes were governed exactly alike.   There was little or no accountability on the part of local officers.   No interest was taken in the election of vestrymen.   One parish knew nothing about the affairs of another.   The West End parishes knew less about those of East London than they knew about Calcutta or Hong Kong.   Within the continuously built area there were several hundred separate local authorities.   Scores of old villages had been swallowed up by the ever-encroaching metropolis, and rural conditions had given place to those of urban life.

There was a certain unmistakable organic unity in the metropolis; yet no political organization corresponding to that unity had been effected.   Numerous affairs essentially important called for united action. But the absence of central agencies left the city to

Need of central organs.

grow of itself, without regulation and without intelligent plans.   When the vast developments of modern industry and commerce began fairly to appear, the necessity for measures recognizing the metropolis as a whole became absolutely imperative.   Fortunately, Parliament could be appealed to in cases of dire emergency; and the British Parliament may indeed be said to have been the governing body of London from the moment when it began to be regarded as something more than a network of contiguous parishes covered with houses.

The earliest recognition of the unity of London was shown by the general government in its provision for the registry of vital statistics. London, according to the Registrar-General, was not merely the ancient City, but the larger populated district. The old so-called bills of mortality, dating from the plague of 1592, prior to which deaths were not officially recorded, were from time to time extended to include larger areas as the outside population grew. In 1838 this wider area came to be definitely known as the Registrar-General's District. It then contained 44,816 acres, or just seventy square miles. It was afterward extended several times, but for many years it has remained fixed at 74,692 acres, or about 122 square miles. This district is practically identical with that which was adopted as the metropolis in 1855 for the purposes of the Metropolitan Board of Works, and which was adopted again in 1870 as the sphere within which the newly formed "school-board for London" should operate. And it has now, by the law which became operative early in 1889, and which detaches its parts from the counties of Middlesex, Kent, and Surrey, been erected into a separate administrative county. The London county line sweeps in an extra hamlet at one point, however, which gives it a total extent of 75,442 acres, or 123 square miles. This, then, must be taken as the present official limit of metropolitan London. The London of the metropolitan parliamentary boroughs has until very lately remained an area nearly identical with the seventy square miles of the reform period; but it now includes 125¼ square miles, and is therefore a little larger than the new county, the boundaries being mainly identical. But the Central Criminal Court District, which is

The London of the Registrar's office.   I

The London of the Board of Works.   II

Of the school-board.   III

The bounds of the new county of London.

"Parliamentary London."

"Judicial London."

regarded as another of the London boundaries, comprises more than 268,000 acres, or 420 square miles.

"Police London." Finally, the Metropolitan Police District contains 440,891 acres or 690 square miles, and includes all the parishes within a radius of 15 miles from Charing Cross. As an illustration of the manner in which the urban population has filled up what were once rural neighborhoods, it is interesting to note the fact that within this Metropolitan Police District, besides the City proper, there are fifty-three parishes of the county of Middlesex, thirty-five of Surrey, eighteen of Kent, fourteen of Essex, and ten of Hertfordshire. This "Greater London." district is now called "Greater London," in distinction from the metropolis, in the weekly returns of the Registrar-General. The multiplicity of boundaries is somewhat confusing. But henceforth London, or the metropolis, will be commonly regarded as the county area, and Greater London will designate in a general way the whole urban population, most of which is included in the Metropolitan Police District. The census of 1881 gave the City of London 50,652 people, London's population. found 3,834,354 within the area now known as the metropolis, or the county of London, and enumerated a total of 4,776,661 in the Greater London of the Metropolitan Police District. The census of 1891 showed that the county then included 4,232,118 people, and that there were within the police circumscription 5,633,000. The estimate of 6,500,000 or 7,000,000 people now living within twenty miles of Charing Cross may not be regarded as extravagant. And popularly speaking these people are all Londoners. Untimately the official bounds of the municipality will very possibly include them. This larger area is not as yet densely peopled, and it will be made to accommodate several millions more.

From about 1805 to 1855, an even half-century,

London's population had grown from a round million to two millions and a half. The situation had become almost intolerable from lack of central management. The home department of the general government maintained a metropolitan police force and kept tolerably good order. Government commissioners of sewers also levied taxes upon the whole community, and provided an imperfect sort of drainage system. Underground sewers were entirely unknown in London until 1831, and they were not numerous or extensive in 1855. Not a single large underground main had been constructed at this last date. Such as they were, the sewers and drainage ditches poured their pollution directly into the Thames at frequent intervals on both banks, and at times the river was so befouled and clogged with filth that navigation was obstructed. The era of modern trade and commerce had set in, and traffic was blocked on the streets for lack of suitable central arteries. There was not in all London at that time a good pavement, nor a broad convenient thoroughfare. The river was without an adequate supply of bridges, and without suitable embankments and retaining walls.

The parishes, of which there were seventy-eight outside the City proper, and within the Registrar-General's metropolitan district, were attending in an irregular way to local concerns, while some parts of the metropolis were "no-man's land," and were without any pretext of local management whatever. The selfishness of the fossilized City corporation was egregious. It never at any time tried to extend its government so as to include the huge outlying population; nor would it consent to any reasonable scheme for the incorporation of the Greater London. Either proceeding would have swamped this inner sanctuary of monopoly and exclusive privilege. The outsiders

CHAP. VIII.

Conditions
in 1855.

Drainage
and streets.

Selfishness
of the City.

were too disorganized to act together. Moreover, too many of their influential fellow-citizens were members of one or another of the city companies. And so reform dragged.

A great beginning, however, was made in the year 1855. In lieu of the complete reform and munici-

Metropolis Management Act of 1855.

palization of the overgrown city, Parliament enacted what has since been known as the Metropolis Management Act. This act contained the rudiments of a municipal constitution. It divided the area outside the City proper into thirty-eight districts, following parish lines and uniting small parishes for the purposes of the act. Twenty-three parishes were regarded as large and populous enough to stand singly,

Rearrangement of local divisions.

and fifty-five smaller ones were grouped into fifteen districts. To these thirty-eight districts were confirmed, under a somewhat more uniform system, the local functions that the parishes had always exercised — these including local sewerage, street-making and paving, street-lighting, sanitary administration, and some other minor matters, to which additions have been made by subsequent enactments. The principal purpose of the act, however, was to create a central authority. This body was called the Metro-

Creation of a central Board of Works.

politan Board of Works. Each parish or district was governed by an elective board, called in the single parishes the Vestry, and in the consolidated areas entitled the District Board; and these bodies were chosen by all ratepayers who were taxed for the care of the poor on a rental value of $200 a year. The vestries and district boards varied in size according to the population of the area, the average being about 75, and the whole number of these local representatives

A body of delegates.

being about 3000. Each district board or vestry was authorized to send a representative to the Metropolitan Board of Works, and the corporation of the City

of London was given three members. Subsequently
the board was enlarged, and the greater districts or
parishes were accorded two or three delegates, making a central body of about sixty members in all.

These thirty-eight parishes and districts remain to-
day in possession of their functions as constituted in
1855. The Metropolitan Board of Works survived Career of the metropolitan board.
until April, 1889, when it was superseded by the new
County Council, which I shall take further occasion
to describe. The central improvements of London
for the period from 1855 to 1889, enormous as they
had been in the aggregate, were the work of the metropolitan board. Its first and most imperative task
was the creation of a system of main sewers. Obviously the petty parish vestries could undertake no
such work. Then it became the board's duty to improve systematically the main thoroughfares. The
river banks, the Thames bridges, the paramount prob- A series of great achievements.
lem of parks and open spaces, the problems of over-
crowding and insanitary houses, and numerous lesser
matters, came under the board's jurisdiction. Its
rounded generation of active work resulted in vast
improvements. London was chaos when the board
found it. It had many of the appointments of a modern metropolis, and was well advanced toward the
assumption of a fully organized municipal life, when
the metropolitan board gave way to its successor.

Before taking up the specific departments of the
board's work, and the whole subject of London's municipal appointments and public services, it will be
well to continue further the discussion of the govern-
mental machinery. The metropolitan board accom- Faults of the metropolitan board.
plished a great work, but in its latter years its ad-
ministration was honeycombed with scandals. Its
indirect election removed it from the people. There
was no interest in its personnel, and its members were

for the most part obscure. The London public knew astonishingly little about it. It was the creature of the vestries, and these vestry local governments had not themselves been successful. The vestries and the district boards were practically unaccountable. The ratepayers, at least until very recently, have almost utterly ignored the election of vestrymen. The levying of rates has been most various in the different parts of the metropolis. There has been much incompetency, in some cases much extravagance, at times great niggardliness, and often much lack of wisdom in the making of such public improvements as have come within the sphere of the parishes and districts.

Faults of the vestries.

Numerous attempts have been made to build further upon the foundation laid in 1855, and to secure a full-wrought municipal government for London. A select committee of Parliament reported in 1861 in favor of the direct election of the Metropolitan Board of Works by the ratepayers, with a view to transforming it into a regular municipal common council. And about once in four or five years ever since 1855 some cabinet minister or prominent member of the House has brought in a bill to create a central elective council, and to supersede the vestries by newly constituted local areas with subordinate councils. Such bills were introduced by Sir George Cornewall Lewis in 1860, by John Stuart Mill in 1867, by Charles Buxton in 1869–70, by Lord Elcho in 1875, by Mr. J. F. B. Firth in 1880, and by Sir William Harcourt as Mr. Gladstone's Home Secretary in 1884.

Various attempts to erect a great municipality.

Sir William Harcourt's important measure proposed to create a great central council of 240 members, merging the old city corporation in the metropolis, and treating the inner City as one of thirty-nine administrative areas, but giving it a large representation in recognition of its historical importance and its heavy

Sir William Harcourt's bill.

property and commercial interests. Among the other districts, representation was proportioned to population and wealth. All the authority possessed by the old Board of Works, by all the parish and district boards, by the authorities of the City corporation, and by other local functionaries was concentrated in the hands of the new central council. This body was expected to revise and consolidate the districts, reducing their number and granting to each a local district council composed of the members of the central body from any given district, and of other elected members. These local councils were to do simply the things delegated to them by the higher authority, and were to be subject always to the control of the central council.

This London proposition adapted the general municipal system of England to the peculiar conditions of the metropolis. The principle of the English system is that of " absolute control through a directly elected authority of all administration and of all expenditure." This principle was not in controversy; it was accepted by all parties. But there had long been a strong party, inspired by the liverymen of the guilds, and now largely identified with the Conservatives, who advocated the partitioning of London into six, or ten, or twelve, or even a greater number of cities, and the giving to each one a separate municipal government of its own. The idea had some seeming justification in the fact of London's vastness, and of certain traditional topographic and natural lines of division. But the real motive was the effectual dismemberment of the great London that threatened to assimilate and absorb the ancient City, and to dispossess its privileged beneficiaries.

Unity versus dismemberment.

What the situation called for was not a series of distinct municipalities, but a sort of federalized municipal

CHAP. VIII.

Defeat of
London proj-
ects in 1880
and 1884.

Reform of
county gov-
ernment.

Local Gov-
ernment Act
of 1888.

government.   There were great common concerns
which required concerted action and vigorous central
administration.   The defeat of measures proposed in
1880 and 1884 was accomplished by the active opposition of the guilds, which were accused, upon seem-
ingly reliable testimony, of spending hundreds of
thousands of dollars in lobbying and sham demon-
strations, and which flooded Parliament with petitions
containing thousands of fictitious names.   The great
bill of 1884 contained the provisions of a magnificent
metropolitan constitution, and its adoption would have
been of incalculable advantage to the millions of
Londoners.

Meanwhile there had been a continual demand for
reform in the county governments of England.   These
governments had been wholly non-representative.   In
every county a number of gentlemen, usually belonging to the landlord class, held the Queen's commission as magistrates or justices of the peace; and they,
meeting four times a year in the so-called "quarter-
sessions," levied the county tax, managed the road
business, granted liquor licenses, and attended to all
the administrative as well as the minor judicial business of the county.   The great towns had all acquired
their representative municipal governments, and were
for most ordinary purposes detached from the counties.   It was at length proposed that elective councils
on about the same plan as those of the municipalities
should be given to the counties, with subordinate district councils in subdivisions of the county.   This
great measure was brought forward by the ministry
in 1888, and it became a law to the satisfaction of all
parties.   It was no part of the original intention of
this measure to reform London administration; but
it was found in drafting the so-called Local Government Bill that it would be wholly impracticable to in-

clude in an elective government intended for the great CHAP. VIII.
rural county of Kent a million or two of Londoners
who had overflown the extreme northwestern corner
of the county; and similar considerations were ap- How London
plicable to Middlesex and Surrey. It was found much became a
county.
more feasible to treat all the great urban communities
of England as separate counties for administrative
purposes. Thus London was made a county, with the
area of the old Metropolitan Board of Works. The
other cities of England were already organized for
administrative work, but the new "administrative
county" of London had to be dealt with specifically in
the bill. It is a curious fact that the Conservatives,
who had so strenuously opposed the earlier plans for
a great London municipal organism, were now the
men who laid the solid framework for such a structure, as a mere incident in the elaboration of a measure intended to initiate local self-government in the The London
rural parts of England. When direct and centralized county as a
municipal
self-government had been given to the towns and cities rudiment.
of England, London was made an exception. More
than fifty years later, when it was no longer possible
to deny some measure of local self-government to the
counties and townships of rural England, London was
for the first time given an elective central authority.
If English legislation is sometimes in defiance of logical symmetry, it sooner or later accomplishes the desired results with a practical wisdom that is rarely
equaled in other countries.

The parishes and districts of 1855, which still re- Framework
main the local government areas of the metropolis, of the London county
and from whose vestries and boards the Metropolitan council.
Board of Works had always been constituted as a
delegate body, were not taken as the basis of apportionment for the new county council. The parliamentary reform bill of 1885 had created fifty-seven

I.— 16

districts besides the City within the metropolitan area, for the purpose of representation in the House of Commons; and these districts were taken as the best temporary divisions for the election of councilors.   Each was accorded two members, while the City proper was allowed four; and thus provision was made for one hundred and eighteen members, to be elected every three years.   The councilors were empowered to add to their body nineteen members having the rank of aldermen and holding their seats for six-year terms, but having no different authority from the ordinary members.   They were further to choose annually, from their own number or otherwise, a chairman, a vice-chairman, and a deputy chairman, thus bringing the whole body up to about one hundred and forty members of a metropolitan parliament.

Districts and membership.

The bill left much to be done in the future.   Thus the City of London and its functions remained practically untouched, and the parish vestries and district boards continued to exercise their accustomed jurisdiction in minor affairs.   Ultimately, of course, these powers will all be conferred upon the central county council, in order that it may re-delegate such authority as it deems best to a revised series of ward or district councils; or else Parliament itself will ordain a new and improved subdivision of London, and constitute minor councils with well-defined duties subject to the county council.   But, as matters stand, the county council is not without an important range of authority.   It supersedes the Metropolitan Board of Works, which had grown to be an administrative body of vast undertakings.   It is also assigned certain administrative duties that had formerly belonged to the county justices.   It is every year demanding from Parliament very extensive additions to its powers, and gains something at almost every session.   If as yet it

Incompleteness of the act of 1888.

Functions of the county council.

is but a framework, it is a substantial and enduring
one; and it will, in the very early future, have become
the most important municipal administrative body in
the world. It is expected that it will in time secure
an enlargement of the official bounds of London to
Its hopeful future.
include an area perhaps as extensive as that of the
police jurisdiction. Its members will ultimately sit
ex officio in reformed district councils for minor administrative purposes. It will invade the sanctuary
of the inner City, and destroy its "flummery" and ancient traditions so far as they carry with them peculiar
immunities and privileges. It will take in hand, one
after another, great public works, and will make London a fitting place for its people to live in, and a convenient place for the vast world commerce that centers
there.

Henceforth, then, the government of London will
be that of the county council, which will gradually absorb the authority now belonging to obscure parish
authorities, and will acquire very much of the jurisdiction now and heretofore exercised directly by departments or bureaus of the imperial government.
The full development of that government is only a
question of time. Nobody doubts what its form and
principle will be. The absolute control of municipal
affairs by one central elective body, representing the
masses of the citizens, will be the permanent and final
The British ideal of per- fect munici- pal govern- ment.
government of this chief of urban communities. Such
is the British ideal of a perfect municipal government.
All administrative and appointive power will be vested
in the council. It will work through standing committees, each committee supervising some branch of
business or administration, at the head of which will be
a skilled executive officer appointed upon his merits.

London's new county government rests upon a
franchise so popular that theoretically nobody who

The franchise in London.

would care to vote is excluded. In the first place, all householders are enfranchised; and this includes every man who rents a place for his family, even if it be only a small room in the garret or the cellar of a tenement-house. It also includes those who live within fifteen miles of the metropolis, but who for any purpose own or occupy metropolitan quarters worth a certain very limited rental. Owners of freehold property in London, no matter where they live, if British subjects, are entitled to vote. Widows and unmarried women who are householders, or occupiers or owners of property, are also authorized to vote for county councilors. The principal basis of the franchise is the household; and the chief disqualifications are receipt of public alms and failure to pay rates that have fallen

Eligibility for the council.

due. Any male resident of the metropolis or vicinity who is entitled to vote is eligible to election. Furthermore, any British subject who owns land in London or who is possessed of a certain amount of property, no matter where he lives, may be chosen a councilor of the county of London. The fact of residence in one district does not disqualify, either in law or in the popular judgment, for candidacy in another district.

Residence in a district not required.

Thus the first council, elected in January, 1889, from fifty-seven districts besides the City, was constituted in utter disregard of the precise residence of members. The successful candidates in East or South London districts were in many instances prominent men who lived in the West End or in rural suburbs. If it were the English fashion, as it is the American, to elect as representatives of a ward or district only men who lived in that ward or district for the general duties of a municipal council, the district or ward plan would be given up in whole or in part, and councilors would be elected upon a general ticket by the whole city; for the strict ward plan can never result

in a representative body of the best type. But nowhere in England is residence in a ward deemed a
necessary qualification.

Great interest was shown in the election of the Mechanism
first council. The machinery of nomination and elec- of nomination was borrowed from the general municipal and tion.
parliamentary systems in vogue throughout the country. Thus, it being desired that John Burns should
be a candidate for the Battersea district, it was only
necessary for purposes of a valid nomination that a
blank should be filled out with John Burns's name,
residence, and calling, and the name of the district;
that it should be signed by a " proposer," a " seconder,"
and eight other resident voters; and that it be filed
with the county's returning officer at least six days
before the date of the election. An unlimited number of such nominations may be filed. The names
are announced, and opportunity is given for candidates to withdraw if they choose. Four days before
the election the revised lists of candidates in all the
districts are posted up conspicuously. The Australian
system of secret voting has long been in vogue in
England, and the government provides the ballot-
papers. Nobody may be voted for except those who
have been duly nominated in the manner specified
above.

Since two councilors are elected from each of the
London districts, the nomination is equivalent to an
election when only two candidates are presented. In The election
the case of Battersea, for example, there were six of 1889.
nominations, and therefore six names appeared on
the ballot-paper. The voter marked two names, and
the two candidates who received the highest number of votes were elected. The candidates averaged
about five in each district, one having eight. In only
one was there no contest: in St. George, Hanover

Square, Colonel Howard-Vincent and Mr. Antrobus were the only nominees, and no election was held. In future elections it will doubtless happen in numerous districts that the incumbents will be returned without opposition, as is the custom to a great extent in municipal elections throughout Great Britain.

Safeguards against corrupt and lavish expenditure.

    All the stringent regulations against the lavish and corrupt use of money that have proved so salutary in purifying English parliamentary elections, have been made applicable to the election of London councilors. Under no circumstances may the election expenses of a councilor aggregate more than twenty-five pounds ($125), except that an additional threepence is allowed for each voter in the district above the first five hundred. All expenditures must be made through authorized agents, and these must report the items to the candidate, who within a month must render a complete return of expenses incurred in his election. No payments may be made on behalf of any candidate for conveyance of voters, for bands of music or parades or other public demonstrations, for clerks or messengers except at the rate of one employed person for each thousand voters, nor for placards or printed matter except through a selected advertising agent. These laws are construed strictly, carry heavy penalties, and are scrupulously observed.

Ability and distinction of councilors.

    This first London council possessed as high an average of ability and distinction as the House of Commons. Sir John Lubbock and the Earl of Rosebery were two of the four members for the City, and such well-known men as Mr. Firth, Mr. Lawson, Mr. Martineau, Colonel Hughes, Colonel Howard-Vincent, Mr. Antrobus, Lord Monkswell, Sir R. Hanson, Lord Compton, and John Burns were in the list, together with many others who had a high local reputation for character and ability. Two ladies were elected — Lady

Sandhurst and Miss Jane Cobden (now Mrs. T. Fisher
Unwin). Unfortunately, it was after a time decided
by the courts that women were not eligible, and these
two eminently capable ladies had to withdraw, together
with another who had been selected as an alderman.
The councilors added to their number by choosing the The first
following persons as aldermen: Lord Lingen, Lord aldermen.
Hobhouse, Quintin Hogg, Sir Thomas Farrer, Frederic
Harrison, John Barker, Edmund Routledge, Frank
Debenham, S. S. Tayler, Arthur Arnold, Hon. R. Gros-
venor, S. Hope Morley, J. Eccleston Gibb, G. W. E.
Russell, the Earl of Meath, Evan Spicer, Mark Beau-
foy, Miss Cons, and the Rev. Fleming Williams. A
council containing so much distinguished material and
approved political ability was certain to have prestige
and success. The aristocracy by no means predomi-
nated in this London council, although it was so liber-
ally represented. The noble lords who held seats were
practical, popular men, with a talent for affairs, and Lords and
they sat beside several scores of plain untitled citizens working-
of London, some of whom are of as humble origin as men.
John Burns, the labor leader, but most of whom are
men of more than commonplace abilities. It may interest New York, Boston, and Chicago readers to be
assured that there were no saloon-keepers or ward
bosses in this London council, over which Lord Rose-
bery presided as chairman, while the scientist-states-
man Sir John Lubbock served as vice-chairman, and
the distinguished London reformer, the late Mr. Firth,
as deputy chairman.

For the first time in their history the citizens of Effect upon
metropolitan London had participated in the election the public.
of a central governing body. They had been aroused
out of their lethargy, and had learned to interest themselves, with new hopes and new convictions, in the
welfare and progress of their huge community. More-

CHAP. VIII.

Publicity for
the first
time.

Enlighten-
ment for the
average Lon-
doner.

Patriotism
of the
council.

over, for the first time in their history they found
themselves able to follow intelligibly the programs
and policies that were being devised for their weal or
woe. The absolute publicity of a great municipal council was a revelation to them. The Metropolitan Board
of Works had courted secrecy and mystery in all its
methods. The vestries had as a rule conducted all their
affairs in ways obscure and inscrutable. The average
Londoner knew only that he paid heavy rates. Nobody
had ever accounted to him for the expenditure of his
money. He had heard that favoritism and jobbery
were rampant in the large financial operations of the
Board of Works, and that the vestries and district
boards were at least unbusiness-like and haphazard
in the performance of their ill-defined functions. He
knew that anomalies and manifestly wrong conditions
were about him everywhere. But he had grown accustomed to these things, and had learned to submit,
because he did not see where to look for remedies.
With the advent of the county council — zealous, dis-
interested, aggressive, eager to champion every right-
eous reform in the affairs of the metropolis — all was
changed as if by magic. At last the plain citizens of
London had something to rally about, viz., their own
elected council. If their representatives in the first
council had proved themselves unworthy of full confidence, London's destined transformation would certainly have been retarded for years. But the council
rose to heights of patriotic service that won even the
reluctant acknowledgments of its enemies; for enemies it had, and very bitter ones. The London reformers advocating a so-called progressive policy
found themselves in a large majority when the ballots
were counted; and the nineteen aldermen whom they
selected, and whose names have just been given, were
of that same municipal, economic, and political faith.

Here, then, was a body of men irrepressibly moved by
the reforming spirit, and determined to magnify their
offices, who had set for themselves the task of so using
their existing powers, and so laboring to obtain more
powers from Parliament, as to crystallize out of the
anti-social and chaotic conditions that prevailed in
their great "province covered with houses" a true
modern municipality, with many direct activities and
many spheres of influence and control. Such a body
must needs have set in opposition against it all the
privileged and selfish interests whose gainful opportunities were disturbed or threatened, besides arousing
the prejudices of those whose environment and affili-
ations make them apprehensive of all movements that
propose to tax the community for the benefit of the
community.

Antagonism of the enemies of reform.

At the end of its three years' work, the first London
council had so conducted itself that its friends could
say without contradiction that "through all these years
of administrative labors, as complex and confusing as
ever fell to any governing body in the world, not one
breath of scandal, no shadow of a shade of personal
corruption, has attached to any single member of the
council." The members had served without a penny
of reward, direct or indirect; yet many of them had
given all or most of their time to the municipal service,
while the whole body of 140, though composed of men
who for the most part had private business or professional duties that could not be abandoned, gave an
average of one third of their working time — *i. e.*, two
whole days each week — to council and committee meetings and labors connected with the public affairs of
the metropolis. It is recorded, not as an exceptional
illustration of county-council industry, but as a fairly
typical instance, that "in the year 1889–90 the parks
committee met 120 times as against twenty meetings

Character and achievements of the first council.

Chap. VIII.

Industry of councilors.

of the similar body attached to the Board of Works, and in 1890–91 it met 210 times, or ten times the number of the Board of Works' meetings." Nor was any of the council's incessant work properly to be criticized as "pernicious activity"; for it assumed its various tasks with a remarkable intelligence and discretion, and apportioned them with excellent system and comprehension.

Election of the second council.

It was not to be expected that the election of a second council—which was fixed for March 5, 1892, the entire body (excepting the nineteen aldermen) retiring every three years—would be without an exciting campaign. The fact that in six of the fifty-eight constituencies there were no contests showed, however, that London might in time settle down to the admirable custom of the provincial towns, which, as I have shown, make it a common practice to reëlect good councilors term after term without any opposition. This election of 1892, which awakened so intense an interest and polled so heavy a vote, was not fought strictly upon municipal issues. A great parliamentary election was expected soon to occur, and the line that separated Liberals from Conservatives was just then too sharply defined to make it humanly possible that

Politics in municipal affairs.

politics should be completely excluded from a municipal campaign. It so happened, however, that the line of cleavage between the great political parties coincided in a rough way with the natural division that had taken place during the previous three years upon legitimate municipal questions and issues. Friends of sound municipal government in London, who dread the mixing of issues and the demoralization that always threatens a city when party politics control local government, did their best to keep party names and party watchwords out of the discussions of the campaign, and they were measurably successful.

They fought the battle under the designations re- CHAP. VIII.
spectively of "Progressives" and "Moderates." The
Progressives defended the general policies of the re- "Progress-
ives" versus
"Moder-
ates."
tiring London council. They stood for taxation re-
form which should make the great landlords, and
holders of ground-rents, pay their share of municipal
revenue. They stood for the extinction of the rights
of the eight private water-companies that now furnish London with an inferior and high-priced supply
of water, and for the creation of a directly owned and
managed municipal supply. They stood for the pol- The issues of
the cam-
paign.
icy of the council in pressing measures for the reform
of the housing conditions of the poor; in general for
an enlargement of the powers of the county council
by additional acts of Parliament; for an energizing
and uplifting of the public municipal life and authority of London; for a more severe administration in
the general interests of morality; and for a variety of
those modern social ameliorations which Birmingham, Glasgow, and other cities have already secured.
Now it happened that the Liberals were for the most
part thoroughly committed to the policy of the Progressives, while it also happened that the Tories or
Conservatives were enlisted as Moderates in the municipal campaign — that is to say, they opposed what
they called the extravagant and utopian projects of the
council. Their campaign was directed by the great Elements of
opposition.
landlords who own most of London, and their allies
were the water-companies and various holders of private monopolies of supply, the great vested liquor
interests, the proprietors of low music-halls, and all
those who found present and past conditions to redound to their own interest and profit. The Progressives announced bolder programs than ever,
aroused intense enthusiasm among the working-men,
and carried the day triumphantly. Thus the second

council, elected to serve until March, 1895, contained
84 Progressives and 34 Moderates. This does not count
the aldermen, whose choice, of course, has been at the
hands of the majority, though the second council endeavored to avoid the reproach of partisanship by selecting several Conservatives when it had to fill a
group of aldermanic vacancies.

The ordinary concerns of municipal life, as I have
said, still remain for the larger part in the hands of
the parishes or the amalgamated districts as arranged
in the Metropolis Government Act of 1855. These are
in control of paving, lighting, sewers, street-cleaning,

garbage disposal, and sanitary inspection, and have
many discretionary powers for usefulness in such regards as housing reform, baths and wash-houses, free
libraries, and other enterprises and ameliorations that
belong to the recognized work of all the best provincial municipalities. Of late, some of these London
vestries have begun to stir themselves, under the contagious influence of the county council's progressive
schemes and doctrines. But most of them have shown
themselves ill adapted to their tasks. Why they have
been so unresponsive to the demand for modern improvements can be explained, in part at least, by a few
simple facts as to their constitution. As compared
with the system existing before 1855, the present arrangement is the embodiment of order, lucidity, and
effectiveness. But when compared with any really
symmetrical and logical system, that which now rami-

fies London is almost baffling in its confusion. If,
however, we avoid its minor intricacies and confine
ourselves to its main outlines, we may hope to com-
prehend it. There were left as administrative or municipal units twenty-three large parishes, and there
were grouped into fifteen other units seventy-eight
smaller parishes. These smaller parishes retained

their elected vestries for certain purposes of civil gov- CHAP. VIII.
ernment, but for the purposes of various improve-
ments each vestry was required to elect its quota of a
district board of works. The dissolution of a group or
two now leaves twenty-nine parish vestries and thirteen Forty-two
district boards as the forty-two units of ordinary mu- units of ad-
nicipal administration in the metropolis. Not to con- ministration.
cern ourselves with the former limitations upon the
franchise, it is enough to say that for some years past
the ratepayers have all been entitled to vote for members of the vestry. The vestries have been large
bodies composed of 120 men in the greater parishes,
and they have numbered about 5000 in the aggregate
for all London. Eligibility to a vestry in London had,
down to 1894, been conditioned upon a property
qualification — or, rather, a ratepaying qualification High prop-
— high enough to exclude working-men. The limit erty qualifi-
remained at an assessed valuation of £40 per an- cation.
num. But London working-men do not pay $200 a
year for house rent. Indeed, many very worthy ones
do not earn more than that amount. In the great
parishes of London — and these municipal divisions
average 100,000 people, while some of them contain a
quarter of a million — five sixths of the men who pay
rates and who would be eligible for Parliament or for Most men
the county council, have never been eligible for a seat ineligible for
in their own local vestry. Since they have been in- vestries.
eligible themselves, they have not been in the habit of
exercising their right to vote. Moreover, it was never
convenient for them to vote; for the vestry elections
had not been conducted like other elections. One
third of the places were filled annually, and the busi- Antiquated
ness was done in the most antiquated manner ima- method of
ginable. In a parish of, let us say, 200,000 people, the vestry elec-
election was usually nothing but a show of hands at a tions.
slimly attended meeting. Frequently not one voter in

a hundred was present. No nominations had been announced in advance. The meeting was held at some hour in the forenoon when working-men could not leave their tasks. The vestrymen of a parish under these circumstances became virtually a close corporation, reëlecting themselves and each other as their terms expired. They were small house-owners and landlords, local shopkeepers, and men of that caliber. They were about as far as possible from fairly representing the sentiments and wishes of their great municipal districts, yet they were levying in the aggregate more than $10,000,000 a year which they were expending in a more or less unaccountable fashion upon streets, sanitary services, and other branches of administration.

Virtually a close corporation.

Wholly unrepresentative.

It has been mentioned as a curious fact that London's central municipal authority was created as an after-thought, in the process of working out a measure designed to give elective governments to the rural counties of England. It must then be recorded as a striking coincidence that the practical downfall of London vestrydom should also have been accomplished as an incident in the passage of a bill providing primarily for real local self-government, on pure democratic lines, in the rural parishes of England and Wales. There are fifteen thousand parishes where privileged vestrydom had always been rampant, and the "squire and parson" had governed as they saw fit. Mr. Henry Fowler, as President of the Local Government Board in Mr. Gladstone's last cabinet, in 1893 introduced the "Local Government Bill, England and Wales," which became a law early in 1894 after a most protracted parliamentary discussion. This measure does for the townships or civil parishes of England what the Municipal Corporations Act of 1835 did for the large towns. It establishes

A striking coincidence.

Reform of rural vestries.

local autonomy upon a system similar in many re- CHAP. VIII.
spects to that of the township system of the United
States, to which so much praise has always been accorded; and it restores those rights of self-government in the small country districts of England that
are supposed to have been exercised in ancient Saxon
days. It provides for elections by ballot, and for
meetings after six o'clock P. M. The election of London   London ves-
vestries, happily for the progress of reform in the   tries included.
lagging metropolis, was dealt with by this bill. The
county council was accorded some supervision over
the parish elections, and all the resident citizens, men   Everybody
and women, were made eligible for election, while the   now eligible.
voting list was to include every name found on the
parliamentary or the county-council rolls. Moreover,
the choice of a parish council became a real election,   Ballot system intro-
conducted under the balloting acts which regulate   duced.
parliamentary and municipal elections. When, at a
parish meeting for the renewal of an instalment of
the vestry, a poll was demanded, it had always been
held on the following day under conditions that pre-
cluded a general participation. Moreover, neither the
Australian ballot system nor the corrupt practices
acts had been applicable in the election of vestries.
All this was changed by Mr. Fowler's great enact-   A fundamental reform in
ment, and in November, 1894, the first election was   1894.
held of members of London's new parish councils.
Thus, at a stroke, the forty or more sub-municipalities that were carrying on most of the detailed work
of town administration for the four millions of dwellers in metropolitan London, were reformed and modernized as to their ruling bodies.   Franchise in
election of
On a former page [1] some explanation was given   poor-law
boards.
of the British municipal franchise as compared with
those for other purposes; and it will be remembered

[1] See pp. 38–46.

that the most complicated and by far the least democratic of all was the franchise for the election of
guardians of the poor. The system of poor-relief
created in 1834 arranged the whole country in a
series of poor-law unions, so called because as a rule
a number of parishes were united to make each poor-
law jurisdiction. There are about 650 of those unions
in England and Wales, and 31 of them are within the
limits of the county of London. The levying of poor-
rates and the dispensing of relief are in the hands,
for each union, of a board of guardians, elected by
owners and occupiers of property; and extra or
"plural" votes have been permitted on a graduated
basis, one vote being allowed for every £50 of assessed valuation up to a maximum of six votes. In
the case of an owner who was also an occupier, it was
possible for one person to cast twelve votes for each
vacancy to be filled in the board of guardians. This
plan obviously gave to property a very excessive representation. Moreover, there were *ex-officio* members
in all the boards of guardians who further increased
the preponderance of the propertied and privileged
classes. Mr. Fowler's Local Government Bill of 1894,
although not primarily intended as a measure dealing
with the poor-law machinery, actually revolutionized
the entire system; for it abolished the plural voting
and *ex-officio* membership, made all women eligible,
reduced the franchise to the most popular basis, making it the same as that for the parish councils, and
made the term of guardians three years. The practical importance of this reconstruction of the boards of
guardians of the poor can hardly be overestimated.

For London the change will have many advantages.
The thirty-one metropolitan poor-law authorities have
huge responsibilities, with 100,000 paupers to maintain, and other duties and outlays which involve the

Marginal notes:

Thirty-one poor-law districts in London.

The system of "plural" voting.

All changed by the act of 1894.

Women now vote and are eligible.

handling of from $15,000,000 to $20,000,000 a year.
These authorities ought, then, to have the confidence
of the people and to be elected as other public servants
are. Moreover, the democratic control of the poor-
law machinery may now be expected to promote the
project of a simplifying of London's local divisions
and jurisdictions. At present the poor-law districts
do not coincide, except here and there, with the parishes
and districts that constitute what we may call the sub-
municipalities. But inasmuch as the peculiar voting
system of the poor-law boards has been abolished,
there would seem to be no reason why in the early
future the two sets of districts should not be assimilated. The whole London tendency is, clearly, toward
the creation of a series of distinct, popularly governed
sub-municipalities, under the ægis of an aggrandized
central municipality. The Fowler act of 1894, transforming the vestries into district councils and dealing analogously with the unions, will eventually have
accomplished almost as much toward London's ultimate municipal system as the Ritchie act of 1888,
which created the county council.

Benefits to
London.

The clash
and tangle of
local juris-
dictions.

A harmoniz-
ing tendency.

Mr. Fowler himself declared, when he introduced his
great bill, that it would constitute the second volume
of local government reform, the measure of 1888 having been the first volume, while the third would follow
in due time, and would include the unification of London, and the entire revision of its central and sectional
governmental system. As a proof of his practical in-
tentions regarding London, he proposed to Parliament
the appointment at once of a royal commission " to consider the proper conditions under which the amalgamation of the city and county of London can be effected,
and to make specific and practical proposals for the
purpose." It was determined that the commission
should be so composed as to insure respect for its

The "third
volume" of
reform.

The com-
mission on
London uni-
fication.

I.— 17

opinions.   Mr. Leonard H. Courtney, a highly distinguished member of parliament, universally esteemed
for his impartiality and excellent judgment, was made
chairman.   Sir Thomas Farrer of the London county
council, the solicitor of the old City corporation, the
mayor of Liverpool (Mr. Robert D. Holt), and the
town clerk of Birmingham (Mr. Edward Orford Smith)
were the other members of the commission.   Thus its
membership combined great knowledge of British municipal administration in general with special qualifications to consider London's peculiar problems.   Much
testimony was heard, and the county council rendered
active aid in promoting a thorough inquiry.   The old
City became disaffected when it found that its antiquated methods and incomprehensible finances were
considered a proper field for investigation, and with-
drew its member from the commission before the work
was completed.   But the moral force of the commission's report was not diminished by the defection of
the old City.   The conclusions reached [1] in August,
1894, and made public a few weeks later, constitute not
only a remarkably statesmanlike plan for the accomplishment of London's task of municipal reconstruction, but form a valuable contribution to the science
of administration as applied to large metropolitan
centers.   A "Greater New York," for example, might
find in it many instructive suggestions; and to the
problems of the future metropolitan Boston it might
seem to have an even closer application.

This so-called unification commission found that
the "large area of London outside the city is really a
great town, and requires town and not county government"; and proceeded to declare that, "bearing this
in mind, we have to apply to an area called a county,
but really a town now endowed with an elementary

Its fortunate personnel.

A valuable report on metropolitan govern-ment.

Suggestions for Boston, New York, etc.

The federa-tive prin-ciple.

[1] See Appendix.

form of government, the dignity and completeness of
the highest form of municipal life." But it also found
that London, while one large town, " for convenience
of administration, as well as from local diversities,
comprises within itself several smaller towns ; and
the application of the principles, and still more of the
machinery, of municipal government to these several
areas must be limited by conditions arising from this
fact." It was then asserted that any controversy remaining would turn upon the partition of powers between this central and these local bodies.

The report then explains its plan of making the A great mu-
county of London a great municipal corporation, and   nicipal cor-
                                                      poration.
transforming the county council into a central town
council, its chairman becoming a lord mayor, and acquiring the dignities that now pertain to the lord
mayor of the old, inner City, with other and more
substantial ones growing out of the fact that he
would be the chief functionary of five million people
rather than of thirty-five thousand. The inner City Strengthen-
becomes reduced, under this plan, to the status of a   ing the sub-
                                                      municipal-
sub-municipality — merely the central one of a series ities.
of local administrative districts. But the commission
urged the importance of allowing as much actual
authority over local affairs as possible to these districts, and of encouraging their self-consciousness and
pride of locality. It found that in point of fact the
larger parishes and existing administrative districts,
under the system of 1855, are already "administered
with varying but in many cases considerable success,
and possess attributes of local life which could not
wisely be weakened or endangered." It names nine- Retention of
teen of these which, in addition to the district it now   existing
                                                      divisions.
calls the " old City," might very well, without much
or any rearrangement of areas, enter at once upon
a municipal career under the new system. Those

A partial list
of London's
sub-munici-
palities.

named in the report are: (1) St. Marylebone, (2) St. Pancras, (3) Lambeth, (4) St. George, Hanover Square, (5) Islington, St. Mary, (6) Shoreditch, St. Leonard, (7) Kensington, St. Mary Abbott's, (8) Fulham, (9) Hammersmith, (10) Mile-end Old Town, (11) Paddington, (12) Bethnal Green, St. Matthew, (13) Newington, St. Mary (Surrey), (14) Clerkenwell, St. James and St. John, (15) Chelsea, (16) Hampstead, St. John, (17) Westminster, St. Margaret and St. John, (18) Poplar, (19) Whitechapel. The report does not attempt to rearrange the other parishes of London, but intimates that they could readily enough be grouped into a few units of administration. Thus the London sub-municipalities might altogether number not far from thirty. The commission would give them elective councils, like those of the provincial municipalities, and would allow them to have mayors, though dispensing with aldermen. Most of their present duties would be left to them, and various others would be added. The commission declares for the principle of assigning to the local administrations everything that they can do as well as the central council could do it. It holds that in any case the departments of administration possessing a common interest for all London would always give the central authority enough to do, and that, as for other matters, it would be best to allow the central body to make rules and by-laws, to inspect and oversee, and to step in where there is default or neglect, but otherwise to leave the actual performance of administrative work to the local councils and their employees.

Perhaps
thirty in all.

Local
mayors.

Principle of
dividing mu-
nicipal work.

Gentle but
firm treat-
ment of the
old City.

The commission proposes that such responsibilities of the old City as are general in their nature should be made over to the new London corporation, and that the corresponding assets and liabilities should follow the same rule. It suggests reasons for allowing the

old City a doubled representation in the central council. It provides for the gradual extinction of the political and municipal prerogatives of the freemen of
the livery companies, and offers the existing city
aldermen the consolation of life seats in the local council of the old City. In short, it abolishes the ancient
corporation with all possible courtesy and consider-   A diplomat-
ation. So diplomatically is the scheme presented that ic process
                                                       of amalga-
it might be said to revive and extend to the whole me- mation.
tropolis the corporate life that has hitherto been pent
up in a single square mile, while still leaving the old
City in control of its local affairs. But whether one
prefers to say that it annexes the county to the City,
or that it merges the City in a municipalized county,
the result is one and the same.

Public opinion has come so strongly to the support   Sustained by
of the proposals of the commission that there can be public opin-
                                                         ion.
little doubt that a law will soon be enacted to carry
out the plan. The great merit of the report lies in its
solid grasp of actual conditions and tendencies. The
measure of 1888 laid the foundation for a central
municipal authority; that of 1894 went far toward preparing the way for the definite establishment of the
sub-municipalities upon uniform and efficient lines;
and the amalgamation of the old City with the administrative county, with the issuance of a municipal
charter to the metropolis, will come as the crowning
task at a very early day. The Conservatives have the
credit for the law of 1888, and the Liberals for that of
1894. The completion of the task of creating a federated metropolitan municipality ought to be carried out by common consent and without obtrusion
of party politics.

The commission has made it clear that there can be An instruc-
                                                     tive demon-
found in practice a reasonable and effective division stration.
of functions between a great central municipal council

I.—17*

and a series of highly organized, directly elected district councils.   It suggests that the members of the central council might advantageously sit *ex officio* in the local bodies of the districts they represent.   It advises that women should be eligible to the district and central councils, and that the franchise should remain, as in the law of 1894, open to all classes of parliamentary and municipal voters.   Mr. Joseph Chamberlain has lately expressed the opinion that half a million people are as many as can well be cared for by a centrally administered municipal government.   He would probably hold that when towns far outgrow that limit the details become too numerous, the interests of localities become too varied, and the whole situation becomes too complex for a system that is kept wholly under one central authority.   There is much to be said on both sides of the question.   If Mr. Chamberlain meant that the great towns lack essential unity, and should therefore be broken into independent municipalities, his position could not be maintained.   There are general concerns belonging to the class of towns having more than a million people that require unity of treatment even more imperatively than those of smaller towns. But there may, on the other hand, be introduced into the management of municipal affairs in the great cities a federal principle that will secure better detailed administration for localities while enhancing the authority and the efficiency of the central municipal government in all matters that have a general bearing. This will be London's contribution to the science of metropolitan government at a time when the rapid expansion of a series of metropolitan areas in Europe and America is creating a new and peculiar problem in administrative organization.

How many people can a municipal government successfully include?

London's solution of a new problem in administration.

CHAPTER IX

METROPOLITAN TASKS AND PROBLEMS

MODERN municipal governments exist in order that they may render certain positive services to the community. The test of their excellence and efficiency must lie in the success with which they perform their practical functions. A discussion, therefore, of municipal services and municipal problems cannot well be detached altogether from a discussion of the mechanism of the municipal government. However, it is quite possible to view the governmental arrangements of a metropolis like London first from the standpoint of organization for municipal purposes, and second from a standpoint which permits us to survey the work to which the administrative machinery must be applied. In the preceding chapter we have considered primarily the question how London has been, is, and is to be organized for the accomplishment of the tasks of a modern metropolitan government. We have now to consider the tasks themselves; for it is obvious that the experiences and problems of metropolitan London must convey some direct lessons, and must throw many side-lights upon the treatment of corresponding metropolitan problems everywhere.

The positive objects of municipal government.

The London problems.

Curiously enough, to the pressing manner in which the drainage problem was forced upon it London owed the fact that it had, until recently, made any

Drainage as the first task.

progress whatever toward a central administration. Metropolitan government, when once established, showed capabilities for serving the interests of its constituent millions of citizens in a great number of ways; but the need of a main-drainage system was the obstinate fact which led to the reluctant admission that there was any such entity as a metro-

Police in national hands. politan London. The general government was in control of the police system, and had no intention to abdicate in favor of a metropolitan municipality. A number of private water-companies,—taking advantage of the helplessness of a vast community that had found no way even to discern, much less to assert,

Water in private hands. its own interests,— had obtained perpetual charters from Parliament, had parceled out the metropolitan district, and were charging the people monopoly rates and making splendid profits on the very simple plan of pumping the unfiltered water of the river Thames through the streets and into the houses. A series of private gas-companies in like fashion were supplying light, and demonstrating the axiom that competition

Gas-supply also private. in the gas business always results in more oppressive monopoly. The fossilized corporation of the inner City, exclusive and self-perpetuating, had much more in common with such private monopolies as the gas-companies and water-companies than it had with the modern municipal governments that exist for the general welfare, and that are answerable to the public for the manner in which they discharge their duties. This inner corporation, while unwilling to admit the

The City's market monopoly. greater London to its privileges, held a monopoly control of market rights for the metropolis, and thus took toll of the whole population in performance of a highly necessary public function. The City corporation also kept some hold upon the river considered as a navigable stream, and was the harbor authority.

As for the docks, and shipping facilities in general, they had naturally, in the absence of an enlightened local administration, taken the form of control by private companies as a semi-monopoly, taxing commerce directly and the community indirectly. The more strictly local and detailed administration outside of the old City was all in the hands of the vestries of many scores of parishes; and these vestries were so constituted and conducted as virtually to exclude the principle of popular representation. Each vestry in its petty sphere was a privileged and self-perpetuating body, eager to imitate the methods of the City corporation and the liveried companies. The vestries levied rates as they pleased, and followed their own variable moods and devices in matters of paving and street lighting.

There were still other "interests" besides those that have been named. The disorganized condition of several million people, living contiguously in a province covered with houses, afforded infinite opportunities; and there emerged all kinds of substitutes for an organized central administration. As Tammany Hall rose to power in New York through its skill and tenacity in seizing hold of the simple fact that New York had no positive, unified central government, so in London the unreformed City corporation, the packed vestries, the greedy water-companies, the ill-regulated gas-companies, the great monopoly land-lord interests, the trustees of innumerable charities ecclesiastical and otherwise, the managers of asylums and institutions, and scores of other elements and interests, each in its own way and for its own purposes, appropriated a portion of the control and authority which should have been exercised either directly at the hands of a central municipal authority, or else under its stern supervision.

CHAP. IX.

The docks a private trust.

Minor administration and vestry "rings."

The usurping "interests."

Tammany,— a London parallel.

Municipal abdication.

Drainage a
neglected
field of
action.

But there was one public service whose mismanagement could not be tolerated, and which offered no compensations or attractions for any of the selfish interests which had apportioned among themselves so many of the other attributes and functions of a metropolitan government. This task was that of drainage. There was no way to make monopoly profits out of it. It was all expense and no income. It must be remembered again that at the opening of the nineteenth century metropolitan London did not have as many as a million people, and the population of the Thames valley above London was only a fraction of that which the census reports now show. But the Thames itself was quite as large a stream then as now, and it is possible that its volume of fresh water may have been somewhat greater. There are several reasons, easily apparent on a moment's reflection, why the question of drainage began to force itself upon many urban communities about the middle of the century. For one thing, the modes and standards of civilized life had grown more fastidious, the relation of cleanliness to health had come to be better understood, the idea of meeting and controlling epidemics by public measures had been fairly broached, and the innovation of underground drains had begun to be regarded as a desirable urban arrangement. But in addition to these considerations, it should be borne in mind that there was now appearing the new phenomenon of rapid town development. Great populations were becoming massed together; and the streams which had sufficed fairly well to carry off the liquid waste that had been poured into them from the small surface drains, had now become taxed beyond the point of decency and safety. London, with the adjacent country, is naturally drained by the river Thames. As population developed in the early dec-

Emergence
of the prob-
lem.

ades of the century, the general government found
it advisable to appoint a number of commissioners,
with limited authority, to exercise supervision over
the sewers and drainage of London. But the problem was far too large for any such treatment. The
condition of the river grew steadily worse. Local underground sewers had begun to be quite generally constructed, and they emptied into the river on either side
at the points of nearest access. The inflowing tides
forced the sludge-laden water far up-stream, and the
outflowing tides brought it back again to plague the
town. At times the nuisance became serious enough
to obstruct navigation.

CHAP. IX.

Conditions
in the middle
of the XIXth
century.

It was under these circumstances that the Metropolis Management Act of 1855 was passed, the Metropolitan Board of Works created, the parish system
considerably reformed and improved, and the tangible
beginning made of a metropolitan municipal government. The first task of the Metropolitan Board of
Works was to construct a system of trunk sewers for
London. The main outlines were simple enough. The
problem of the Board of Works was that of gathering
all the sewage of London north of the Thames into a
series of great intercepting or trunk sewers which were
to converge at a convenient point, whence by means of
one great sewer tunnel the whole fluid mass should be
conveyed to a point of outfall on the river-bank some
miles below the city. For that part of London south
of the Thames a similar system was to be created.
Local street sewers were to be constructed and maintained by the parish vestries and district boards, under
plans conforming with those of the metropolitan system; and the drainage of each local district was to be
collected by some arm of the metropolitan board's
ramification of trunk sewers. The system was carried out efficiently. Trunk sewers at different levels

Creation of
the metro-
politan
board.

The main
drainage
project.

CHAP. IX.

Efficiently
carried out.

pierced all the metropolitan districts on both sides of the river, and two huge tunnels, one on the north side and the other on the south side, were constructed to carry the total effluent for a distance of some fifteen miles, the outfall on the north side being at Barking and that on the south side being at Crossness.

Cost of the
undertaking.

During the whole period of its active existence, from 1855 to the time when its duties and responsibilities were turned over to the London county council in 1889, the Metropolitan Board of Works had expended more than $35,000,000 upon its scheme of main drainage, while the parishes and districts had also expended in the aggregate a sum probably much greater for street sewers. The original plan of the metropolitan board was that of temporary storage at the outfall

Working of
the inter-
mittent sys-
tem.

points, in order to discharge each half-day's accumulation upon the outflowing tide. This system had its evident advantages; but experience proved that there were disadvantages to an extent quite unforeseen. The storage system at times of rainfall resulted in a choking of the sewers and an overflow of sewage at innumerable places in London, with the most disastrous consequences. At the point of convergence of the trunk sewers north of the Thames, it was necessary to erect a great pumping station which should lift the collected sewage a distance of eighteen or twenty feet in order that it might reach the Barking outfall at a point suffi-ciently elevated to make possible its discharge on the

Pumping
works.

turning tide; but the total result of the intermittent system was an almost chronic failure of the mammoth pumping works at the Abbey-Mills junction to keep the collected mass in the receiving-tanks low enough to prevent the flooding of the sewer system. It became evident that the scheme of intermittent discharge ought if possible to be abandoned. The frequency of overflow had made it necessary to provide a system of relief sewers, discharging directly into the river. And thus, at all times of heavy rainfall, a large proportion of the ordinary sewage found its way to the stream in the very heart of the metropolis.

Besides the constant study of the problem made by the metropolitan board and its engineers, there were several special examinations of the subject of metropolitan sewage disposal made by royal commissions. The last of these inquiries was conducted by a commission which was appointed in 1882, and which reported in 1884 after exhaustive investigation of the experience of other great cities. The report was by no means consoling. It declared that under no circumstances, neither by a continuous nor by an intermittent system, ought any crude sewage to be discharged into the Thames; and it went so far as to condemn the discharge into the river of the partially clarified effluent after a process of precipitation of the solid materials — although it recommended such treatment as an alleviating expedient. The Metropolitan Board of Works accordingly proceeded to construct huge intercepting outfall works at Barking and at Crossness, and to endeavor with the aid of a staff of chemists and sanitary experts to find an effective and not too costly method for the separation of the sludge before discharging any liquid sewage into the river. Not to recount in detail the various experiments made, the board finally adopted as its system a treatment of the inflowing sewage first with slaked lime and then with sulphate of iron. About one grain of sulphate of iron and four grains of lime were added to every gallon of ordinary sewage as the material flowed on toward the great settling-tanks, in which the chemicals assisted the precipitation of the solids.

The county council found the Barking works in practical operation, while the Crossness establishment

CHAP. IX.

Improvements made by county council.

System as completed in 1894.

The fleet of sludge steamers.

Sludge not available as a fertilizer.

was only begun.   It has succeeded in greatly improving the efficiency of the system.   Instead of using the subsidence reservoirs alternately, it allows the sewage to flow slowly through the series, passing over weirs and culverts as it moves on, depositing its sludge from tank to tank until at length it emerges deodorized and comparatively clear and unobjectionable, and is allowed to pass off into the river.   The county council completed the Crossness works in June, 1894, and since that time in ordinary weather the entire flow of London sewage, exceeding 200,000,000 gallons per day, passes through the separating process at one or the other of these two great intercepting establishments before it enters the river.   It is still true that a portion of the rainfall, in varying amounts and not wholly unmixed with sewage, finds its way directly into the river by means of the relief sewers ; but this quantity is less than it formerly was, and the completion of additional pumping and main-tunnel facilities will at an early day make it feasible to carry off the entire London drainage, even in exceptional seasons, by way of the separation works at the two outfall stations.

These outfall works have not been constructed without considerable outlay.   The Barking establishment has cost approximately $2,500,000, and the corresponding one at Crossness represents a cost of more than $1,500,000.   But these two stations by no means complete the working plant.   A very essential auxiliary is the municipal fleet of great sludge steamers that carry the soft mud from the precipitation-tanks out to the deep sea.   It has been demonstrated that no successful use of the sludge can at present be made for agricultural purposes.   The experiment was tried for a time, but abandoned.   In order to make it possible to distribute sludge as a commercial ferti-

lizer, it must be compressed into cakes or blocks. But
even then it has a low value, and its utilization was
found to pay only a fraction of the expense of compression and transportation. Since the completion
of the Crossness works, the system has required a fleet
of six steamers for the removal of the sludge, each
ship carrying a thousand tons on every trip. The
arrangements for loading and discharge and for the
whole movement of the fleet have been reduced to a   Loading and
system of great convenience and absolute precision.   emptying
                                                      sludge ships.
The soft mud is driven by force-pumps through crane-
like tubes directly into the hold of the ship. The
cargo is carried fifty miles down-stream to a very
deep channel, when the discharging valves are opened
below water-level, and the mass of sludge unloads
itself while the ship keeps on her course for a distance
of ten miles. Every conceivable test of close observation and chemical analysis has failed to detect any influence or effect of this discharge either in the water
or on the adjacent shores.

The county council has brought to bear upon every
detail of the management of the drainage system a zeal
at once for improvement and for economy. The old
Board of Works, neither in the one respect nor the
other, could compare for a moment with the sewage   Drainage
committee of the county council. Constant additions   problem
                                                      solved for
and reconstructions are bringing the network of col- the present.
lecting sewers toward a condition of modern completeness. Thus, for the present, the problem of London's
drainage may be considered as solved; for the existing
system is susceptible of enlargement from time to
time as the volume of sewage increases. The ramification of main sewers can be extended through a wider
area, and can serve another million people in the outer
ring, as it undoubtedly will within half a dozen years.
The pumping facilities can be increased accordingly,

additional outfall tunnels can be constructed, the precipitation works can be enlarged, more ships can be
added to the fleet of sludge-carriers, while continued
experience can devise means to make the precipitation
more complete, and thus still better to protect the river
against pollution.

But even yet the final system of sewage disposal
has not been adopted. Mr. Binney, the engineer of
the county council under whose direction the entire
system is now administered, made a report in 1891,
with the advice and assistance of Sir Benjamin Baker,
touching the whole subject in its broadest aspects. If
what may be called " Main-Drainage London " now
embraces a population of 5,000,000, there are already
about 7,000,000 people within the district which the
drainage system must soon include; and within forty
years, by all conservative calculations, not less than
12,000,000 people will have to be served by the one
metropolitan sewerage and sewage-disposal system.
Forty years is not a long time in the history of a great
city. That period has elapsed quickly enough since
the metropolitan board laid down the lines of London's present drainage. It is therefore needful that
in the provision of essential public services the future
should be well considered. Messrs. Binney and Baker
made a careful study of the estuary of the Thames,
and proposed a system which might combine sewage
farms with the direct discharge of crude sewage into
the sea. The proposed scheme would be a costly one,
the capital outlay being estimated at from $40,000,000
to $50,000,000; for it would require outfall tunnels
from forty to sixty miles long, according to the route
selected. One proposal would extend the existing
main tunnel from Barking in a direct line toward the
mouth of the Thames, some twenty miles further, and
there distribute the sewage to the amount of perhaps

Demands of the future.

When London will have 12,000,000 people.

Sewage-farms.

200,000,000 gallons a day over the surface of irrigated sewage-farms on the Birmingham or Berlin model. But 200,000,000 or 300,000,000 additional gallons must be removed in the early future, and a great tunnel eighteen feet in diameter has been proposed that would follow a somewhat circuitous route in order to take advantage of natural grades, and extend well out under the shoals of the Foulness Sands to a point of discharge in deep water.

For so great and so rich a community as metropolitan London will be in the second decade of the twentieth century, the cost of executing sewer works such as those proposed by Mr. Binney will, relatively speaking, not be half so great as was the cost of the existing system. It was estimated by Sir Robert Rawlinson in an elaborate paper published by him some years ago on "London Sewerage and Sewage," that the entire volume of this fluid waste was then worth nearly $9,000,000 a year for manurial purposes, and that the true system for London to adopt was that of the direct irrigation of land. Sir Robert's opinion is impregnably sound. The economic loss involved in a system for the chemical separation of sludge, with its removal to the deep sea by means of a fleet of ships in constant service (making a round trip of a hundred and twenty miles, which may in future have to be increased to one hundred and fifty or two hundred miles), would appear on reflection to be very great both in the expensiveness of the method and in the irreparable waste of material that is abstracted from the land and ought to be returned to it. If the present method does not require so great a capital, it involves expensive processes. These entail an actual financial burden as heavy as the interest payments that would be required for an enormous capital investment.

I.— 18

CHAP. IX.

Direct discharge of sewage in deep sea.

Economic considerations.

Manurial value of London's sewage.

Cost of sludge freighting.

Precipitating the sludge clarifies but does not purify.

But there is a further consideration that remains to be mentioned. The present system of chemical precipitation, while it removes most of the solid matter suspended in the inky fluid and leaves a comparatively clear-looking effluent, by no means purifies the released liquid. In explaining the new Glasgow system of sewage treatment, I have shown how the effluent after the sludge has been precipitated is carried through a series of coke and sand filters. And thus the final result on discharge into the river is a water that has been not merely relieved of its muddiness, but also rendered both chemically and bacteriologically pure by a process of filtration. With a little additional care, perhaps without any change whatever in the system, the final Glasgow effluent might safely be pumped into the reservoirs that furnish the town's supply of drinking-water. It is true that the settling of the mud or sludge is a great gain. But the discharged fluid at Barking or Crossness is still saturated with chemical solutions of organic waste, and is as impure as water could possibly be. No system of discharge on ebbing tides can prevent the back-flow of this poisonous liquid; and the fresh water coming down from the upper reaches of the Thames is not sufficient in volume to purify it or to nullify its effects. It was for this reason that the commission of 1884 declared that any permanent scheme must provide for the further purification of this liquid by some process; and they preferred to advise its application to land. When manurial values are considered, it is true that the apparently clear water flowing into the river from the Crossness and Barking works contains far more of the nitrogenous soil-enriching elements than are carried out to sea in the 2,500,000 tons of sludge that are now annually freighted away from the two outfall stations. I have not scrupled thus to discuss the

Filtration, as begun at Glasgow, purifies.

The Barking effluent pollutes the Thames.

Manurial value of the clarified sewage.

problem of London's sewage at length, because not one of the nine or ten great American communities that are assuming metropolitan proportions has as yet begun to grapple conclusively with the problem of the final and satisfactory disposition of its sewage. London's case is more urgent; and our American cities may yet profit, if they will, by the results of London's costly experiments and investigations.

CHAP. IX.

Lessons for America.

It happens that there is a somewhat intimate connection between the future of London's water-supply and that of its modes of sewage treatment. Two great topics regarding the present and future supply of the London population with water are now under controversial discussion. One of these controversies relates to the control of the supply, while the other relates to its sources, quantity, and quality. Let us consider the second question first. In 1891 it was ascertained that the population supplied by the metropolitan water-companies was 5,500,000; and it will soon have reached 6,000,000. The net daily supply in that year averaged 171,000,000 gallons, or 31 gallons per capita for all purposes. Of this amount somewhat more than 100,000,000 gallons a day was pumped from the Thames, perhaps 50,000,000 from the river Lea, and the rest either from large wells or basins dug in gravel beds along the Thames, or else from very deep wells sunk into the chalk strata in the territory lying east and southeast of London. Much criticism has been directed against the supply both on account of its insufficient quantity and also on account of its alleged impurity. The county council ever since its establishment has given constant attention to the subject, with a view to its own assumption of London's water-supply. The council has made exhaustive investigations on its own account,

Controversies touching London's water-supply.

Quantity of existing supply.

Sources of supply.

Public inquiries.

and the general government has also dealt with the question through a royal commission which reported in September, 1893, after an inquiry of a year and a half. The county council, represented by its chief engineer, Mr. Binney, took the ground in extensive arguments before the royal commission that London's present sources of supply should be altogether abandoned as no longer suitable as regards either quantity or quality; and that London should follow the example of Manchester, Birmingham, Liverpool, and Glasgow in seeking a new and inexhaustible supply from distant sources. To some mountainous region in Wales, it is supposed, London would be compelled to build its aqueducts if it should eventually conclude to abandon its present sources.

County council and royal commission.

The royal commission, however, made a highly optimistic report in favor of the Thames and the other subsidiary sources of the present supply. The commission agreed with the London water-companies that it would be sufficient to make a forecast of forty years, whereas the county council had contended for the consideration of a fifty-year period. The commission concluded that in the year 1931 the area now supplied by the metropolitan water-companies — which in 1891 was 845 square miles, and which then contained 5,700,-000 people — would have an aggregate population of 11,250,000. The question which it set for itself to answer then stood as follows: "Can a sufficient supply of water of sufficiently good quality be obtained from the Thames and Lea valleys for the use of eleven and a quarter million persons without serious prejudice to the other inhabitants of those valleys?" The commission dealt in an interesting manner with the question, What is a reasonable per capita daily allowance of water in view of the growing needs of a civilized town population? They finally agreed upon 35 gallons as a

A report in favor of the Thames.

Amount needed in 1931.

A per capita daily allowance of 35 gallons.

safe basis of calculation, declaring their belief that this figure erred on the side of lavishness if it erred at all. They found, then, that "Water London" in 1931 must have a daily supply in round figures of 392,000,-000 gallons.

The volume of water flowing down the channel of the Thames varies much, according to the conditions of rainfall; but the commission, after some sifting of testimony, found it to average 1,350,000,000 gallons a day in that part of the river where the water-companies' intakes are situated. Regarding the Thames, the commission reached the unanimous conclusion that 300,000,000 gallons a day could be withdrawn for water-supply without disturbance of navigation. It was shown that in any case the navigable condition is maintained by a series of locks and weirs; and so long as the stretches of the stream thus ponded up are kept full, it is a matter of comparatively little consequence how much additional water is flowing over the dams. The only stretch where navigation could be affected extends for a mile or two below the lowest weir, which is at Richmond; and only at the lowest point of the ebb-tide would the depth of the stream be diminished even there. It was proposed, in compensation, that a reservoir should be constructed in the Richmond Park, into which 50,000,000 gallons would flow twice a day with each rising tide, only to be released at low tide as a substitute for fresh water withdrawn by the metropolitan intakes at a point above the weir.

That portion of the commission's inquiry which was directed to the question how great a supply might be derived from deep wells sunk in the tracts of chalk country in the Lea valley and on the south side of the Thames, was especially thorough and interesting. As a conclusion it was reported that

What the Thames could yield.

Effect upon navigation.

Compensation tidal reservoir.

A supply from wells in the chalk strata.

I.—18*

about 70,000,000 gallons a day might safely be withdrawn from those admittedly pure and desirable sources without injury to streams or agriculture. Thus, with 50,000,000 gallons from the river Lea, the commission had provided for 420,000,000 gallons a day, equal to a supply of thirty-five gallons per capita for 12,000,000 people. Mr. Binney, the county council's chief engineer, was of opinion that every drop of fresh water flowing down the Thames was needed for its purifying effect upon the sewage constantly entering the stream below the city. The commissioners maintained that Mr. Binney had given undue weight to this consideration. They might have suggested what is, after all, the most important point to be borne in mind: that the true solution would be the withdrawal of all sewage and other sources of pollution. The smaller communities in the Thames valley above London are one after another adopting sewage-farms, and it will be feasible eventually to divert London's drainage away from the river. When that is accomplished, the flood-tides will bring nothing offensive that can require the neutralizing effects of fresh water. Moreover, the great bulk of the river's average daily flow would in any case remain unappropriated. The commission's plans contemplate a great series of storage reservoirs at Staines, some miles above London.

As to the purity of the water now supplied to London, the commission took much testimony with reassuring results. It was found that although the existing practice of the companies was far from uniform, the filtration of the supply had recently become general; and, as regards most of the water furnished, the work of filtration had proved effective. The commission was aided by experts in biology, who demonstrated to its satisfaction that sand filtration not only

Objections by the council's engineer.

A part of the true solution.

Quality of London's water.

Value of filtration.

removes deleterious chemical substances, but, what is far more important, frees water from harmful bacteria. The evidence on this point collected by the London commission antedated the most conclusive demonstration that has now been made,— namely, the absolute success of the new filtration works at Hamburg [1] in removing cholera microbes from the Elbe water, which, as pumped into the subsidence-basins, had millions of cholera germs in every cubic inch. The recent experience of all the German towns deriving their water-supply from the rivers Rhine and Elbe confirms to the point of an absolute demonstration the position taken in 1893 by the royal commission on the water-supply of the English metropolis. It may therefore be considered as proved that for a good while to come London may continue to drink the water of the Thames; and the question of an ultimate supply from the mountains of Wales or elsewhere may safely be left for consideration twenty or forty years hence.

An immediate and a pressing question, however, is that of the proprietorship and administration of the water-supply. Eight water-companies now divide between them the sources, the territory to be supplied, and the emoluments, which are very considerable. The New River Company, which dates from the time of King James I., supplies the central part of the metropolis on the north side of the river, and serves about 1,200,000 people, furnishing about 33,000,000 gallons a day. The East London Water Works Company was formed in the year 1805, having absorbed two companies of much earlier origin, and it also is supplying approximately 1,200,000 people with 40,000,000 gallons a day, its territory being that great and populous region extending from Whitechapel and Stepney

Chap. IX.

Testimony sustained by recent German experience.

Question of public ownership.

The London water-companies.

[1] See "Hamburg's New Sanitary Impulse," by Albert Shaw, in the "Atlantic Monthly" for June, 1894.

to West Ham, known as East London. The Chelsea
Company was chartered in 1723, and supplies about
300,000 people with nearly 10,000,000 gallons a day.
The West Middlesex Company was incorporated in
1806, and it supplies about 600,000 people at the West
End with 16,000,000 gallons a day. The Grand Junction Company also has its sphere of operations in a
number of the extensive parishes of West London, and
it supplies 350,000 people with 17,000,000 gallons —
much the most liberal per capita supply of any London
company. It dates from 1798. The Lambeth Water
Works Company and the Southwark and Vauxhall

Company divide between them most of London south
of the Thames, including also great suburban areas
in the county of Surrey that lie beyond the London
metropolis. The Lambeth Company was first incorporated in 1785, and the Vauxhall Company began
operations in 1805, although both companies have
had several subsequent charters which extended their
franchises to greater areas. The Lambeth Company
in 1891 supplied a population of 655,000 people with
20,000,000 gallons a day, and the Vauxhall Company
supplied about 850,000 people with 24,000,000 gallons.
Finally, the Kent Water Works Company, incorporated in 1809, operates in a number of far eastern
parishes south of the Thames, and in 1891 was supplying 460,000 people with 12,500,000 gallons daily.

These companies, by the terms of their charters,
have been allowed to levy certain statutory rates based
upon the rental valuation of the houses supplied.
The arrangement is an antiquated one, dating from a
period when frequent revaluations of property were
unknown. The actual consequences have been, during several past decades, that with every increase in the
assessed valuation of a house or piece of property the
water-company supplying that house has been able to

increase the amount of the yearly water tax, although upon the average there has been actual diminution in the quantity of water supplied from year to year to each house. The number of houses to be supplied has increased more rapidly than the supplies which the companies found available for distribution. As a result, down to 1887, or later, only about half the houses in London were receiving a continuous supply. They were compelled to store in tanks or cisterns enough water to meet the wants of those portions of the day or night when their supply was turned off by the company. Public feeling against the companies has grown so intense that they have made strenuous efforts to give an improved service; and within the past five years the continuous supply has been extended to the great majority of London houses. It still remains true, however, that the companies are in the absurd position of being able to levy a fixed statutory rate on the pound of assessed valuation, and thus to collect an increased sum every five years, wherever the assessed value of property advances.

Insufficient service.

An oppressive system.

It was alleged several years ago that it cost the companies less than £700,000 a year to supply London with water, for which the people of London had to pay the companies £1,700,000. The receipts have now increased to nearly £2,000,000, or $10,000,000. The companies are paying dividends on a share capital of some $75,000,000, and it is alleged by the experts of the county council that the aggregate plants of the eight companies could be duplicated and greatly improved by the expenditure of $50,000,000. No one would have the audacity to dispute the proposition that the people of London could easily provide themselves, through the agency of their representative county council, with a much more satisfactory system than the present one, while reducing the water rates at least

Income and capital.

What public management would save.

fifty per cent. The county council has been negotiat-
ing for the purchase of the properties and rights of
the existing companies, but thus far no basis of agreement has been reached because the companies have
insisted upon an aggregate valuation of from $150,-

Valuing the
works.
000,000 to $250,000,000, nearly all of which is repre-
sented by the revenue-producing values of the public
franchises which have cost the companies nothing.

    The solution of the question would be a very simple
one if it were not for the House of Lords. The House

How the
companies
are pro-
tected.
of Commons would readily pass a measure giving the
county council authority at its option either to nego-
tiate for the existing works, or to establish an independent system, forbidding the companies to increase
their takings from the Thames, and sanctioning the
use of the river by the council. This would bring the
companies to terms at once; for the people of London
could readily provide themselves with a duplicate system at one third of the price that the companies have
demanded for their antiquated establishments. Public
control of London's water is, of course, only a question of time. Nothing is more readily apparent to

A conspiracy
of "inter-
ests."
any foreign observer of English affairs than the fact
that there exists what is virtually a huge conspiracy
of "interests," monopolies, and privileged groups, all
of which rely ultimately upon the aid and countenance of the House of Lords, and its constitutional
right to veto the legislation of the people's representatives in Parliament. But the position of the House
of Lords itself has now become somewhat critical; and

A weakening
opposition.
that distinguished body can hardly find it convenient
to lend itself too insistently to a scheme for compelling
the people of London to pay an extra hundred million
dollars to a group of private companies in order to
buy back what they have never sold,— namely, the
natural right to supply themselves with the most es-

sential of all commodities. Justice in this case is so
clear that it must soon prevail over monopoly claims.

One of the most important functions that the county
council acquired in its capacity as heir to the undertakings of the Metropolitan Board of Works, was
that of the maintenance and improvement of a main
thoroughfare system. A street-map of London as the
city was in 1840 or 1850 would be necessary to make
plain all the improvements that have been wrought,
especially in the central districts lying within four or
five miles of Charing Cross. As the metropolis grew,
the pressure of traffic upon its central thoroughfares
naturally became enormous. It was necessary, at
great cost, to widen and straighten important streets,
and to open new thoroughfares. Thus great improvements were made in the lines of streets that lead from
Charing Cross to the Bank. It became imperative to
create other arteries between the City and the West
End; and the Holborn Viaduct, with High Holborn
and New Oxford streets, was constructed. Queen
Victoria street and the magnificent Thames embankments constituted still another new route created with
the outlay of millions. The Northumberland Avenue,
the Gray's Inn Road, the Charing Cross Road, and
dozens of other now important thoroughfares, have
been cut through solid masses of buildings, involving
heavy financial operations in condemning property,
clearing sites, constructing the streets, and reselling
the new street frontage.

London, like many other old cities, had a tangled
network of streets that for the most part began nowhere and ended nowhere. Upon this network it
became necessary to superimpose a system of main
thoroughfares as avenues of communication. This
work had begun, either under the authorities of the

London's
system of
chief thor-
oughfares.

Great re-
forms of the
metropoli-
tan board.

New central
arteries.

Main arteries
of traffic.

City corporation or under special parliamentary commissions, long before the day of the metropolitan
board; but this body accomplished the major part.
Including the splendid river boulevards and retain-
ing-walls known as the Albert, Victoria, and Chelsea
embankments, I find that the metropolitan board
from 1856 to 1887 had expended about $75,000,000
upon these main street improvements, during which
time the outlying parts of the metropolis had added
to the ordinary street system about 2000 miles of new
thoroughfares, lined with several hundred thousand
new houses. But the cost of these local streets had
been locally defrayed; and it is to the expense of
main arterial improvements that I refer. Including
what the City and special commissions have spent,
not less than $100,000,000 has gone into this work of
reforming the vicious street system of London since
1850. And still the task is far from completed. New
lines of communication must yet be made to relieve
the glut of traffic on east and west routes north of the
Thames.

Cost of chief street improvements.

Only a competent central authority like the new
council can manage these gigantic municipal reforms
in the suitable way. But while these main improvements have been in progress, it should be said in justice to the vestries and district boards that the network of lesser streets has been wonderfully changed
for the better, and that London as a whole is now
also a well-paved city. It devolves upon the council,
as upon its predecessor the Board of Works, to regulate the width and formation of new streets, the lin-
ing of the buildings, the naming of streets, and the
numbering of houses. Unfortunately the metropolis
was already far too large when this power was given
to a central authority. There are fine avenues in the
newer suburbs; but throughout most of the metropo-

The lesser street sys- tem — good paving.

lis the lesser streets must remain in a condition that to an American seems painfully chaotic. An important work had been done by the metropolitan board in constructing Thames bridges, but the supply was wholly insufficient. The county council now maintains ten great bridges across the Thames, while four (the Blackfriars, the Southwark, the London, and the new Tower bridge) are cared for by the old City corporation out of the revenues of its ancient Bridge House Estate. The county council is completing an enormous tunnel under the river at Blackwall, at a cost of $5,000,000, and has obtained terminal sites for another tunnel. In lieu of a bridge for the East Londoners at Woolwich, the council operates a free ferry for passengers and vehicles. The opening of this ferry was one of the first acts of the county council. That it supplied a serious want was demonstrated by the fact that 4,000,000 people a year were soon making use of it. Indeed, the statistics that show the increase of traffic across the Thames are very remarkable. The council is entering upon the work of reconstructing Vauxhall bridge at a cost of $2,500,000, and a long series of new bridges to be built and old ones to be made over forms part of the forecast of municipal undertakings for the coming twenty years.

The council since its succession to the street-improvement work of the metropolitan board has not been lacking in ambition to accomplish great projects of reform. It has definitely mapped out schemes of a central character that would cost millions upon millions. One of these is a widening of the Strand in its narrowest sections, and another is a great new thoroughfare to connect Holborn street with the Strand. The task of most immediate urgency is the construction of a system of approaches to the new Tower bridge. But while the council has proceeded to exe-

CHAP. IX

The Thames bridges.

Blackwall tunnel.

Woolwich free ferry.

Further bridge work.

Improvement programs.

cute numerous street-improvement projects of a less costly nature, it has taken the position with regard to all large schemes that it will hold them in abeyance Awaiting until it wins its battle in Parliament for a new system of taxation that will place a part of the burden of permanent improvements upon the owners of the property that is chiefly benefited. The Board of Works executed its huge improvements, on a recklessly extravagant scale, at the expense of the ratepayers of the metropolis; and not a penny was paid by the wealthy landowners, the value of whose property was in many instances more than doubled. All London improvements have hitherto proceeded on the principle that the public must pay full damages to any owner who can show himself injured, while the public may not recoup itself at all by assessing part of the cost of the improvement on those who are enriched by it.

Awaiting taxation reform.

The London rates are all paid by the occupiers,— *i. e.*, by the tenants,— and the cost of permanent improvements, no less than ordinary administrative outlays, must all be defrayed out of ordinary rates levied upon occupiers in proportion to the rental value of the premises they rent. Unbuilt areas, held by landlords for speculative increase of values, are not rated at all. It is not denied that some large though indeterminate part of the rates paid by occupiers must in the long run affect the rent charges, and must therefore act indirectly as a tax upon the landlords and house-owners. But the occupiers do not believe that the burden is thus shifted; and certainly in the case of huge improvements that forthwith enrich the landowners of a distinct metropolitan street or area, it is both absurd and oppressive to charge the cost upon the ratepayers of the whole vast community. In America we should collect all or most of the cost by means of "special assessments" levied against benefited

The exempted landlords.

Is the burden shifted?

property. The approaches to the new Tower bridge constitute a particularly aggravated case, and the county council has declared that it will not proceed to construct them until Parliament sanctions the "betterment" principle.

Again, it is the House of Lords that stands in the way. The House of Commons in the session of 1893–94 passed a London improvement bill which authorized the council to assess neighboring property for a part of the cost of certain specified improvements; but the House of Lords amended the bill by throwing out this special-taxation clause. The Commons refused to accept the amendment, and the subject was left in abeyance, with the practical certainty that the Lords would not be able to resist public opinion on the "betterment" question for more than a year or two longer. The value of London real estate increases by millions every year not through any effort on the part of landowners as such, but through the general advancement of a community whose real wealth-makers are its working-people, from the prime minister to the humblest laborer or apprentice boy, toiling with brain or hand in the accomplishment of the varied tasks of our modern civilization. A local-taxation system which unsparingly reaches the poorest working-man, but exempts the landowner, and regards the "unearned increment" as something more inviolable than wages or human life, is an abomination. While in so many regards the London people are in the very forefront of progress, they are in other respects the most laggard, the most benighted, and the most wronged and oppressed by conspiracies of privilege and monopoly, of all the denizens of modern cities. They are destined to shake off their bonds, but the struggle will be severe. And there is some ground for anxiety lest the reaction may carry them too far toward socialism. But the "betterment" principle does not even savor of socialism or of economic heresy.

When the county council was first organized in 1889, the standing committee on which the largest number of members desired to serve was that upon *Interest in* the "housing of the working-classes." The subject *the housing question.* of London housing had been much agitated for several years, and the necessity for reforms had been quite universally admitted. The county council, under the great housing act of 1890, became the authority in which was vested the work of carrying out all such schemes as that of the radical treatment of insanitary areas. The earliest task of the committee was that of a careful survey of the facts; and it had soon mapped out several scores of slum spots of greater or less extent which in its judgment demanded drastic *The council's inquiries.* remedial treatment. The masterly and methodical inquiries which Mr. Charles Booth had prosecuted in respect to the housing, the poverty, and all the conditions of labor and employment of the London population, lent both impulse and information to the practical studies upon which the council entered.

The committee also made it a part of its duties to find scattered instances of unhealthy dwellings, and to report these to the district and parish authorities. *Contagious zeal.* The reforming zeal of the enthusiasts of the county council proved contagious, and the medical health officers of the parochial and district boards began to coöperate with efficiency. It was largely due to the *The act of 1890.* county council that Parliament in 1890 consolidated, revised, and in various ways improved the body of legislation relating to housing reforms which had been accumulating on the statute-books for forty years. The first part of this act of 1890 relates to the treatment of considerable areas, the second part to the condemning and demolition of individual houses, and the third part to the public provision of workmen's dwellings. The council in its preliminary survey of housing conditions in the metropolis had found that a portion of the parish of Bethnal Green in East London was in a miserable state of dilapidation. An area of some fifteen acres was covered with ancient two-story cottages facing on streets barely eighteen feet wide, and with the diminutive back-yard spaces completely filled with outbuildings and workshops. Bethnal Green had once been a thriving community of Huguenot weavers who had taken refuge in England from persecution in France, and had domiciled themselves in what was then a little village in the suburbs of London. But Bethnal Green had been swallowed up in the growth of the metropolis, and its tiny cottages had become packed with a slum population of the worst sort. The county council found five or six thousand people living in this area of fifteen acres, crowded into seven hundred and fourteen low cottages. It was determined that the neighborhood should be reconstructed in such a manner as to furnish an object-lesson. The council's scheme was sanctioned in July, 1891, and then the tedious process of acquiring the property was begun. Claims to the amount of $2,500;000 were presented by the owners of this pestilential slum, but official appraisers reduced the inordinate claims, and the council came into possession for somewhat less than $1,500,000. Then ensued the work of rearrangement. The Housing of the Working Classes Act of 1890 requires that every scheme for the demolition of insanitary dwellings by London authorities shall be accompanied by a scheme for rehousing in a suitable way as many people as are affected by the demolition; and that in London such compensatory housing shall be either upon the sites

A shocking slum in East London.

Bethnal Green's condemnation.

Buying up the property.

Demolition of seven hundred houses.

I.— 19

Attractive
plans of re-
construc-
tion.

that have been cleared, or else in the same district and within convenient distances. The reconstruction project for Bethnal Green, known as the "Boundary Street Scheme," has an attractive street plan that suggests a Parisian *Place de l'Étoile* on a diminutive scale. In the center is a band-stand, surrounded by a public garden of an acre or more, with a street encircling it. From this circle seven streets radiate, and connect the area with the street system of the general district. In place of the old eighteen-foot streets, the county council has laid out streets that are from forty to sixty feet wide.

The coun-
cil's building
regulations.

In planning its new tenement-houses, the council conformed scrupulously with the principles and provisions that its committee on building by-laws had embodied in its new measure for the regulation of building in the metropolis. It would be difficult to select any topic with which the county council has had to deal that is more important than that of the proper regulation of new housing; and its proposals as embodied in a bill which Parliament will undoubtedly sanction must be productive of the most salutary results. So far as the new building regulations relate to sanitary conditions, they deal with court and back-yard areas, with the height of buildings, with the depth and use of basements, and with the height of ceilings, and they enter with great minuteness into every detail as to admission of light and air to

Sanitary re-
quirements.

rooms occupied as human habitations. They prescribe the minimum size of living-rooms, and in general they lay down a system which would of itself make practically impossible any very dangerous congestion of population in the neighborhoods constructed under its regulations.

To return to the Bethnal Green scheme, then, it may be said that while the rows of new municipal houses are not to be all exactly alike, the standard plan that has been adopted provides for tenements of five stories, with a height from the sidewalk of about forty-five feet, the front line being set back some eight feet from a forty-foot street, and the area space in the rear being from forty to forty-five feet wide, to allow abundance of light and air and to afford playroom for children. The tenements are all divided into family apartments of two rooms and three rooms. There are no one-room apartments, and none larger than those containing three rooms; but the sanitary conveniences have been planned with great skill, and when the entire scheme of reconstruction is completed this county-council village in East London will contain the best-planned dwellings for very poor people that can be found in London.

Chap. IX.

The new homes in Bethnal Green.

For several decades, under semi-philanthropic auspices, there has progressed a movement in London for the construction of what are called "model" tenement-house blocks. The best-known of these structures are the Peabody Fund tenement-houses. The ordinary type of working-man's home in London is the small, old-fashioned house commonly of two stories, sometimes of three. The model tenement introduces in London the innovation of the five- or six-story flatted structure built for many families, and housing from 100 to 1000 people. There are now some 600 buildings in London that belong to this class, with a total capacity of perhaps 120,000 people. The houses provided from time to time out of the proceeds of the Peabody Fund now shelter a population of 20,000. Many of these 600 buildings have been constructed by commercial companies with a suggestion of philanthropy about them, but with more regard to dividends than to the real welfare of the working-classes; and not a few of them are

'Model" tenement blocks in London.

Peabody Fund houses.

defective in their sanitary arrangements, and are to be condemned on the ground that the death-rate in them is very considerably higher than the average for all London. The Peabody houses are excellent, and show a favorable death-rate. But as to this system of great, *Disapproval of this type.* swarming, tenement hives, the best London opinion does not approve of it; and the housing reformers no longer look to it as providing a solution for the problem of the better housing of London's working-people.

Metropolitan London is essentially a congeries of old villages which in the last fifty years have grown together and been encompassed in an ever expanding *A congeries of villages.* sea of houses. The breathing-places have been almost wholly covered with additional structures, and the passages are narrow. If the streets could be widened, and larger court spaces restored, the gradual rehousing of the population under a modified system of apartment buildings like those of the county council in Bethnal Green would be advantageous. Even yet, however, the greatest need is for measures of *Need of measures to check bad building in suburbs.* prevention. Nowhere is the suburban tendency more striking than in London ; and the chief care of the housing reformers should be to protect future generations against the greed of speculators who are now acquiring the building sites in outlying districts, laying them out with narrow streets, and covering them with flimsily constructed small houses. In many cases the scenes of these speculative operations lie beyond the jurisdiction of the county council, but the local authorities in the so-called " outer ring " are coming under the influence of the county council in many ways, and they may yet be induced to prescribe proper regulations.

In 1891, under representations made by the county council, Parliament passed the Public Health Act for London, the provisions of which fell to the supervision of the housing committee, which has since that time performed its work under the name of the "public health and housing committee." Its duties include the inspection of workshops and factories to see that they do not offend against sanitary regulations, and are extended to various other tasks in the interest of the health and safety of the community. To no topic has this committee given more attention than to that of the provision of workmen's suburban trains by the great railways which have their terminal stations in the heart of the metropolis, and whose lines cross the "outer ring" at twenty points or more. The railways have received many public privileges, and their rates and the details of their management fall to a certain extent under control of Parliament and the general government. The public health and housing committee of the county council takes the broad view that the best service it can render to the working-men of London is to make it possible for them to live in the outskirts. Rapid, cheap, and convenient transit is therefore the watchword of the county council. To this end it has made exhaustive statistical reports upon the existing supply of working-men's morning and evening suburban trains on the London railways; has communicated with the railway companies, urging more favorable terms for working-men; and has shown great energy in promoting bills in Parliament regarding the insertion of clauses providing for working-men's trains in all bills that in any wise confer privileges upon railway companies. The council has also procured statistical data from continental cities, which it has brought into comparison with corresponding London statistics, in order to show how much more favorable are the provisions for working-men's suburban transit in Berlin and other European cities than in London.

I.— 19*

Workmen's suburban trains.

Cheap and rapid transit demanded.

Statistical data.

The true
solution of
density
problems.

In its efforts to facilitate the existing suburban tendency, the county council has really placed itself in harmony with all the forces that are unconsciously working toward the true solution of the problems of density and overcrowding. Forty years ago it was practically impossible for a poor man, even for a clerk in a City bank, to live beyond walking distance from his work. Such stage-coaches as then plied between London and the suburban towns were far too expensive for men of humble means to use as a daily luxury. To-day London is served by many thousands of cheap

The rise of
transit facil-
ities.

omnibuses, which cover all parts of the metropolitan district with astonishing efficiency. Besides the omnibus service there are systems of tram lines or street railways in North London, South London, and East London — aggregating 125 street miles of trackage, and considerably promoting the inward and outward daily movements of population. The inner and outer circles of underground railways are also an important adjunct; and, finally, the great railway lines provide means of transit for the more distant suburbs.

Re-grouping
of popula-
tion-masses.

The effect of all these transit facilities, imperfect though the system is as yet, has begun to be shown in a remarkable rearrangement of the population. A few decades ago the inner City contained a population of 100,000. The census of 1891 showed only 37,000, and

Rapid de-
cline of the
central dis-
tricts.

the ebb-tide has not yet ceased to flow. What is true of the City of London in a high degree is true of the other central parishes and districts only in smaller measure. Thus in the decade from 1881 to 1891, Westminster lost 20 per cent. of its population; the Strand district, 18.2 per cent.; St. Giles, 12.1 per cent.; Marylebone, 8 per cent. In general, since 1861 there has been a gradual decline in the inhabitancy of that central area — comprising both the fashionable West End districts and the unfashionable parishes of East London — which contains the innermost million of the London population. This central area in 1861 contained nearly 1,200,000 people. In 1891 it could claim barely 1,000,000 people. Its falling off has been at an increasing rate, the percentages of decline for the three decades being respectively 2.7, 4.6, and 7.2 per cent. Meanwhile, the rest of London inside the county council area has been growing. In 1861 this outer zone of the metropolis contained 1,600,000 people, and in 1891 it contained 3,200,000.

These three millions and more may be said, in a general way, to be the population served by the omnibuses and tram lines. Whereas their numbers had grown by 30 per cent. between 1861 and 1871, and by 29 per cent. in the next decade, they grew by less than 18 per cent. between 1881 and 1891. But this was only because the so-called "outer ring," lying beyond the jurisdiction of the county council but inside the metropolitan police area, was receiving the surplus population. This "outer ring" has been growing since 1861 at the rate of 50 per cent. each decade. It had scarcely 400,000 inhabitants in 1861, and more than 1,400,000 in 1891. Half a million people had been added to the population of this zone of outer parishes between 1881 and 1891. These people, now exceeding a million and a half, may in an approximate fashion be regarded as Londoners who are dependent upon the suburban trains of the great railways, in so far as their daily work takes them from circumference to center.

It has been customary to call the police area "Greater London"; but in point of fact there is now growing up outside of the police area still another outermost zone of London suburbs, at a distance of from fifteen to twenty-five miles from Charing Cross, which is taken as the center of the metropolis. It may

CHAP. IX.

Loss of 200,000 people in thirty years.

Growth of outer zone.

The area of omnibuses and street-cars.

The zone of suburban trains.

A new "outermost" belt.

CHAP. IX.

be predicted that computations after the next census in 1901 will show that this outermost belt, not now comprised in any of the different London circumscriptions, has lately been growing by the process of metropolitan overflow at a higher rate per cent. than any of the series of concentric zones lying nearer the center.

The metropolitan overflow.

This remarkable new suburban movement, it may be noted in passing, belongs to the area of improved transit facilities; and it is not by any means peculiar to London. It is almost equally apparent in Germany, Austria, and other continental countries, and is perhaps most potential of all in the United States. The census of 1891 showed that Liverpool had absolutely declined by 6.3 per cent. in ten years. But the Registrar-General reported that this decline did not indicate any falling off in the prosperity and development of Liverpool, but only showed how restricted were the boundaries of the city, inasmuch as the contiguous suburbs beyond the municipal limits had in ten years increased their population by more than sixty per cent. And it was further explained that a similar process was affecting Manchester and other large English centers.

Universality of suburban movement.

Interesting case of Liverpool.

But to return to the metropolis, and the statistics of its shifting population-density, it may be stated that over against the accelerating decline in the central districts and parishes may be noted in the last census period a gain of from 45 to 65 per cent. in such outlying metropolitan districts as Wandsworth, Hampstead, and Fulham, while in the "outer ring" many districts show a gain of more than 100 per cent. Thus in the immediate vicinity of London, and a part of the Greater London of the metropolitan police district, are big communities like West Ham, Leyton, Willesden, and Croydon. Leyton in the ten years of the census period had increased by 133 per cent., having grown from 27,000 to 63,000 people. Willesden's gain

Districts of most rapid growth in London.

West Ham, Willesden, Leyton, and Croydon.

had been 122 per cent., from 27,600 to 61,300. Tottenham, another London suburb, had grown 95 per cent., from 36,500 to 71,300. West Ham, the hugest of the suburban towns in the first "outer ring," had gained 60 per cent., having grown from 129,000 to 205,000. Croydon, the next largest of the municipalities lying outside the county council's line but inside the metropolitan police district, had nearly 103,000 people in 1891, as against less than 79,000 in 1881. These instances must suffice to demonstrate the tendency.

Relation of transit to housing.

The growth of transit facilities, keeping pace with the population developments of the past generation, has made it possible for London to retain the general characteristics of its housing system. Thus with all the overcrowding that doubtless exists in the central districts, the census of 1891 found nearly 800,000 houses inside the boundary line of the metropolitan police district, 150,000 houses having been added in ten years. The average number of occupants was seven to each house. In the more central portions there were eight persons to a house, while in the outer belt the average was six persons. The average of the inner districts was increased by the model-tenement blocks and other large houses sheltering several families. At least three fourths of the population of London would now appear to be tolerably well sheltered. It is estimated, however, that there are approximately a million people whose conditions of shelter are positively deleterious to health, decency, and civilization; and that for their purposes there ought to be a reconstruction on approved plans of about 400,000 rooms. The Bethnal Green project is but the beginning of a series of ambitious housing schemes that will do much to reform the central parts of London during the next quarter-century.

A million people who need to be rehoused.

Relative
density.

The sphere
of London
trams and
omnibuses.

Proposed
purchase of
street rail-
ways.

Meanwhile, the improvement of transit facilities will afford the principal relief. Within the bounds of the metropolis the population-density is from 50 to 60 per acre; although we have seen that in the Bethnal Green area the density was 400 per acre, while it exceeds 1000 per acre in the large model-tenement blocks. The "outer ring," on the other hand, contains so much vacant space that it will yet be many years before the average density has reached 10 per acre. The administrative county, or metropolitan area, while of irregular shape, may be said to lie within an average distance of five or six miles from Charing Cross, except for a long extension southeastward, the bounds of which are ten or twelve miles from Charing Cross. The area comprised within the five or six miles' radius may be called the territory of tramways, omnibuses, and underground railways; and this composite system of transit is now carrying perhaps 600,000,000 passengers a year, or an average of 2,000,000 a day for each secular working-day in the year. The number is of course constantly increasing. An area of about 125 square miles is thus served by modes of transit which are fairly efficient but susceptible of great improvement. Every reform in the main thoroughfare system of the metropolis assists materially in the daily ebb and flow of population. This fact is so well appreciated that the county council has in contemplation a number of street-improvement projects, in addition to those which it has already carried out as successor to the policy of the Metropolitan Board of Works. Street improvements will facilitate the development of the tramway system, and the county council is moving definitely in the direction of the purchase of all the lines now operated by private street-railway companies within the county of London.

The twenty-one-year franchises held by the dozen

greater and smaller companies that operate street railways in London began to expire in 1891, and will fall
in successively during a period of ten or twelve years.
The county council, following the example of the provincial municipalities, will acquire all these lines. The
process of purchase has been retarded by tedious appeals to the highest tribunals, growing out of the
refusal of the companies to accept the awards of arbi-
trators; but such delays are only temporary. By a
process of gradual extension and consolidation, the
usefulness of the system to the people of the metropolis can be immensely enhanced. The "City and South
of London" underground railway — which has tun-
neled beneath the Thames, is operated by electricity,
and is provided at all stations with passenger lifts or
elevators — has given a successful demonstration of
the possibilities of a series of subterranean lines extending in different directions from the center of
London. It was opened at the end of 1890, and is a
great improvement over the useful but uncomforta-
ble underground steam service of the "Metropolitan"
and "Metropolitan District" companies. The newest
electric underground project is the Central London
Railway which is now building.

It is the newer regions, lying for the most part at a
distance of more than five miles from central London,
that constitute the territory dependent upon the suburban service of the great railways and the finger-tips
of the underground lines. The ten main railway companies whose lines center in London operate about
2500 suburban trains each day, and carry hundreds
of thousands of people. They all furnish a service of
working-men's trains, limited to certain hours in the
morning and evening. The county council is endea-
voring to secure for this service a larger number of
trains, a wider limit of hours, a more uniform classifi-

CHAP. IX.
cation of rates, and the introduction of something approximating toward a zone tariff system. There is some reason to believe that the London railways may eventually be induced to make radical changes in the principles upon which their suburban service is conducted, with a view to the more rapid development of the suburbs and the consequent growth of their passenger traffic. The county council has shown that suburban railway service is provided for working-men in the continental cities at much lower prices than in London. Its persistent agitation of this subject is meeting with favorable responses, and most of the railways centering in London are introducing various improvements in their special suburban transit for working-men.

An improving service.

As I have already explained, the public health and housing committee of the county council is charged with jurisdiction over certain portions of the metropolitan health administration. The ordinary duties that belong to the enforcement of the health acts are, however, assigned to the parish and district boards. Under the new Local Government Act of 1894, the position of these local authorities is strengthened so far as their sanitary work is concerned. Each of them maintains a medical officer of health and a corps of sanitary inspectors. Until very recently their work of inspection was incompletely performed. Some great parishes, having from a hundred thousand to a quarter of a million people, employed only one or two inspectors. But a change for the better has taken place, and under the moral influence and official oversight of the county council, the parish and district boards have vastly improved and developed their sanitary organization. They are responsible for the cleansing of streets, for the removal and disposition of garbage,

Sanitary work in London districts.

Hopeful progress visible.

and for all minor tasks and processes that belong to good municipal housekeeping. These tasks are as yet most unevenly performed in the different districts, but there is striking progress visible almost everywhere.

That part of health administration which is concerned with infectious diseases belongs to a Metropolitan Asylums Board, which reports directly to the central British government,— i. e., to the Local Government Board,— and which is composed of seventy-two managers of whom eighteen are nominated by the Local Government Board, and fifty-four are appointed by the various boards of guardians in the thirty London poor-law districts. This asylums board was formed in 1867, at a time when it was urgently necessary to provide smallpox and fever hospitals and to bring all the arrangements for the control of epidemics under some central authority. There were other obvious reasons why there should be some federation of the local poor-law boards, particularly the demand for a general administration of asylums and institutions for certain classes of unfortunates. The responsibilities devolving upon this board are too serious to admit of any neglect ; and although the metropolis ought not to maintain a separate authority for such tasks, one may, nevertheless, commend the vigor and efficiency which has recently characterized the work of this organization for the control of infectious maladies.

Metropolitan Asylums Board.

The central poor-law authority.

The hospitals of the board have since 1891 been more than doubled in capacity, and every feature of the work of isolating infectious diseases begins to show some of that progress that has so strikingly marked the municipal sanitary administration of Glasgow, Birmingham, and other provincial towns. In 1892 there were 27,000 scarlet-fever cases in London, of which 14,000 cases were treated at home, while 13,000 were removed to the hospitals of the asylums

Infectious diseases in London.

board.   There were nearly 7800 cases of diphtheria, of which it appears that about 5100 were removed to the board's hospitals.   As for smallpox, the asylums board isolates sporadic outbreaks so effectively that the disease no longer assumes epidemic form in any of the London districts.   Typhus has been almost totally stamped out.   The asylums board maintains a well-organized ambulance service ; has asylums for imbeciles ; manages a training-ship for boys turned over to its care by the poor-law authorities of the various districts ; and performs certain other services.

As a result of public improvements and reforms in the sanitary administration, imperfect though these reforms have been, the death-rate of London has been reduced from more than thirty as the average annual rate per thousand during the half-century from 1800 to 1850, down to the present average rate of about twenty.   This means, in a population of 5,000,000, the saving of 50,000 lives a year.   It means, of course, the prevention of a vastly greater number of cases of sickness, a marked increase in the average duration of life, and an important conservation of the physical strength and wealth-producing energy of the people. The saving of 500,000 lives in every decade in the one city of London as a result of improved public arrangements, is a triumph for sanitary science that may well encourage further efforts.

Reduction of death-rate.

A triumph of sanitary science.

The maintenance of lunatic asylums for the metropolis is one of the duties that was laid upon the county council by the act of 1888, and its hospitals for this purpose have been enormously extended during the brief period of its existence.   The care of the insane for a great community of five or six million people is no trivial undertaking; and until the advent of the county council the task was not altogether well performed. There has been a remarkable change for the better.

Lunatic asylums.

Public baths and wash-houses and free libraries, which have become so popular as departments of municipal administration in the provincial towns, belong to the domain of the London vestries and district boards. Until a recent date these bodies had shown little concern for the social welfare of their neighborhoods, and only a few scattered districts had adopted the Free Libraries Act, while baths and wash-houses were scarcely known within the metropolitan area. But more than half of the London districts have now established free public libraries. Many of these districts have built, or have begun to build, commodious town-halls, in which the vestries or district boards have their offices, connected with which are assembly-rooms and central district libraries and reading-rooms, besides which, in some cases, there are contiguous public baths. In several of the districts there are systems of branch libraries and reading-rooms in addition to the central establishment. A movement of this kind once fairly begun is seldom arrested in its progress. The standard has been established; those London districts not provided with libraries will begin to demand them. The same remark may be applied to the public baths and wash-houses. Their erection in a few districts has given the metropolitan masses a new idea, and the multiplication of these beneficent institutions throughout the metropolis has already begun. The provision of common lodging-houses is a matter that comes under the jurisdiction of the county council. It has ventured to establish one or two institutions on the Glasgow model, with results that are admittedly important enough to justify a gradual extension of the policy.

The Progressives of the county council are aware that their whole program cannot be carried out at once, but their future policy includes among other

(margin notes)
Public baths and libraries.

Progress of free-library movement.

Baths and wash-houses.

Model lodging-houses.

CHAP. IX.

The London
gas-com-
panies.

things the municipalization of public lighting. At
present London is supplied with gas by three companies, one of which, the London Gaslight and Coke
Company, is a mammoth concern, monopolizing the
entire metropolis north of the Thames, while the Commercial Gas Company and the South Metropolitan
Company divide between them the district south of
the river. The prices charged to London consumers
have been at times regulated by acts of Parliament.
They are considerably higher, however, than prices that
would be charged under municipal operation.   It has
been very conservatively estimated that if the county
council should buy up the London gas-companies,
even at the highest price that could be demanded, the

Financial
argument
for munici-
palization.

immediate result would be a saving to the people
of London of more than $5,000,000 a year, a sum that
now goes as dividends to private shareholders. This
sum could either be returned to the public in the form
of a reduced charge for gas, or it could be covered
into the municipal treasury and expended upon desirable works of public utility. Meanwhile, a number of
the vestries and district boards have acquired powers
under the electric lighting acts, and have established

Public elec-
trical works.

plants for lighting their own streets and for furnishing electric illumination to such private consumers as
may desire it. The tendency toward a municipal assumption of the gas and electric lighting supply of
the metropolis is a very strong one. The presence in
the London streets of gas-companies, water-companies,
and various other private interests has proved a serious
obstacle in the way of maintaining satisfactory pavements.   The provision of subways for pipes and wires
of various sorts has made considerable progress, but

Objections
to use of
streets by
companies.

there are cases on record where the gas and water
companies have refused to avail themselves of subways that were placed at their disposal, and have torn

up newly paved streets in order to lay their pipes in the ground in accordance with their antiquated methods. Incidents of this kind are helping to accelerate the growth of a London sentiment against the use of public streets for any purpose by private water-companies, gas-companies, tramway companies, electric light and power companies, telephone companies, or any other private interests whatsoever.

Great attention has been given in recent years to the acquisition of ground for parks. Formerly the principal public gardens and open spaces of London were appurtenances of the Crown, and were under control of the commissioners of her Majesty's works and public buildings. This remains true of Hyde Park, with St. James's and Green, of Richmond, Hampton Court, and the Kew Gardens, of Regent's Park and of Greenwich — all noble pleasure-grounds that are freely at the service of the London masses. But the county council has fallen heir to a number of parks that had been either created by the metropolitan board or transferred to it. Thus in 1887 the Victoria, Battersea, and Kennington parks had been transferred from the control of her Majesty's commissioners to the metropolitan board; and among the other well-known parks, commons, and open spaces that came under the council's charge are Southwark, Finsbury, Blackheath, Hackney, Clapham, Hampstead Heath, Stoke Newington, Shepherd's Bush, Tooting Beck, Plumstead, Streatham, Wormwood Scrubs, Wandsworth, Vauxhall, and Brixton. A large amount of legislation enacted within the past quarter-century has had for its object the creation and preservation of open spaces, the transformation of disused cemeteries into park spaces, and the encouragement in all possible ways of park-making in and about the

The parks of London.

The council's inheritance of public grounds.

Preservation of open spaces.

I.— 20

CHAP. IX.

metropolis.   The result has been surprising in the aggregate.   The City corporation has lately made

Aid of the City and guilds.

good use of some of its wealth in the purchase for public parks of several extensive tracts beyond the limits of the metropolis.   The guilds and certain private associations are also zealously helping to atone for past neglect, and to provide the present and future metropolis with recreation-grounds and breathing-spaces.   But there is daily reason for regret that the need of parks was not sooner foreseen, and that so many ancient tracts of common land have been swallowed up beyond recovery in the expanding wilderness of brick and mortar and narrow streets.   Much remains to be done in the opening of park spaces in metropolitan London.

When the county council was organized in 1889, the parks and open spaces committee proved to be only less

Zeal of the new council.

popular than the committee on the housing of the working-classes.   A remarkably large number of the county councilors asked to be placed upon the parks committee.   As constituted, it speedily proved its efficiency; so that its work obtained praise in many quarters where the county council and its programs were generally criticized and opposed.   Within three years

Doubling the parks in three years.

it had succeeded in expanding the park area controlled by the council from fifteen hundred acres to three thousand acres, and this development was due to the acquisition of a great number of additional spaces well distributed throughout the various portions of the metropolis.

Even more remarkable than the increase of park area was the transformation which this committee wrought in the care and condition of the parks.   Spaces which

Attractions in the parks.

had been anything but attractive have come under the magic touch of the landscape gardener.   The council's policy of making the parks minister in the

highest possible degree to the pleasure and recreation
of the people has found expression in a hundred ingenious ways. But most remarkable of all has been
the manner in which the committee on parks has made
provision for the athletic culture of young Londoners
of both sexes, and for their natural and healthful de- Provision of
play-
votion to outdoor sports. Cricket-grounds and foot- grounds.
ball grounds, literally by the thousand, have been laid
out, besides many hundreds of tennis-courts, and various golf and hockey grounds. The council committee
has not merely provided these opportunities for recreation, but it has gone so far as sedulously to super-
vise the use of the cricket-grounds and other play- Supervising
the sports of
grounds, to the end that the largest possible number young Lon-
of young people may get the best attainable results don.
of pleasure and physical development from their use.
The council has imitated the continental cities in making provision of music in the parks, and its numerous Music in the
subsidized bands are giving more than a thousand parks.
open-air concerts each season. I have only indicated
in a very summary fashion a part of the work of this
zealous committee which administers the parks and
open spaces. It has succeeded in making the parks
so attractive that several million persons each year
are now deriving pleasure either from participation
in the games, attendance at the concerts, or in other
similar ways. The preservation of several very large
outlying tracts of wooded parkland, together with the Future generations pro-
opening up of numerous larger and smaller public tected.
pleasure-grounds in every district of the huge metropolis, has now made it certain that the growth of London
can never shut off the children of future generations
from access to grass and trees and open-air sports.

On the creation of a popularly elected school-board
for the metropolis in 1870, and its great work of

education, it may be said in a word that the board has more than 400 schools, with nearly 500,000 children enrolled as pupils.   Prior to 1871 all the elementary schools of London were denominational and private, being partly supported by grants from the government.   There were then about 300,000 pupils enrolled in all London; and a large proportion of the schools were utterly inefficient, and attendance was irregular. Probably not 200,000 children were receiving efficient and regular instruction.   There are now at least 750,-

000 enrolled in schools of good character and standing, approved by the government inspectors.   Thus the general educational condition of London has been revolutionized within twenty-five years.   Compulsory education is not a merely nominal provision in London, for school attendance is enforced by an army of 272 " visitors."

The school-board was the first public body that the metropolitan population was permitted to elect by direct vote.   It has fifty-five members, elected in eleven large districts.   The entire board is renewed every three years, and the principle of minority representation prevails.   Thus, in the Tower Hamlets district, which elects five members, the voter might " plump " his five votes for a single candidate, or might distribute them to two, three, four, or five candidates.   To illustrate the working of the system in that district, a few years ago Sir Edmund Hay Currie and Mrs. Annie Besant were candidates favoring the "progres-

sive" as opposed to the "reactionary" policy.   The radicals and anti-denominationalists concentrated their votes upon these two candidates and elected them, whereas if they had pushed a full ticket of five names they would have been defeated.   The plan gives every considerable element an opportunity to secure representation.

The ultimate policy of the London School Board has not yet been determined. The progressive element is holding up before the people of London a school policy that corresponds with the municipal reform program of the progressive majority in the county council. Thus it is proposed to heighten the efficiency of the board-schools in every possible way ; to increase the compensation of teachers ; to annex a gymnasium and a swimming-bath to every public school ; to put pianos and other means of pleasure and culture in the school-rooms ; and even, as regards the schools in the poorest neighborhoods, to provide free meals for the scholars, thousands of whom come to school without having partaken of a breakfast. The conservative policy, on the other hand, which has carried the day at the triennial elections more frequently than that of the progressives, would seem to regard the parochial and private schools as the normal educational system, while the public board-schools are but a supplementary arrangement which exists in order to furnish the necessary modicum of elementary education to such children as would otherwise receive no instruction whatever. Economy is the key-note of this party when in control of school administration. The great electoral contest of November, 1894, was embittered by the prominent introduction of the question of religious instruction in the schools.

Speaking broadly, it may be said that all elements concerned with school administration in London are making progress in their views, and that the so-called reactionists of to-day are merely occupying the ground upon which the progressives stood ten years ago. The outlook for a constant development in the extent and character of the instruction afforded by the London School Board, and in the socialistic range of its activities on behalf of the poorer children of the metropo-

Margin notes: CHAP. IX. — The progressive school policy. — The reactionist policy. — Growth of new ideas.

I.— 20*

lis, is as bright as the school reformers could well desire. The board has begun to arouse itself to the need of great improvements in its system of evening classes for the benefit of boys and girls whose day-school work has ended with their twelfth or thirteenth year. These continuation classes deal with practical subjects, and give promise of a great widening of their usefulness in the early future.

Evening schools.

Several acts of Parliament for the promotion of technical education throughout Great Britain have placed the London county council in a position to organize and to develop a vast educational work under its own direct control. From the royal exchequer the London county council, in common with the councils of the other chief towns of Great Britain, receives a certain proportion of excise receipts and other dues as a "Technical Education Exchequer Fund." With these contributions from the general government, and with appropriations out of its own revenues, the county council is in position to expend about half a million dollars a year in promoting the technical education of the young people of London. It has entered upon this great work with commendable prudence and wisdom. Under the chairmanship of one of its most brilliant and indefatigable members, Mr. Sidney Webb, the council has formed a grand committee as a "Technical Education Board," having added to the twenty councilors of the committee some fifteen leading representatives of existing educational institutions and agencies for the promotion of technical instruction in London.

The council's work of technical education.

Half a million to spend.

The Technical Education Board.

It is the policy of this technical education board to knit together into one harmonious system all worthy institutions and classes already existing in London, and to found new institutions only as their need should become apparent for the rounding out of the

system.   The board's first task was one of careful inquiry and tabulation.   Its secretary, Mr. Llewellyn
Smith, drew up an exhaustive analytical report upon   Federation
the whole status of practical and technical instruction   of existing
institutions.
in the metropolis.   The report was accompanied by
diagrams showing the distribution throughout the
London districts of the chief industries.   Mr. Charles
Booth's inquiries promoted this interesting analysis.
As a result of investigation, the technical education
board decided upon the plan of (1) granting funds
upon certain conditions to existing institutions; (2)   Scheme of
establishing a system of scholarships; and (3) provid-   promotion.
ing instruction for certain groups and classes of people not already reached by existing agencies.

The origin and history of the guilds or livery companies of London would seem to make it obviously
appropriate that they should use a portion of their   London
large revenues in establishing technical schools to ad-   guilds and
practical
vance the interests of those trades and crafts whose   education.
names the guilds have borne through so many generations.   This idea has in fact commended itself strongly
to the members of the City companies.   Some years
ago a number of them, in conjunction with the City
corporation, founded the City and Guilds of London   City and
Institute, agreeing to support it by large yearly con-   Guilds of
London
tributions.   This institute has already accomplished   Institute.
a great work for technical instruction throughout the
United Kingdom.   It maintains (1) a great central
school of technology in South Kensington, London;
(2) a practical technical college in another part of the
city; and (3) a school of applied art in South London.
Besides these central institutions, it subsidizes classes
in various technical subjects in all parts of the country, under the principle of grants of money based upon
the result of examinations.   Side by side with the
work of the City and Guilds of London Institute, has

been that of the so-called Science and Art Department of the general government. This department
maintains great central schools of science and art in
connection with the vast museums of South Kensington, and also subsidizes classes — most of them in the
industrial applications of the principles of science and
art — throughout Great Britain and Ireland. A third
important agency in the work of technical instruction is the series of polytechnic institutes and people's
palaces that has sprung into being in different parts
of London.   Two or three of these great institutions
are now supported wholly by contributions from the
wealthier London guilds.   Others have derived their
support in part from private benefactions, and in
part from charity funds which are at the disposal of
certain public commissioners.   These commissioners
administer the revenues of a great number of old
parochial endowments which have been revised, consolidated, and reduced to modern uses, under the terms
of an act of Parliament which Mr. James Bryce some
years ago introduced and carried to a successful conclusion. The polytechnic institutes, besides affording
recreation in a vast number of ways to their thousands of members, provide also a very wide range of
evening educational work, chiefly in technical subjects
and practical trades.   Besides these conspicuous agencies, there might be mentioned a long list of institutions which in their own manner and measure have
for some time been engaged in practical instruction of
a kind which falls under the cognizance of the new
technical education board.

The connection of the board with all these London
institutions is twofold.   First, it has secured a county
council representation upon their various governing
bodies, and second, it has brought into the membership of the board itself a number of men most promi-

nently identified with the control of the several institutions. There has thus been effected a statesmanlike federation of all the interests and agencies which are working toward the joint advancement of London's industries and London's workers, under the new method of furnishing education in technical processes and principles. Of all departments of administration which are now engaged in the task of making London better, happier, and more prosperous, I am inclined to the opinion that the technical education board, with the institutions which it fosters, is the department that bids fair to accomplish the largest share in the aggregate result.

CHAP. IX.

Statesmanlike methods of technical board.

One of the London topics always under controversy is the control of the police. The metropolitan police organization falls under the direct control of the home department of the general government. The old City has a police force of its own. The metropolitan organization includes some fifteen thousand men, while the City's force numbers perhaps fifteen hundred. The royal commission on the unification of London proposes that the City police shall be amalgamated with the metropolitan force, but does not propose to transfer the police control from the general government to the county council. The London reformers in general have strenuously insisted upon the necessity of the direct municipal control of the police, as in Birmingham, Manchester, and all the provincial towns. It might be argued, on the other hand, that the position of the metropolis is different from that of the provincial towns, inasmuch as Manchester and Birmingham have no interests to protect except those that are strictly local; while the metropolis includes, besides the local interests of its inhabitants, an aggregation of interests pertaining to the whole British empire.

Question of police control.

London reformers demand municipal police system.

London's position as imperial capital.

The question of London police control is not in fact a very important one. The shrewdest municipal progressists in Paris, Berlin, and Vienna have no desire to burden the municipality with police control. They willingly accept the argument that, since the policing function is in theory and origin a general rather than a local one, the general government of a nation or an empire may well retain the direct control of the police of the capital town, even though it may find it altogether expedient to delegate to provincial towns the ordinary administration of their local police departments. As for London, a number of considerations of practical convenience help to sustain the argument for municipal control, and the ultimate solution may be found to lie in a twofold system, the great bulk of the police force passing over to the control of the municipal council.

Views in Paris, Berlin, and Vienna.

It is one of the demands of the London reformers that permission should be given by Parliament to the county council to establish a modern system of metropolitan markets. The old corporation has remained in possession as the market authority for London, and its establishments, while in many respects highly interesting and in some regards modern and efficient, fall very far short of the reasonable requirements of the vast community, and can scarcely be regarded as highly popular in their administration.

The London markets.

The London docks are altogether in the hands of private companies. They constitute an extensive system upon which more than a hundred million dollars of capital has been expended; but the competition of rival companies has led to much expenditure that a unified public system of docks could have avoided. Private enterprise in London dock management compares very unfavorably with public enterprise as exhibited in the management of the Liverpool docks,

The dock system.

An objectionable private monopoly.

and in the harbor and dock management of various other English ports. The London dock companies some years ago passed from the stage of competition to that of combination; and practically the entire dock interest is now managed by a joint committee of the boards of the leading companies as a huge monopoly or trust. The methods employed by the companies are not conducive in the highest sense to the commercial interests of London; while their effect upon the condition of labor in East London was painfully exemplified several years ago in the now historic dock strikes. The municipal acquisition of the docks is therefore a reasonable clause in the program of the London reformers.

The London county council has lately been conspicuous for certain economic heresies. No policy had been more offensive to the orthodox economists and administrators of England than that of the direct employment of labor in any kind of public work, when the circumstances admitted of the use of the contract system. The county council has not wholly abandoned the contract system, but its sphere of direct employment grows wider from year to year. By repeated experiments it has demonstrated its ability to underbid the lowest bidder. That is to say, it has in a large number of instances rejected all bids for such tasks as sewer construction, the erection of a building, or the re-turfing of a park, and has proceeded to employ its own workmen and to carry out the task under the eye of its own architects or surveyors or engineers. In every instance it has completed the work for a much smaller sum than the lowest of the rejected bids; and it has declared the finished work to be more satisfactory in character than any which could be expected from a contractor.

Furthermore, the council has endeavored to set a

CHAP. IX.

Municipal acquisition demanded.

Contract system opposed.

Success of direct employment.

CHAP. IX.
Council as model employer.

good example to all the world as a model employer. Its labor policy has been largely due to the zeal of a labor leader in its own body, namely, Mr. John Burns. Throughout all its varied undertakings the council has endeavored to reduce the hours of labor, and has found it possible to secure for every worker one day of rest in seven. Its solicitude extends from the flushers of sewers to hospital nurses and to keepers and attendants in the insane asylums. Its policy of better wages and shorter hours has unquestionably increased the pay-roll by a quarter of a million dollars a year; but this sum has been offset, in the estimation of the council, by the greatly enhanced efficiency of its army of employees, who are now serving it with an unprecedented zeal and intelligence. Again, the coun-

Attendant economies.

cil's liberality in the matter of wages paid to the rank and file of its workmen has been accompanied by a weeding out of high-salaried supernumeraries. Still further, the council has effected great economies in its purchase of departmental supplies, and has saved large sums by abolishing the favoritism and the wastefulness in the letting of contracts which had grown to scandalous proportions in the hands of its predecessors. Another of the council's innovations is the strict enforcement of a clause in all its contracts which compels the contractor to pay standard wages, and a second clause which absolutely forbids the sub-letting of contracts, and which therefore exterminates the sweating system so far as the municipal business is concerned. Finally, the council has introduced a sys-

Retiring pensions to employees.

tem of small retiring pensions for all faithful municipal employees, including those employed in ordinary labor, as well as its most highly esteemed functionaries such as the members of the Metropolitan Fire Brigade.

It is unanimously agreed that the members of the Fire Department should receive every possible con-

sideration. The county council has improved their
wages, has found a way to increase their holidays,
and is now proceeding to construct commodious residential quarters, in connection with the fire stations,
for the families of about 400 married men. To quote
from the annual review in 1894 of Sir John Hutton,
the esteemed chairman of the council:

CHAP. IX.
Provisions
for the Fire
Department.

> The present strength of the Fire Brigade stands at 846; the
> number of land fire-engine stations is 56; of street stations, 53;
> and of fire-escape stations, 180, together with a large number of
> manual fire-engines, hose-carts, ladder-trucks, vans, ladders,
> and 35 miles of hose in efficient condition.

Statistics of
fire service,
etc.

London does not suffer from many serious fires.
For instance, in 1891 there were only seven of any
consequence, whereas in 1881, when London was less
populous, there were nine. There are American towns
of 50,000 people that in some years have as great a
number of disastrous fires as London, which has just
a hundred times as great a population.

The Fire Departments of New York and Chicago
employ a considerably larger force of men than that
of London, while those of Philadelphia, Boston, and
Brooklyn are three fourths as large. It costs more
than twice as much to maintain the New York department, while the Chicago and Boston departments cost
somewhat more than that of London, and the Philadelphia and Brooklyn departments are nearly as expensive. There has, under the county council, been
an enormous increase in the number of fire hydrants
in London, which at the end of 1894 were approaching
20,000, only a small fraction of that number having
been in existence in 1888. By way of comparison,
Chicago had 6400 hydrants in 1890, Philadelphia
had 7400, and New York had 8500. The system of
electric alarms has also been made very complete in

London's
department
compared
with those of
American
cities.

Number of
hydrants.

CHAP. IX.

London. Sir John Hutton complains that London is becoming quite too much a paradise for the insurance companies, and some of the extreme collectivists begin to suggest a municipal insurance department to benefit by the improved efficiency of the Fire Brigade.

A paradise for insurance companies.

The financial operations of the county council are extensive and complicated because it acts in the capacity of a borrowing authority for all the local governing bodies of the metropolis. This arrangement, obviously, enables the vestries and other local agencies to obtain money at better rates than they could secure for themselves. In 1894 the council's total outstanding bonded debt was £33,000,000 ($165,-000,000), of which less than £19,000,000 was its own net obligation, while £14,000,000 represented loans made to minor bodies. Most of the council's debt is an inheritance from the Board of Works, and represents main drainage, street improvements, etc. The council has been spending on capital account about $5,000,000 a year, while extinguishing maturing indebtedness at about half that rate. If the debts of the old City, and all kinds of local obligations that pertain to public bodies exercising jurisdiction within the limits of the metropolis, were aggregated, the total would perhaps be £45,000,000, or $225,000,000 — a per capita debt of £9, or $45. The per capita debt of Manchester exceeds $100; that of Liverpool is about $75 and that of Birmingham is $80. But these provincial towns have incurred most of their municipal indebtedness for investments that are productive assets and that provide for their own interest and sinking-fund charges, so that a large local debt signifies no added burden for the ratepayer, but quite the contrary. The remunerative assets of all these towns have a per capita value far exceeding the total indebt-

The council as loan agency.

London's debt.

Aggregate debts of London authorities.

Compared with other towns.

edness for all purposes.   In London, however, the
situation is wholly different.   Private interests derive
profit in London from the sources which feed municipal revenue in the other towns, and the burden of
the London debt falls squarely upon the shoulders of
the ratepayers.   London now borrows at 2½ per cent.
interest, though its bonds at this rate have not yet
commanded par.   Sir John Hutton, in view of the remarkable success of the Paris municipal loans, issued
in small bonds for which the popular demand is far
beyond the supply, is advocating in the London council a similar system of direct popular loans in the form
of bonds of very small denominations.

As to current revenue and expenditure, the following summary statement made in 1894 aggregates the
transactions of all the London governing bodies, great
and small :

> The government of London costs, in round figures, £11,000,000
> ($55,000,000) a year, which is equal to a rate of nearly seven
> shillings in the pound.   Receipts from rates meet 71.67 per cent.
> of the total expenditure.   Imperial grants amount to 11.50 per
> cent., and income from fines, dues, rent and other sources, makes
> up the remainder.   Over £2,500,000 is spent on London's poor,
> and £1,900,000 in educating the children at board schools.   Ves-
> tries and district boards spend over £2,000,000, the county
> council spends £1,900,000, and the police cost £1,700,000.

Of the nearly $10,000,000 expended in 1893 by the
council, the maintenance of the sewers and sewage
system cost about $1,200,000, the Fire Brigade $700,-
000, the management of parks nearly $500,000, and
the asylums department about $300,000.   The techni-
cal education board has attained the position of a
heavy spending department, and the other outlets for
public money are not few.

It is difficult to translate the British rating system
into terms of local taxation that would permit close

English
rates and
American
taxes.

comparison with American tax-rates. In the United States local taxes are paid by owners upon the assessed capital value of property, while in England they are paid by occupiers upon the assessed yearly rental value of the premises inhabited or otherwise used. We may, however, take the case of a house that is assessed at £20 ($100) rental in London, and assume that a like house would be assessed at $1800 in an American city. The sum total of all local London rates averages seven shillings in the £, and the amount paid to the rate-collectors on houses of this valuation would be £7 or $35 a year. A two per cent. tax levy in an American city — two per cent.

The burden
about equal.

being perhaps an average total rate — would amount to $36 for a house assessed at $1800. So far as I am able to compare, I am led to the conclusion that the actual rates of local taxation in English and American cities are not widely divergent. In one country the owner is taxed, and in the other the tenant is made to pay. I shall not venture to express an opinion as to the real and final distribution of the burden. It is a

The English-
man gets
more for his
money.

debatable topic. But that the citizens of English towns obtain far more than Americans for the money they pay to the local tax-gatherer is a proposition that is too obvious to admit of any discussion.

In conclusion, then, it may justly be maintained that there is much in the governmental arrangements of London that is instructive and admirable, and still more that is commendable in the spirit of reform and progress that is now awake and active there. But perhaps the chief lessons for us in America are lessons of warning. If London, within the lifetime of

Lessons of
warning.

men still in their prime, had taken due precautions, what errors might have been averted! London is now creating a park system, and acquiring land that has quadrupled in value within thirty years. London is widening and straightening streets, and incurring thereby the expense of appropriating frontage that costs twice as much now as it would have cost a few years ago. The people of London have been compelled to pay hundreds of millions as a penalty for their neglect to provide a public water-supply. They suffer an inestimable loss in convenience and actual money through the haphazard nature of passenger transportation facilities. An intelligent system might have been devised if the matter had received due attention thirty years ago. If London had provided suitable building regulations forty or fifty years ago, and forbidden faulty and insanitary construction, enormous subsequent expenses of demolition would have been averted. If the ground-rent system had not been allowed to grow insidiously through the past generations, the general character of London, architecturally and in other respects, would have been radically improved. Our American cities, studying the experience of Old World centers like London, cannot exercise too great forethought in preparing for the greatness that inevitably awaits them.

CHAP. IX.

Cost of past
negligence.

The need of
forethought.

APPENDICES

APPENDIX I

THE ENGLISH MUNICIPAL CODE[1]

THE municipal corporation of a borough shall bear the name of the mayor, aldermen, and burgesses of the borough, or, in the case of a city, the mayor, aldermen, and citizens of the city.

BURGESSES

A person shall not be deemed a burgess for any purpose of this act unless he is enrolled as a burgess.

A person shall not be entitled to be enrolled as a burgess unless he is qualified as follows:

(a) Is of full age; and

(b) Is on the fifteenth of July in any year, and has been during the whole of the then last preceding twelve months in occupation, joint or several, of any house, warehouse, counting-house, shop, or other building (in this act referred to as a qualifying property) in the borough; and

(c) Has during the whole of those twelve months resided in the borough, or within seven miles thereof; and

(d) Has been rated in respect of the qualifying property to all poor rates made during those twelve months for the parish wherein the property is situate; and

(e) Has, on or before the twentieth of the same July, paid all such rates, including borough rates (if any), as have become payable by him in respect of the qualifying property up to the then last preceding fifth of January.

Every person so qualified shall be entitled to be enrolled as a burgess, unless he —

(a) Is an alien; or

(b) Has, within the twelve months aforesaid, received union or parochial relief or other alms; or

(c) Is disentitled under any act of Parliament.

THE COUNCIL

The municipal corporation of a borough shall be capable of acting by the council of the borough, and the council shall exercise all powers vested in the corporation by this act, or otherwise.

[1] The Municipal Corporations (Consolidation) Act of 1882 provides a general constitution for all the municipalities of England and Wales. Legislation for Scotland and Ireland makes similar provisions. I have selected such parts of the Code as explain the system.

The council shall consist of the mayor, aldermen, and councilors.

The councilors shall be fit persons elected by the burgesses.

A person shall not be qualified to be elected or to be a councilor unless he —

(*a*) Is enrolled and entitled to be enrolled as a burgess; or

(*b*) Being entitled to be so enrolled in all respects, except that of residence, is resident beyond seven miles but within fifteen miles of the borough, and is entered in the separate non-resident list directed by this act to be made; and

(*c*) In either of those cases is seized or possessed of real or personal property or both, to the value or amount, in the case of a borough having four or more wards, of the annual value of thirty pounds, and in the case of any other borough of fifteen pounds.

Provided, that every person shall be qualified to be elected and to be a councilor, who is, at the time of election, qualified to elect to the office of councilor; which last-mentioned qualification for being elected shall be alternative for and shall not repeal or take away any other qualification.

But if a person qualified under the last foregoing proviso ceases for six months to reside in the borough, he shall cease to be qualified under that proviso, and his office shall become vacant, unless he was at the time of his election and continues to be qualified in some other manner.

A person shall be disqualified for being elected and for being a councilor, if and while he —

(*a*) Is an elective auditor or a revising assessor, or holds any office or place of profit, other than that of mayor or sheriff, in the gift or disposal of the council; or

(*b*) Is in holy orders, or the regular minister of a dissenting congregation; or

(*c*) Has, directly or indirectly, by himself or his partner, any share or interest in any contract or employment with, by, or on behalf of the council.

But a person shall not be so disqualified, or be deemed to have any share or interest in such a contract or employment by reason only of his having any share or interest in —

(*a*) Any lease, sale, or purchase of land, or any agreement for the same; or

(*b*) Any agreement for the loan of money, or any security for the payment of money only; or

(*c*) Any newspaper in which any advertisement relating to the affairs of the borough or council is inserted; or

(*d*) Any company which contracts with the council for lighting or supplying with water or insuring against fire any part of the borough; or

(*e*) Any railway company, or other company incorporated by act of Parliament or royal charter, or under the Companies' Act, 1862.

The term of office of a councilor shall be three years.

On the ordinary day of election of councilors in every year one third of the whole number of councilors for the borough or for the ward, as the case may be, shall go out of office, and their places shall be filled by election.

The third to go out shall be the councilors who have been longest in office without reëlection.

ALDERMEN

The aldermen shall be fit persons elected by the council.

The number of aldermen shall be one third of the number of councilors.

A person shall not be qualified to be elected or to be an alderman unless he is a councilor or qualified to be a councilor.

If a councilor is elected to, and accepts, the office of alderman he vacates his office of councilor.

The term of office of an alderman shall be six years.

On the ordinary day of election of aldermen in every third year one half of the whole number of aldermen shall go out of office, and their places shall be filled by election.

The half to go out shall be those who have been aldermen for the longest time without reëlection.

THE MAYOR

The mayor shall be a fit person elected by the council from among the aldermen or councilors or persons qualified to be such.

An outgoing alderman is eligible.

The term of office of the mayor shall be one year, but he shall continue in office until his successor has accepted office and made and subscribed the required declaration.

He shall receive such remuneration as the council think reasonable.

He shall, subject to the provisions of this act respecting justices, have precedence in all places in the borough.

The mayor may from time to time appoint an alderman or councilor to act as deputy mayor during the illness or absence of the mayor.

The appointment shall be signified to the council in writing, and be recorded in their minutes.

A deputy mayor may, while acting as such, do all acts which the mayor as such might do, except that he shall not take the chair at a meeting of the council, unless specially appointed by the meeting to do so, and shall not, unless he is a justice, act as a justice or in any judicial capacity.

OFFICERS OF COUNCIL

The council shall from time to time appoint a fit person, not a member of the council, to be the town clerk of the borough.

The town clerk shall hold office during the pleasure of the council.

He shall have the charge and custody of, and be responsible for, the charters, deeds, records and documents of the borough, and they shall be kept as the council direct.

A vacancy in the office shall be filled within twenty-one days after its occurrence.

In case of the illness or absence of the town clerk, the council may appoint a deputy town clerk, to hold office during their pleasure.

All things required or authorized by law to be done by or to the town clerk may be done by or to the deputy town clerk.

The council shall from time to time appoint a fit person, not a member of the council, to be the treasurer of the borough.

The treasurer shall hold office during the pleasure of the council.

A vacancy in the office shall be filled within twenty-one days after its occurrence.

The offices of town clerk and treasurer shall not be held by the same person.

The council shall from time to time appoint such other officers as have been usually appointed in the borough, or as the council think necessary, and may at any time discontinue the appointment of any officer appearing to them not necessary to be reappointed.

The council shall require every officer appointed by them to give such security as they think proper for the due execution of his office, and shall allow him such remuneration as they think reasonable.

Every officer appointed by the council shall at such times during the continuance of his office, or within three months after his ceasing to hold it, and in such manner as the council direct, deliver to the council, or as they direct, a true account in writing of all matters committed to his charge, and of his receipts and payments, with vouchers, and a list of persons from whom money is due for purposes of this act in connection with his office, showing the amount due from each.

Every such officer shall pay all money due from him to the treasurer, or as the council direct.

If any such officer—

(a) Refuses or wilfully neglects to deliver any account or list which he ought to deliver, or any voucher relating thereto, or to make any payment which he ought to make; or

(b) After three days' notice in writing, signed by the town clerk or by three members of the council, given or left at his usual or last-known place of abode, refuses or wilfully neglects to deliver to the council, or as they direct, any book or document which he ought so to deliver, or to give satisfaction respecting it to the council or as they direct, a court of summary jurisdiction having jurisdiction where the officer is or resides may, by summary order, require him to make such delivery or payment, or to give such satisfaction.

But nothing in this section shall affect any remedy by action against any such officer or his surety, except that the officer shall not be both sued by action and proceeded against summarily for the same cause.

MEETINGS AND PROCEEDINGS OF COUNCIL

The rules in the second schedule shall be observed.

The schedule is as follows:

(1) The council shall hold four quarterly meetings in every year for the transaction of general business.

(2) The quarterly meetings shall be held at noon on each ninth of November, and at such hour on such other three days before the first of November the next following as the council at the quarterly meeting in November decide or afterward from time to time by standing order determine.

(3) The mayor may at any time call a meeting of the council.

(4) If the mayor refuses to call a meeting after a requisition for that purpose, signed by five members of the council, has been presented to him, any five members of the council may forthwith, on that refusal, call a meeting. If the mayor (without so refusing) does not within seven days after such presentation call a meeting, any five members of the council may, on the expiration of those seven days, call a meeting.

(5) Three clear days at least before any meeting of the council, notice of the time and place of the intended meeting, signed by the mayor, or, if the meeting is called by members of the council, by those members, shall be fixed on the town hall. Where the meeting is called by members of the council, the notice shall specify the business proposed to be transacted thereat.

(6) Three clear days at least before any meeting of the council, a summons to attend the meeting, specifying the business proposed to be transacted thereat, and signed by the town clerk, shall be left or delivered by post in a registered letter at the usual place of abode of every member of the council, three clear days at least before the meeting.

(7) Want of service of the summons on any member of the council shall not affect the validity of a meeting.

(8) No business shall be transacted at a meeting other than that specified in the summons relating thereto, except in case of a quarterly meeting, business prescribed by this act to be transacted thereat.

(9) At every meeting of the council, the mayor, if present, shall be chairman. If the mayor is absent, then the deputy mayor, if chosen for that purpose by the members of the council then present, shall be chairman. If both the mayor and the deputy mayor are absent, or the deputy mayor, being present, is not chosen, then such alderman, or, in the absence of all the aldermen, such councilor, as the members of the council then present choose shall be chairman.

(10) All acts of the council, and all questions coming or arising before the council, may be done and decided by the majority of such members of the council as are present and vote at a meeting held in pursuance of this act, the whole number present at the meeting, whether voting or not, not being less than one third of the number of the whole council.

(11) In case of equality of votes, the chairman of the meeting shall have a second or casting vote.

(12) Minutes of the proceedings of every meeting shall be drawn up and fairly entered in a book kept for that purpose, and shall be signed in manner authorized by this act.

(13) Subject to the foregoing provisions of this schedule, the council may from time to time make standing orders for the regulation of their proceedings and business, and vary or revoke the same.

COMMITTEES AND OTHER MATTERS

The council may from time to time appoint out of their own body such and so many committees, either of a general or special nature, and consisting of such number of persons as they think fit, for any purposes which, in the opinion of the council, would be better regulated and managed by means of such committees; but the acts of every such committee shall be submitted to the council for their approval.

A member of the council shall not vote or take part in the discussion of any matter before the council or a committee in which he has, directly or indirectly, by himself or his partner, any pecuniary interest.

No act or proceeding of the council, or of a committee, shall be questioned on account of any vacancy in their body.

A minute of proceedings at a meeting of the council, or of a committee, signed at the same or next ensuing meeting by the mayor, or by a member of the council or of the committee, describing himself as, or appearing to be, chairman of the meeting at which the minute is signed, shall be received in evidence without further proof.

Until the contrary is proved, every meeting of the council, or of a committee, in respect of the proceedings whereof a minute has been so made, shall be deemed to have been duly convened and held, and all the members of the meeting shall be deemed to have been duly qualified; and where the proceedings are proceedings of a committee, the committee shall be deemed to have been duly constituted, and to have had power to deal with the matters referred to in the minutes.

BY-LAWS

The council may, from time to time, make such by-laws as to them seem meet for the good rule and government of the borough, and for prevention and suppression of nuisances not already punishable in a summary manner by virtue of any act in force throughout the borough, and may thereby appoint such fines, not exceeding in any case five pounds, as they deem necessary for the prevention and suppression of offenses against the same.

Such a by-law shall not be made unless at least two thirds of the whole number of the council are present.

Such a by-law shall not come into force until the expiration of forty days after a copy thereof has been fixed on the town hall.

Such a by-law shall not come into force until the expiration of forty days after a copy thereof, sealed with the corporate seal, has been sent to the secretary of state; and if within those forty days the Queen, with the advice of her Privy Council, disallows the by-law, or part thereof, the by-law, or part disallowed, shall not come into force; but it shall be lawful for the Queen, at any time within those forty days, to enlarge the time within which the by-law shall not come into force, and in that case the by-law shall not come into force until after the expiration of that enlarged time.

Any offense against such a by-law may be prosecuted summarily.

ACCOUNTS AND AUDIT

There shall be three borough auditors — two elected by the burgesses, called elective auditors, and one appointed by the mayor, called the mayor's auditor.

An elective auditor must be qualified to be a councilor, but may not be a member of the council, or the town clerk, or the treasurer.

The mayor's auditor must be a member of the council.

The term of office of each auditor shall be one year.

The appointment of the mayor's auditor shall be made on the ordinary day of election of the elective auditors.

On a casual vacancy in his office an appointment to fill it shall be made within ten days after the occurrence of the vacancy.

The treasurer shall make up his accounts half yearly to such dates as the council, with the approval of the Local Government Board, from time to time appoint, and subject to any such appointment to the dates in use at the commencement of this act.

The treasurer shall within one month from the date to which he is required to make up his accounts in each half year, submit them, with the necessary vouchers and papers, to the borough auditors, and they shall audit them.

After the audit of the accounts for the second half of each financial year, the treasurer shall print a full abstract of his accounts for that year.

The town clerk shall make a return to the Local Government Board of the receipts and expenditure of the municipal corporation for each financial year.

The return shall be made for the financial year ending on the twenty-fifth of March, or on such other day as the Local Government Board, on the application of the council, from time to time prescribe.

The return shall be in such form and contain such particulars as the Local Government Board from time to time direct.

The return shall be sent to the Local Government Board within one month after the completion of the audit for the second half of each financial year.

If the town clerk fails to make any return required under this section, he shall for each offense be liable to a fine not exceeding twenty pounds, to be recovered by action on behalf of the Crown in the High Court.

The Local Government Board shall in each year prepare an abstract of the returns made in pursuance of this section, under general heads, and it shall be laid before both houses of Parliament.

REVISING ASSESSORS

In every borough whereof no part of the area is coextensive with or included within the area of a parliamentary borough, there shall be two revising assessors elected by the burgesses.

Every person shall be eligible who is qualified to be a councilor and is not a member of the council, or the town clerk, or treasurer.

The term of office of each revising assessor shall be one year.

Every revising assessor shall, as soon as conveniently may be after his election, and from time to time as occasion requires, appoint, by writing signed by him, a person eligible to the office of revising assessor, to be his deputy, to act for him in case of his illness or incapacity to act.

ARRANGEMENT OF WARD DIVISIONS

If two thirds of the council of a borough agree to petition, and the council thereupon petition the Queen for the division of the borough into wards, or for the alteration of the number and boundaries of its wards, it shall be lawful for Her Majesty from time to time, by order in council, to fix the number of wards into which the borough shall be divided; and the borough shall be divided into that number of wards.

Notice of the petition, and of the time when it pleases Her Majesty to order that the same be taken into consideration by her Privy Council, shall be published in the "London Gazette" one month at least before the petition is so considered.

When an order in council has been so made, the secretary of state shall appoint a commissioner to prepare a scheme for determining the boundaries of the wards and apportioning the councilors among them.

In case of division into wards, the commissioner shall apportion all the councilors among the wards.

In case of an alteration of wards, he shall so apportion among the altered wards the councilors for those wards as to provide for their continuing to represent as large a number as possible of their former constituents.

In either case, each councilor shall hold his office in the ward to which he is assigned for the same time that he would have held it had the borough remained undivided or the wards unaltered.

In case of division into wards the returning officer at the first election for each ward held after the division shall, notwithstanding anything in this act, be the mayor or a person appointed by the mayor.

If by reason of any division or alteration under this section any doubt arises as to which councilor shall go out of office, the doubt may be determined by the council.

The division of a borough into a greater number of wards shall not affect the qualification of aldermen or councilors.

The number of councilors assigned to each ward shall be a number divisible by three; and in fixing their number the commissioner shall, as far as he deems it practicable, have regard as well to the number of persons rated in the ward as the aggregate rating of the ward.

The commissioner shall make the scheme in duplicate, and shall deliver one of the duplicates to the town clerk, and shall send the other to the secretary of state, to be submitted by him to Her Majesty in council for approval.

The scheme shall be published in the "London Gazette," and shall come into operation at the date of that publication, and thenceforth the boundaries of wards and apportionment of councilors determined and made by the scheme shall be observed and be in force.

QUALIFICATIONS, VACANCIES, AND NON-ACCEPTANCE PENALTIES

Every qualified person elected to a corporate office, unless exempt under this section or otherwise by law, either shall accept the office by making and subscribing the declaration required by this act within five days after notice of election, or shall, in lieu thereof, be liable to pay to the council a fine of such amount not exceeding, in case of an alderman, councilor, elective auditor, or revising assessor, fifty pounds, and in case of a mayor one hundred pounds, as the council by by-law determine.

If there is no by-law determining fines, the fine, in case of an alderman, councilor, elective auditor, or revising assessor shall be twenty-five pounds, and in case of a mayor fifty pounds.

The persons exempt under this section are :

(*a*) Any person disabled by lunacy or imbecility of mind, or by deafness, blindness, or other permanent infirmity of body ; and

(*b*) Any person who, being above the age of sixty-five years or having within five years before the day of his election either served the office or paid the fine for non-acceptance thereof, claims exemption within five days after notice of his election.

A fine payable under this section shall be recoverable summarily.

A person elected to a corporate office shall not, until he has made and subscribed before two members of the council, or the town clerk, a declaration as in the eighth schedule, act in the office except in administering that declaration.

A person elected to a corporate office may at any time, by writing signed by him and delivered to the town clerk, resign the office, on payment of the fine provided for non-acceptance thereof.

In any such case the council shall forthwith declare the office to be vacant, and signify the same by notice in writing, signed by three members of the council and countersigned by the town clerk, and fixed on the town hall, and the office shall thereupon become vacant.

No person enabled by law to make an affirmation instead of taking an oath shall be liable to any fine for non-acceptance of office by reason of his refusal on conscientious grounds to take any oath or make any declaration required by this act or to take on himself the duties of the office.

Any person ceasing to hold a corporate office shall, unless disqualified to hold the office, be reëligible.

The mayor and aldermen shall, during their respective offices, continue to be members of the council, notwithstanding anything in this act as to councilors going out of office at the end of three years.

If the mayor, or an alderman, or councilor —

(*a*) Is declared bankrupt, or compounds by deed with his creditors, or makes an arrangement or composition with his creditors, under the Bankruptcy Act, 1869, by deed or otherwise ; or

(*b*) Is (except in case of illness) continuously absent from the borough, being mayor, for more than two months, or, being alderman or councilor, for more than six months ;

He shall thereupon immediately become disqualified and shall cease to hold the office.

In any event the council shall forthwith declare the office to be vacant, and signify the same by notice signed by three members of the council, and countersigned by the town clerk, and fixed on the town hall, and the office shall thereupon become vacant.

Where a person becomes so disqualified by being declared bankrupt, or compounding, or making an arrangement or composition, as aforesaid, the disqualification, as regards subsequent elections, shall, in case of bankruptcy, cease on his obtaining his order of discharge, and shall, in case of a compounding or composition as aforesaid, cease on payment of his debts in full, and shall, in case of an arrangement as aforesaid, cease on his obtaining his certificate of discharge.

Where a person becomes so disqualified by absence, he shall be liable to the same fine as for non-acceptance of office, recoverable summarily, but the disqualification shall, as regards subsequent elections, cease on his return.

On a casual vacancy in a corporate office, an election shall be held by the same persons and in the same manner as an election to fill an ordinary vacancy ; and the person elected shall hold the office until the time when the person in whose place he is elected would regularly have gone out of office, and he shall then go out of office.

In case of more than one casual vacancy in the office of councilor being filled at the same election, the councilor elected by the smallest number of votes shall be deemed to be elected in the place of him who would regularly have first gone out of office, and the councilor elected by the next smallest number of votes shall be deemed to be elected in the place of him who would regularly have gone out of office, and so with respect to the others ; and if there has not been a contested election, or if any doubt arises, the order of rotation shall be determined by the council.

Non-acceptance of office by a person elected creates a casual vacancy.

If any person acts in a corporate office without having made the declaration by this act required, or without being qualified at the time of making the declaration, or after ceasing to be qualified, or after becoming disqualified, he shall for each offense be liable to a fine not exceeding fifty pounds, recoverable by action.

A person being in fact enrolled in the burgess roll shall not be liable to a fine for acting in a corporate office on the ground only that he was not entitled to be enrolled therein.

The acts and proceedings of a person in possession of a corporate office, and acting therein, shall, notwithstanding his disqualification or want of qualification, be as valid and effectual as if he had been qualified.

An election of a person to a corporate office shall not be liable to be questioned by reason of a defect in the title, or want of title, of the person before whom the election was had, if that person was then in actual possession of, or acting in, the office giving the right to preside at the election.

A burgess roll shall not be liable to be questioned by reason of a defect in the title, or want of title, of the mayor or any revising authority by whom it is revised, if he was then in actual possession and exercise of the office of mayor or revising authority.

If there is no town clerk, and no deputy town clerk, or there is no treasurer, or the town clerk, deputy town clerk, or treasurer (as the case may be) is incapable of acting, all acts by law authorized or required to be done by or with respect to the town clerk or the treasurer (as the case may be) may, subject to the provisions of any other act, be done by or with respect to a person appointed in that behalf by the mayor.

REGISTRATION OF VOTERS

Where the whole or part of the area of a borough is coextensive with or included in the area of a parliamentary borough, the lists of burgesses are to be made out and revised, and claims and objections relating thereto are to be made, in accordance with the provisions of the Parliamentary and Municipal Registration Act, 1878.

When the parish burgess lists have been revised and signed, the revising authority shall deliver them to the town clerk, and a printed copy thereof, examined by him and signed by him, shall be the burgess roll of the borough.

The burgess roll shall be completed on or before the twentieth of October in each year, and shall come into operation on the first of November in that year, and shall continue in operation for the twelve months beginning on that day.

The names in the burgess roll shall be numbered by wards or by polling districts, unless in any case the council direct that the same be numbered consecutively without reference to wards or polling districts.

Where the borough has no wards, the burgess roll shall be made in one general roll for the whole borough.

Where the borough has wards, the burgess roll shall be made in separate rolls, called ward rolls, one for each ward, containing the names of the persons entitled to vote in that ward, and the ward rolls collectively shall constitute the burgess roll.

A burgess shall not be enrolled in more than one ward roll.

Where a duplicate of a burgess list is made under section 31 of the Parliamentary and Municipal Registration Act, 1878, it shall have the same effect as the original, and may be delivered instead thereof.

Every person enrolled in the burgess roll shall be deemed to be enrolled as a burgess, and every person not enrolled in the burgess roll shall be deemed not to be enrolled as a burgess.

The town clerk shall cause the parish burgess lists, the lists of claimants and respondents, and the burgess roll, to be printed, and shall deliver printed copies to any person on payment of a reasonable price for each copy.

The overseers of each parish shall at the same time that they make the parish burgess list make a list of the persons entitled in respect of the occupation of property in that parish to be elected councilors, as being resident within fifteen miles although beyond seven miles from the borough.

The provisions of this act as to the parish burgess lists, and claims and objections relating thereto, and the revision of those lists, shall, as nearly as circumstances admit, apply to the lists made under this section.

The town clerk shall arrange the names entered in these lists, when revised, in alphabetical order as a separate list (in this act called the separate non-resident list), with an appropriate heading, at the end of the burgess roll.

ELECTION OF COUNCILORS

Where a borough has no wards, there shall be one election of councilors for the whole borough.

Where a borough has wards, there shall be a separate election of councilors for each ward.

At an election of councilors, a person shall be entitled to subscribe a nomination paper, and to demand and receive a voting paper, and to vote, if he is enrolled in the burgess roll, and not otherwise.

No person shall subscribe a nomination paper in or for more than one ward, or vote in more than one ward.

Nothing in this section shall entitle any person to do any act therein mentioned who is prohibited by law from doing it, or relieve him from any penalty to which he may be liable for doing it.

The ordinary day of election of councilors shall be the first of November.

At an election of councilors for a whole borough the returning officer shall be the mayor.

At an election for a ward the returning officer shall be an alderman assigned for that purpose by the council at the meeting of the ninth of November.

Nine days at least before the day for the election of a councilor, the town clerk shall prepare and sign a notice thereof, and publish it by fixing it on the town hall, and, in case of a ward election, in some conspicuous place in the ward.

MODE OF NOMINATION

The nomination of candidates for the office of councilor shall be conducted in accordance with the rules of Part II. of the third schedule.

The rules of Part II. of the third schedule are as follows:

(1) Every candidate for the office of councilor must be nominated in writing.

(2) The writing must be subscribed by two burgesses of the borough, or, in the case of a ward election, of the ward, as proposer and seconder, and by eight other burgesses of the borough or ward, as assenting to the nomination.

(3) Each candidate must be nominated by a separate nomination paper, but the same burgess, or any of them, may subscribe as many nomination papers as there are vacancies to be filled, but no more.

(4) Each person nominated must be enrolled in the burgess roll or entered in the separate non-resident list required by this act to be made.

(5) The nomination paper must state the surname and other names of the candidate, with his abode and description.

(6) The town clerk shall provide nomination papers, and shall supply any burgess with as many nomination papers as may be required, and shall, at the request of any burgess, fill up a nomination paper.

(7) Every nomination paper subscribed as aforesaid must be delivered by the candidate, or his proposer or seconder, at the town clerk's office, seven days at least before the day of election, and before five o'clock in the afternoon of the last day for delivery of nomination papers.

(8) The town clerk shall forthwith send notice of every such nomination to each candidate.

(9) The mayor shall attend at the town hall on the next day after the last day for delivery of nomination papers for a sufficient time, between the hours of two and four in the afternoon, and shall decide on the validity of every objection made in writing to a nomination paper.

(10) Where a person subscribes more nomination papers than one, his subscription shall be inoperative in all but the one which is first delivered.

(11) Each candidate may, by writing signed by him, or, if he is absent from the United Kingdom, then his proposer or seconder may, by writing signed by him, appoint a person (in the schedule referred to as the candidate's representative) to attend the proceedings before the mayor on behalf of the candidate, and this appointment must be delivered to the town clerk before five o'clock in the afternoon of the last day for delivery of nomination papers.

(12) Each candidate and his representative, but no other person, except for the purpose of assisting the mayor, shall be entitled to attend the proceedings before the mayor.

(13) Each candidate and his representative may, during the time appointed for the attendance of the mayor for the purposes of this schedule, object to the nomination paper of any other candidate for the borough or ward.

L.—22

(14) The decision of the mayor shall be given in writing, and shall, if disallowing an objection, be final; but, if allowing an objection, shall be subject to a reversal on petition questioning the election or return.

(15) The town clerk shall, at least four days before the day of election, cause the surnames and other names of all persons validly nominated, with their respective abodes and descriptions, and the names of the persons subscribing their nomination papers as proposers and seconders, to be printed and fixed on the town hall, and in the case of a ward election, in some conspicuous place in the ward.

(16) The nomination of a person absent from the United Kingdom shall be void, unless his written consent given within one month before the day of his nomination in the presence of two witnesses is produced at the time of his nomination.

(17) Where the number of valid nominations exceeds that of the vacancies, any candidate may withdraw from his candidature by notice signed by him, and delivered at the town clerk's office not later than two o'clock in the afternoon of the day next after the last day of delivery of nomination papers. Provided, that such notices shall take effect in the order in which they are delivered, and that no such notice shall have effect so as to reduce the number of candidates ultimately standing nominated below the number of vacancies.

(18) In and for the purposes of the provisions of this act relating to proceedings preliminary to election, the burgess roll or ward roll which will be in force on the day of election shall be deemed to be the burgess roll or ward roll, and a person whose name is inserted in one of the lists from which the burgess roll or ward roll will be made up, shall be deemed to be enrolled in that roll although that roll is not yet completed.

CONDUCT OF ELECTION

If the number of valid nominations exceeds that of the vacancies, the councilors shall be elected from among the persons nominated.

If the number of valid nominations is the same as that of the vacancies, the persons nominated shall be deemed to be elected.

If the number of valid nominations is less than that of the vacancies, the persons nominated shall be deemed to be elected, and such of the retiring councilors for the borough or ward as were highest on the poll at their election, or, if the poll was equal or there was no poll, as are selected for that purpose by the mayor, shall be deemed to be reëlected to make up the required number.

If there is no valid nomination, the retiring councilors shall be deemed to be reëlected.

If an election of councilors is not contested, the returning officer shall publish a list of the persons elected not later than eleven o'clock in the morning on the day of election.

If an election of councilors is contested, the poll shall, as far as circumstances admit, be conducted as the poll at a contested parliamentary election is, by the Ballot Act, 1872, directed to be conducted, and subject to the modifications expressed in Part III. of the third schedule, and to the other provisions of this act, the provisions of the Ballot Act, 1872, relating to a poll at a parliamentary election (including the provisions relating to the duties of the returning officer after the close of the poll) shall apply to a poll at an election of councilors.

Every person entitled to vote may vote for any number of candidates not exceeding the number of vacancies.

The poll shall commence at eight o'clock in the forenoon and close at eight o'clock in the afternoon of the same day.

But if one hour elapses during which no vote is tendered, and the returning officer has not received notice that any person has within that hour been prevented from coming to the poll by any riot, violence, or other unlawful means, the returning officer may, if he thinks fit, close the poll at any time before eight o'clock.

Where an equality of votes is found to exist between any candidates, and the addition of a vote would entitle any of those candidates to be declared elected, the returning officer, whether entitled or not to vote in the first instance, may give such additional vote by word of mouth or in writing.

Nothing in the Ballot Act, 1872, as applied by this act, shall be deemed to authorize the appointment of any agents of a candidate at a municipal election; but if, in the case of a municipal election, an agent of a candidate is appointed, and notice in writing of the appointment is given to the returning officer, one clear day before the polling day, then the provisions of the Ballot Act, 1872, with respect to agents of candidates, shall, as far as regards that agent, apply in the case of the election.

CHALLENGING VOTERS

At an election of councilors, the presiding officer shall, if required by two burgesses, or by a candidate or his agent, put to any person offering to vote, at the time of presenting himself to vote, but not afterward, the following questions, or either of them:

(*a*) Are you the person enrolled in the burgess (or ward) roll now in force for this borough (or ward) as follows (read the whole entry from the roll)?

(*b*) Have you already voted at the present election (add, in case of an election for several wards, In this or any other ward)?

The vote of a person required to answer either of these questions shall not be received until he has answered it.

If any person wilfully makes a false answer thereto he shall be guilty of a misdemeanor.

Save as by this act authorized, no inquiry shall be permitted at an election as to the right of any person to vote.

ELECTION OF ALDERMEN

The ordinary day of election of aldermen shall be the ninth of November, and the election shall be held at the quarterly meeting of the council.

The election shall be held immediately after the election of the mayor, or, if there is a sheriff, the appointment of the sheriff.

An outgoing alderman, although mayor elect, shall not vote.

Every person entitled to vote may vote for any number of persons not exceeding the number of vacancies, by signing and personally delivering at the meeting to the chairman a voting paper containing the surnames and other names and places of abode and descriptions of the persons for whom he votes.

The chairman, as soon as all the voting papers have been delivered to him, shall openly produce and read them, or cause them to be read, and then deliver them to the town clerk to be kept for twelve months.

In case of equality of votes, the chairman, although as an outgoing alderman or otherwise not entitled to vote in the first instance, shall have the casting vote.

The persons, not exceeding the number of vacancies, who have the greatest number of votes, shall be declared by the chairman to be, and thereupon shall be, elected.

ELECTION OF MAYOR

The ordinary day of election of mayor shall be the ninth of November.

The election of mayor shall be the first business transacted at the quarterly meeting of the council on the day of election.

An outgoing alderman may vote, although the person for whom he votes is an alderman.

In case of equality of votes, the chairman, although not entitled to vote in the first instance, shall have the casting vote.

ELECTION OF AUDITORS

The ordinary day of election of elective auditors shall be the first of March, or such other day as the council, with the approval of the Local Government Board, from time to time appoint.

The ordinary day of election of revising assessors shall be the first of March.

An elector shall not vote for more than one person to be elective auditor or revising assessor.

Elections of elective auditors and of revising assessors shall be held at the town hall, or some one other convenient place appointed by the mayor.

Save as in this section provided, all the provisions of this act with respect to the nomination and election of councilors for a borough not having wards shall apply to the nomination and election of elective auditors and revising assessors.

WOMEN ELECTORS, AND VARIOUS PROVISIONS

For all purposes connected with and having reference to the right to vote at municipal elections, words in this act importing the masculine gender include women.

The council may divide the borough or any ward into polling districts, and thereupon the overseers shall, as far as practicable, make out the parish burgess lists so as to divide the names in conformity with the polling districts.

Any notice required to be given in connection with a municipal election may, as to elective auditors and revising assessors, be comprised in one notice, and may, as to ward elections, comprise matter necessary for several wards.

On a casual vacancy in a corporate office, the election shall be held within fourteen days after notice in writing of the vacancy has been given to the mayor or town clerk by two burgesses.

Where the office vacant is that of mayor, the notice of the meeting for the election shall be signed by the town clerk.

In other cases the day of election shall be fixed by the mayor.

If the mayor is dead, or is absent or otherwise incapable of acting in the execution of his powers and duties as to elections under this act, the council shall forthwith choose an alderman to execute those powers and duties in the place of the mayor.

In case of the illness, absence, or incapacity to act of the alderman assigned to be returning officer at a ward election, the mayor may appoint to act in his stead another alderman, or, if the number of aldermen does not exceed the number of wards, a councilor not being a councilor for that ward, and not being enrolled in the ward roll for that ward.

If a person is elected councilor in more than one ward, he shall, within three days after notice thereof, choose, by writing signed by him and delivered to the town clerk, or in his default the mayor shall, within three days after the time for choice has expired, declare for which of those wards he shall serve, and the choice or declaration shall be conclusive.

A municipal election shall not be held in any church, chapel, or other place of public worship.

If a municipal election is not held on the appointed day or within the appointed time, it may be held on the day next after that day or the expiration of that time.

If a municipal election is not held on the appointed day, or within the appointed time, or on the day next after that day or the expiration of that time, or becomes void, the municipal corporation shall not thereby be dissolved or be disabled from electing, but the High Court may, on motion, grant a mandamus for the election to be held on a day appointed by the court.

Thereupon public notice of the election shall, by such person as the court directs, be fixed on the town hall, and shall be kept so fixed for at least six days before the day appointed for the election; and in all other respects the election shall be conducted as directed by this act respecting ordinary elections.

If a parish burgess list is not made or revised in due time, the corresponding part of the burgess roll in operation before the time appointed for the revision shall be the parish burgess list until a burgess list for the parish has been revised and become part of the burgess roll.

If any person forges or fraudulently defaces or fraudulently destroys any nomination paper, or delivers to the town clerk any forged nomination paper, knowing it to be forged, he shall be guilty of a misdemeanor, and shall be liable to imprisonment for any term not exceeding six months, with or without hard labor.

An attempt to commit any such offense shall be punishable as the offense is punishable.

If a mayor or revising assessor neglects or refuses to revise a parish burgess list, or a mayor or alderman neglects or refuses to conduct or declare an election, as required by this act, he shall for every such offense be liable to a fine not exceeding one hundred pounds, recoverable by action.

If —

(a) An overseer neglects or refuses to make, sign, or deliver a parish burgess list, as required by this act; or

(b) A town clerk neglects or refuses to receive, print, and publish a parish burgess list or list of claimants or respondents, as required by this act; or

(c) An overseer or town clerk refuses to allow any such list to be inspected by a person having a right thereto; he shall for every such neglect or refusal be liable to a fine not exceeding fifty pounds, recoverable by action.

An action under this section shall not lie after three months from the neglect or refusal. A moiety of any fine recovered therein shall, after payment of the costs of action, be paid to the plaintiff.

CORRUPT PRACTICES

In this part —

"Bribery," "treating," "undue influence," and "personation" include respectively anything done before, at, after, or with respect to a municipal election, which, if done before, at, after or with respect to a parliamentary election, would make the person doing the same liable to any penalty, punishment, or disqualification for bribery, treating, undue influence, or personation, as the case may be, under any act for the time being in force with respect to parliamentary elections.

"Corrupt practice" means bribery, treating, undue influence, or personation.

"Candidate" means a person elected, or having been nominated, or having declared himself a candidate for election, to a corporate office.

"Canvasser" means any person who solicits or persuades, or attempts to persuade, any person to vote or abstain from voting at a municipal election, or to vote or abstain from voting for a candidate at a municipal election.

"Voter" means a burgess or a person who votes, or claims to vote, at a municipal election.

Any person guilty of a corrupt practice at a municipal election shall be liable to the like actions, prosecutions, penalties, forfeitures, and punish-ishments, as if the corrupt practice had been committed at a parliamentary election.

Where it is found by the report of an election court that a corrupt prac-tice has been committed by or with the knowledge and consent of a candi-date at a municipal election, that candidate shall be deemed to have been personally guilty of a corrupt practice at the election, and his election, if he has been elected, shall be void; and he shall (whether elected or not) during seven years from the date of the report be subject to the following disqualifications:

He shall be incapable of —

(*a*) Holding or exercising any corporate office or municipal franchise, or being enrolled or voting as a burgess.

(*b*) Acting as a justice or holding any judicial office.

(*c*) Being elected to or sitting or voting in Parliament.

(*d*) Being registered or voting as a parliamentary voter.

(*e*) Being employed by a candidate in a parliamentary or municipal election.

(*f*) Acting as overseer or as guardian of the poor.

If any person is on indictment or information found guilty of a corrupt practice at a municipal election, or is in any action or proceeding adjudged to pay a penalty or forfeiture for a corrupt practice at a municipal election, he shall, whether he was a candidate at the election or not, be subject during seven years from the date of the conviction, or judgment, to all the disquali-fica ions mentioned in this section.

If, after a person has become disqualified under this part, any witness on whose testimony he has become disqualified is, on his prosecution, convicted of perjury in respect of that testimony, the High Court may, on motion, and on proof that the disqualification was procured by means of that perjury, order that the disqualification shall cease.

If it is found by an election court that a candidate has by an agent been guilty of a corrupt practice at a municipal election, or that any offense against this part has been committed at a municipal election by a candidate, or by an agent for a candidate with the candidate's knowledge and consent, the candidate shall during the period for which he was elected to serve, or for which, if elected, he might have served, be disqualified for being elected to and for holding any corporate office in the borough, and if he was elected his election shall be void.

A municipal election shall be wholly voided by such general corruption, bribery, treating or intimidation, at the election as would by the common law of Parliament void a parliamentary election.

A burgess of a borough shall not be retained or employed for payment of reward by or on behalf of a candidate at a municipal election for that borough or any ward thereof as a canvasser for the purposes of the election.

If any person is retained or employed in contravention of this prohibition, that person and also the person by whom he is retained or employed shall be guilty of an offense against this part, and shall be liable on summary conviction to a fine not exceeding ten pounds.

An agent or canvasser retained or employed for payment or reward for any of the purposes of a municipal election shall not vote at the election, and if he votes he shall be guilty of an offense against this part, and shall be liable on summary conviction to a fine not exceeding ten pounds.

If a candidate or an agent for a candidate pays or agrees to pay any money on account of the conveyance of a voter to or from the poll, he shall be guilty of an offense against this part, and shall be liable on summary conviction to a fine not exceeding five pounds.

The costs and expenses of a prosecutor and his witnesses in the prosecution of any person for bribery, undue influence, or personation at a municipal election, with compensation for trouble and loss of time, shall, unless the court otherwise directs, be allowed, paid, and borne as in cases of felony.

The clerk of the peace of the borough, or, if there is none, of the county in which the borough is situate, shall, if so directed by an election court, prosecute any person for bribery, undue influence, or personation at the election in respect of which the court acts, or sue or proceed against any person for penalties for bribery, treating, or undue influence, or any offense against this part at the election.

The votes of persons in respect of whom any corrupt practice is proved to have been committed at a municipal election shall be struck off on a scrutiny.

The enactments for the time being in force for the detection of personation and for the apprehension of persons charged with personation at a parliamentary election shall apply in the case of a municipal election.

ELECTION PETITIONS

A municipal election may be questioned by an election petition on the ground —

(*a*) That the election was as to the borough or ward wholly voided by general bribery, treating, undue influence, or personation; or

(*b*) That the election was voided by corrupt practices or offenses against this part committed at the election; or

(*c*) That the person whose election is questioned was at the time of the election disqualified; or

(*d*) That he was not duly elected by a majority of lawful votes.

A municipal election shall not be questioned on any of those grounds except by an election petition.

An election petition may be presented either by four or more persons who voted or had a right to vote at the election, or by a person alleging himself to have been a candidate at the election.

Any person whose election is questioned by the petition, and any returning officer of whose conduct a petition complains, may be made a respondent to the petition.

The petition shall be in the prescribed form, and shall be signed by the petitioner, and shall be presented in the prescribed manner to the High Court in the Queen's Bench Division, and the prescribed officer shall send a copy thereof to the town clerk, who shall forthwith publish it in the borough.

It shall be presented within twenty-one days after the day on which the election was held, except that if it complains of the election on the ground of corrupt practices, and specifically alleges that a payment of money or other reward has been made or promised since the election by a person elected at the election, or on his account or with his privity, in pursuance or furtherance of such corrupt practices, it may be presented at any time within twenty-eight days after the date of the alleged payment or promise, whether or not any other petition against that person has been previously presented or tried.

At the time of presenting an election petition, or within three days afterward, the petitioner shall give security for all costs, charges, and expenses which may become payable by him to any witness summoned on his behalf, or to any respondent.

The security shall be to such amount, not exceeding five hundred pounds, as the High Court, or a judge thereof, on summons, directs, and shall be given in the prescribed manner, either by a deposit of money or by recognizance entered into by not more than four sureties, or partly in one way and partly in the other.

Within five days after the presentation of the petition the petitioner shall in the prescribed manner serve on the respondent a notice of the presentation of the petition, and of the nature of the proposed security, and a copy of the petition.

On the expiration of the time limited for making objections, or, after objection made, on the objection being disallowed or removed, whichever last happens, the petition shall be at issue.

The prescribed officer shall, as soon as may be, make a list, in this act referred to as the municipal election list, of all election petitions at issue, placing them in the order in which they were presented, and shall keep at his office a copy of this list, open to inspection in the prescribed manner.

The petitions shall, as far as conveniently may be, be tried in the order in which they stand in the list.

An election petition shall be tried by an election court consisting of a barrister qualified and appointed as in this section provided, without a jury.

A barrister shall not be qualified to constitute an election court if he is of less than fifteen years' standing, or is a member of the Commons House of Parliament, or holds any office or place of profit under the Crown, other than that of recorder.

A barrister shall not be qualified to constitute an election court for trial of an election petition relating to any borough for which he is recorder, or in which he resides, or which is included in a circuit of Her Majesty's judges on which he practises as a barrister.

An election petition shall be tried in open court, and notice of the time and place of trial shall be given in the prescribed manner not less than seven days before the day of trial.

(Here follow very elaborate directions regarding procedure in trial of election petitions.)

WORKING-MEN'S DWELLINGS

If a municipal corporation determines to convert any corporate land into sites for working-men's dwellings, and obtains the approval of the Treasury for so doing, the corporation may, for that purpose, make grants or leases for terms of nine hundred and ninety-nine years, or any shorter term, of any parts of the corporate land.

The corporation may make on the land any roads, drains, walls, fences, or other works requisite for converting the same into building land, at an expense not exceeding such sum as the Treasury approve.

The corporation may insert in any grant or lease of any part of the land (in this section referred to as the site) provisions binding the grantee or lessee to build thereon as in the grant or lease prescribed, and to maintain and repair the building, and prohibiting the division of the site or building, and any addition to or alteration of the character of the building, without the consent of the corporation, and for the revesting of the site in the corporation, or its reëntry thereon, on breach of any provision in the grant or lease.

In this section the term working-men's dwellings means buildings suitable for the habitation of persons employed in manual labor and their families; but the use of part of a building for purposes of retail trade, or other purposes approved by the council, shall not prevent the building from being deemed a dwelling.

POLICE

The council shall from time to time appoint, for such time as they think fit, a sufficient number not exceeding one third of their own body, who, with the mayor, shall be the watch committee.

The watch committee may act by a majority of those present at a meeting thereof, but shall not act unless three are so present.

The watch committee shall from time to time appoint a sufficient number of fit men to be borough constables.

A borough constable shall be sworn in before a justice having jurisdiction in the borough, and when so sworn shall, in the borough, in the county in which the borough or any part thereof is situate, and in every county being within seven miles from any part of the borough, and in all liberties in any such county, have all such powers and privileges, and be liable to such duties and responsibilities, as any constable has and is liable to for the time being in his constablewick, at common law or by statute, and shall obey all such lawful commands as he receives from any justice having jurisdiction in the borough or in any county in which the constable is called on to act.

The watch committee may from time to time frame such regulations as they deem expedient for preventing neglect or abuse, and for making the borough constables efficient in the discharge of their duties.

The watch committee, or any two justices having jurisdiction in the borough, may at any time suspend, and the watch committee may at any time dismiss, any borough constable whom they think negligent in the discharge of his duty, or otherwise unfit for the same.

When a borough constable is so dismissed, or ceases to belong to the constabulary force of the borough, all powers vested in him as a constable by this act shall immediately cease.

The watch committee shall, on the first of January, the first of April, the first of July, and the first of October in every year, send to the secretary of state a copy of all rules from time to time made by the watch committee or the council for the regulation and guidance of the borough constables.

A borough constable may, while on duty, apprehend any idle and disorderly person whom he finds disturbing the public peace, or whom he has just cause to suspect of intention to commit a felony, and deliver him into the custody of the borough constable in attendance at the nearest watch-house, in order that he may either be secured until he can be brought before a justice, or where the constable in attendance is empowered and thinks fit to give bail for his appearance before a justice.

If a borough constable is guilty of neglect of duty, or of disobedience to a lawful order, he shall, for every such offense, be liable on summary conviction to imprisonment for any time not exceeding ten days, or, in the discretion of the court, to a fine not exceeding forty shillings, or to be dismissed from his office.

GRANT OF CHARTERS

If on the petition to the Queen of the inhabitant householders of any town or towns or district in England, or of any of those inhabitants, praying for the grant of a charter of incorporation, Her Majesty, by the advice of her Privy Council, thinks fit by charter to create such town, towns, or district, or any part thereof specified in the charter, with or without any adjoining place, a municipal borough, and to incorporate the inhabitants thereof, it shall be lawful for Her Majesty by the charter to extend to that municipal borough and the inhabitants thereof so incorporated the provisions of the Municipal Corporations Acts.

Every petition for a charter under this act shall be referred to a committee of the Lords of Her Majesty's Privy Council (in this part called the Committee of Council).

One month at least before the petition is taken into consideration by the Committee of Council, notice thereof and of the time when it will be so taken into consideration shall be published in the "London Gazette," and otherwise in such manner as the committee direct for the purpose of making it known to all persons interested.

Where Her Majesty by a charter extends the Municipal Corporation Acts to a municipal borough it shall be lawful for Her Majesty, by the charter, to do all or any of the following things :

(*a*) To fix the number of councilors and to fix the number and boundaries of the wards (if any), and to assign the number of councilors to each ward ; and

(*b*) To fix the years, days, and times for the retirement of the first aldermen and councilors ; and

(*c*) To fix such days, times, and places, and nominate such persons to perform such duties, and make such other temporary modifications of the Municipal Corporations Acts, as may appear to Her Majesty to be necessary or proper for making those acts applicable in the case of the first constitution of a municipal borough.

A scheme shall, before being settled by the Committee of Council, be referred for consideration to the secretary of state and the Local Government Board, and, if and so far as it is intended to affect any authority which is a harbor authority within the meaning of the Harbors and Passing Tolls, etc., Act, 1861, to the Board of Trade.

A scheme shall in every case provide for placing the new borough within the jurisdiction of the council as the sanitary authority.

If the Committee of Council are satisfied that a local authority or other petitioners have properly promoted or properly opposed a scheme before them, and that for special reasons it is right that the reasonable costs incurred by the authority or other petitioners in such promotion or opposition should be paid as expenses properly incurred by the local authority in the execution of their duties, the Committee of Council may order those costs to be so paid, and they shall be paid accordingly.

A charter creating a municipal borough which purports to be granted in pursuance of the royal prerogative, and in pursuance of or in accordance with this act, shall after acceptance be deemed to be valid and within the powers of this act and Her Majesty's prerogative, and shall not be questioned in any legal proceeding whatever.

Every such charter shall be laid before both houses of Parliament within one month after it is granted, if Parliament is then sitting, or if not, within one month after the beginning of the then next sitting of Parliament.

APPENDIX II

THE LONDON (PROGRESSIVE) PLATFORM

(ADOPTED BY THE LONDON LIBERAL AND RADICAL UNION, IN 1892)

A STATEMENT OF A PROGRESSIVE POLICY FOR THE LONDON COUNTY COUNCIL MAY BE DIVIDED INTO THREE SECTIONS:

(*a*) DEMANDS FOR NECESSARY POWERS.
(*b*) DECLARATIONS OF MUNICIPAL POLICY.
(*c*) DEFINITE PLEDGES OF JUSTICE, ECONOMY, AND UTILITY IN ADMINISTRATION.

THE aim of the Progressive party in London should continue to be so to secure the administration of the limited powers of government which have been conceded to London as to give every Londoner the best advantage possible out of the public services; to compel public attention to the unjust limitation of the powers of self-government in London, and to the unjust way in which the revenue is now raised; and to resist additions to the county council rate wherever possible until Parliament has provided that the right people should bear it.

Their policy is at once a ratepayer's policy, for it is directed entirely to relieve the occupiers of their unjust burden, and to check its increase in the mean time; and a people's policy, for it is directed to making London a better place to live in for every section of its population.

Many of the succeeding paragraphs rather express what has been done and is being aimed at by the present London county council than contain any new proposals; and the London Liberal and Radical Union desire to express their recognition of the great work which the London county council has accomplished even within the limited powers already at its disposal.

(*a*) THE DEMANDS FOR NECESSARY POWERS COMPRISE THE FOLLOWING:

1. That the Local Government Act, 1888, should be amended by conceding to London all the powers of municipal government now enjoyed by any of the cities of Great Britain.

2. That the London county council should have full powers to hold inquiries and to promote bills for all purposes of water-supply, gas-supply, electric lighting, docks, markets, tramways, subways, burial-grounds, and for all purposes relating to the river Thames within its jurisdiction.

3. That the London county council should have full powers to promote such bills as may be necessary from time to time for the amendment of the Metropolis Management Act, the Metropolitan Police Acts, Buildings Acts, Rating and Assessment Acts, and generally as to metropolitan government and finance.

4. That the London county council should obtain the control of the police.

5. That all doubts and restrictions as to the council's powers of purchasing and working tramways be cleared away.

6. That the London county council should obtain a central control of assessment and valuation, a central registration office, a labor bureau, and a London statistical department (none of which yet exist).

7. That the London county council, instead of the police, should become the licensing authority for stage and hackney carriages, their conductors and drivers, hawkers and peddlers, and lodging-houses.

8. That a district councils bill should be passed (in accordance with the report on district councils accepted by the council of this Union), and that it should provide that the London county council shall have the necessary powers of central control.

9. That the London county council should have power to take over the duties of the burial boards.

10. That the London county council should have further control over London charities.

11. That the London county council should be authorized to keep a register of all owners, both freeholders and leaseholders, of land and buildings in the metropolis, and that such owners be required to register therein.

(b) THE POINTS OF A PROGRESSIVE MUNICIPAL POLICY INCLUDE:

I.— CONTROL OF CERTAIN GREAT CORPORATE UNDERTAKINGS

1. The municipalization of the water-supply: to be obtained by the creation of a statutory water committee of the London county council, elected yearly, with power either to introduce an alternative or additional supply or to take over the existing undertakings at a price corresponding to their depreciated utility.

The council ought also to have the power to forbid the taking of water for London drinking purposes from tainted reaches of the Thames or Lea, to compel the restoration of proper compensation water to these rivers where (as with the Lea) there is not left sufficient flow to carry off the foul matter, and to veto the taking in any case of more than a reasonable proportion of the total flow of either river (as noted by the royal commission).

2. The control of the gas-supply: to be obtained by the regulation of the quality and price of gas on a basis more efficient than the present system, and by the creation of a similar statutory committee with power either to provide a municipal supply or to take over the companies on terms fair to the ratepayers.

3. The control of the markets: to be obtained by power to enact by-laws to prevent such nuisances as constantly occur (*e. g.*, at Covent Garden and Billingsgate), and to compel the existing markets (so long as they continue) to provide efficient accommodation, especially for food-supply; and by full power to establish and carry on public markets in all parts of London without regard to existing monopolies, and to take over existing markets where thought necessary.

4. The control of the river and the docks: to be obtained by by-law powers controlling all matters of public concern, and by controlling or superseding to that extent the Thames Conservancy, with power to the county council to create new docks or to take over existing ones; or to promote a public dock board for these purposes.

5. The control of the tramways: to be obtained by such by-law regulations as exist in other cities (*e. g.*, in Edinburgh), and by the abolition of the present limitations on the powers of purchase intended to be given by Parliament.

As soon as the London county council can obtain possession of a workable line, it should be worked upon the principles now in successful operation at Huddersfield.

6. The control of all the open spaces of London: by means of regulations providing (*e. g.*) for their convenient use for purposes of public meeting, pending the transfer to the council of the spaces now (nominally) vested in the Crown, including powers over London graveyards.

In the case of those parks and open spaces already vested in council, its policy should be, as now, to make them of the utmost use for the recreation of the people, by making all reasonable arrangements for sports, conveniences, and refreshments, and by providing music.

II.— PRINCIPLES OF MUNICIPAL ACTION

1. That the county council should not only treat its own workers fairly, but should set a good example to other employers in respect of the hours of labor, rate of wages, and conditions of employment generally.

2. That the county council should continue the policy it has already initiated of arranging for its employees a normal eight hours' day and a six days' week, and trade-union rate of wages.

3. That it should assist the public, so far as it can without excessive cost, to make more use of the existing possessions of London by pressing for increased facilities at cheap rates on all tramways, subways, and railways: by pressing for adequate facilities as to workmen's trains; by utilizing and adding to the open spaces; and by assisting to regulate the present chaotic arrangements as to hospital, infirmary, dispensing, and other medical aid.

4. That it should defend the interests of the public by demanding in the committees of Parliament a full equivalent for the public in return for monopoly concessions,— *e. g.*, where vacant spaces or open grounds are taken

for new undertakings, a proper equivalent in land should be dedicated to public uses.

5. That, while acting in harmony with all local bodies, it should watch the common interests of the whole community of the metropolis, specially as to the housing of the people, the public health, and finance.

6. That the council should make due provision for the erection and management of municipal common lodging-houses, together with power to make free night-shelters.

7. That the council shall not have power to resell the freehold of any land which may come into its possession.

8. That it shall uphold, as against the City, the necessity of one government for London, and demand that the county and City should be merged in one municipality at the earliest practicable time.

9. That the council should insist on the relief of the ratepayers—

(a) By obtaining betterment contributions to improvement schemes.

(b) By charging a proper quota of the annual London budget upon the owners of rental and ground values.

(c) By the creation of a municipal death duty.

(d) By the equalization of all rates throughout London.

(e) By the division of rates between owner and occupier.

(f) By the appropriation to the proper public uses of the metropolis of the funds of the City companies and charities.

(g) By the equitable rating of vacant land, and the collection of a fair share of the rates from the owners of vacant houses.

(c) DEFINITE PLEDGES OF JUSTICE, ECONOMY, AND UTILITY IN ADMINISTRATION

1. That the rule forbidding contracts to be given to any firm which does not pay the rate of wages and observe the conditions of labor which are accepted as fair in their trade, shall be strictly upheld.

2. That where recognized schedules of wages cannot be enforced, the council shall, where possible, frame a schedule and annex it to its contracts.

3. That sub-contracting shall be rigorously suppressed.

4. That, so far as practicable, the council shall employ its own workers direct.

5. That while paying sufficient remuneration to secure the best skill in the interests of London, the council should jealously control the increase of large salaries.

6. That with a view to provide for the unemployed, the council should distribute the work it would naturally undertake in such a way that it may come in, as far as possible, at times when the demand for labor is decreasing; and should use its influence and powers to induce other local authorities to adopt a like course.

7. That the council should institute a better system of financial control over the spending departments, in the interests of economy.

8. That the council should publish an annual budget, and forbid (except under absolute necessity) all extraordinary estimates.

9. That until a more just arrangement can be made as to London rating, or until the principle of betterment can be enforced, the council should decline to promote any costly schemes of metropolitan improvement which it is possible to defer.

10. That the council should continue to contribute a reasonable amount annually to the increase of open spaces and the better enjoyment of those which exist.

11. That the council should use its powers to provide greater facilities for polling at elections.

12. That the council should put in force the regulations for tenement-houses, and should use its best endeavors to compel the enforcement of the sanitary law and the factory and workshop acts.

13. That the council should make and enforce by-laws for the better protection of the public against nuisances.

14. That the council should exercise a vigilant watchfulness in the interests of the public safety over theaters and places of entertainment and public meeting, over neglected property, and over new buildings.

15. That the council should insist on an ample provision of light and air, and should discourage the overcrowding of the people in large blocks where proper conditions are not obtained.

16. That (while discouraging large and costly schemes on the basis of Cross's act) the council should vigorously enforce the housing acts against the owners of slum property.

17. That the county council shall use its powers to provide proper dwellings, at rents sufficient to secure them from loss, in those parts of the metropolis and suburbs where proper housing for the working population has been swept away or does not exist.

18. That pending the construction of the Blackwall Tunnel, the council shall increase the accommodation for transit by free ferry across the Thames below bridge.

19. That the council should take steps to procure the removal of all gates and bars which obstruct the London streets.

20. That the council should make further arrangements for the publication of its reports, statistics, etc., and for the regular gratuitous supply of all its publications to the public libraries of London.

21. That the council should support such a reform of the law as will make clear the right of women to be county councilors.

22. That the council should support such a reform of the law as will provide for the payment of all members of the council for their services.

APPENDIX III

THE UNIFICATION OF LONDON

REPORT[1] OF THE ROYAL COMMISSION OF 1894, WHICH WAS APPOINTED TO
RECOMMEND A SCHEME FOR THE COMPLETE MUNICIPAL UNITY OF THE
METROPOLIS THROUGH THE AMALGAMATION OF THE OLD CITY AND
THE COUNTY OF LONDON

THE act of 1888, in creating the London county council, combined in that body two distinct characters, and invested it with two distinct classes of duties and powers. It not only constituted London outside the City a separate county, under a county council, exercising the functions hitherto performed by the justices in quarter sessions, but also transferred to this council the powers and duties previously vested in the Metropolitan Board of Works, so that the London county council stands out among other county councils, as regards both the extent and limitation of its authority. Over the county of London,— London outside the City,— its powers are very extensive. Where it has no power of direct administration itself, it controls in various ways the action of the local authorities, the vestries, and district boards. At the City boundary many, if not most, of these powers are stopped, and we come into the jurisdiction of a separate municipality — the City of London, which also exercises some powers beyond its own precincts — and into a new county — the county of the City of London. For some purposes, however, such as main drainage, the two areas are combined under the county council into one, the administrative county of London, comprising both the county of London and the City of London with the county of the City of London. The task set before the commission is the amalgamation of these areas and jurisdictions.

That such an amalgamation is desirable if it is practicable we understand to be assumed in the terms of the reference to us, "to consider the proper conditions under which the amalgamation of the City and county of London can be effected, and to make specific and practical proposals for that purpose." This assumption did not command the assent of our late colleague, Mr. H. Homewood Crawford, the City solicitor, and he and those who represented the City before us as witnesses protested against their appearance on or before the commission being regarded as an admission that the amalgamation was desirable.

[1] Several portions, of limited extent, are omitted from this republication of the Royal Commission's report, as not necessary to an understanding of the principles or the policy laid down in the document.

UNIFICATION IN ACCORDANCE WITH HISTORIC DEVELOPMENT

A consideration of the evidence we have received confirms the opinion
suggested by the course of previous inquiries and of legislation, or, in other
words, by the historic development of the metropolis, that the government
of London must be intrusted to one body, exercising certain functions
throughout all the areas covered by the name, and to a number of local
bodies exercising certain other functions within the local areas which collectively make up London, the central body and the local bodies deriving
their authority as representative bodies by direct election, and the functions assigned to each being determined so as to secure complete independence and responsibility to every member of the system.

If the two great principles of the Municipal Corporations Act, 1835,—
viz. (1) extension of area and (2) reform of constitution,— had been applied to the City of London half a century ago, much subsequent legislation might have been spared, and there would obviously have been no necessity for the present commission.   To complete the work then left undone,
and, as far as possible, on similar lines, in order to bring London into harmony with the other municipal corporations of the country, seems to be
the proper solution of the problem with which we have to deal.

Independently of its position as the capital and seat of government, the
important points of difference between London and any other large city are,
first, its enormous size, and, secondly, the complexity of the jurisdictions
affecting it.   The term London is at present so indefinite as to cover at
least ten different areas, though the London with which we are concerned
is, as above stated, the administrative county, comprising the county and
the City and county of the City.   Many other cities and towns are also
counties in themselves, and the difference between counties at large and
counties of cities is rather one of degree than one of principle.   Many
boroughs which are not counties of cities were made separate administrative counties (county boroughs) under the Local Government Act, 1888, and
are thus in administrative matters exempt from the jurisdiction of the authorities of the counties in which they are situated.

The recent treatment of the large area of London outside the City as a
county, while adequately recognizing its essential unity, gave undue prom-
inence to county rather than to city characteristics.   London is really a
great town, and requires town and not county government.   In those cities
and boroughs that are also counties of themselves, the county government
is so merged and blended with the municipal constitution that the former
in practice is almost obliterated.   Bearing this in mind, we have to apply
to an area, called a county, but really a town, now endowed with an elementary form of government, the dignity and completeness of the highest
form of municipal life.

Our task, however, does not end here.   We have already dwelt on the
necessary coexistence of a central body exercising functions over the whole
area of the metropolis, and of local bodies with functions exercised within

local areas, and we have been much impressed by the fact that whether we undertake the organization of the government of the greater area, or of the smaller areas comprised within it, we are in all cases dealing with areas which possess the characteristics of town life, and the organization of their joint and several government should be settled accordingly. London, we repeat, is one large town, which for convenience of administration, as well as from local diversities, comprises within itself several smaller towns; and the application of the principles, and still more of the machinery, of municipal government to these several areas must be limited by conditions arising from this fact.

It seems possible that the hesitation which marks the report of the commissioners of 1837 may have been due to the fact that they imperfectly appreciated the double aspects of unity and separability of London as a whole; and this view of the problem has indeed been developed in later years by the course of inquiry and legislation. It has now grown into so general an acceptance, that all the witnesses before us, we believe without exception, concurred in recognizing the necessity for the existence of a central body exercising functions common to London as a whole, and of local bodies exercising functions restricted to their localities, both the one and the other being directly elected by their respective constituents, thus having independent origin if not exercising independent jurisdictions.

Any controversy that remains turns upon the partition of powers between this central and these local bodies.

POSITION OF "THE CITY"

It will be at once apparent that the principal difficulty in effecting a reorganization of the government of London as a whole lies in the existence of the City as now limited, containing barely one square mile (671 acres) out of the 118 miles (75,442 acres) covered by the administrative county; with a population insignificant at night — only 37,700 out of 4,232,000 in the whole county — but in the day-time more thronged than the most crowded district of the rest of London; a ratable value out of all proportion to its size, forming $\frac{1}{8}$ instead of $\frac{1}{12}$ of the whole; and with an historic reputation for splendor and wealth which is the pride, rather than the envy, of the rest of the metropolis.

It is not surprising that any change, however agreeable to the course of municipal development throughout the kingdom, and however full of promise of enhanced splendor in the future, which proposes to carry over this heritage of tradition and renown from the limited area hitherto specially enjoying it to the whole metropolis that has grown up around it should be viewed with mistrust and repugnance by those who may be called upon to share what they have hitherto exclusively administered with the mass of their fellow-citizens.

But this was identically the same difficulty which confronted the commissioners of 1835 in dealing with cities second only to the City of London in all that makes London famous.   Liverpool and Bristol, no less than London, had a commercial center with large estates and peculiar privileges confined to a small number of citizens, many of whom were not resident; but these and many other towns had their boundaries extended so as to take in the suburbs at their gates; and if there was in any case unwillingness to accept this extension at first, no sooner had the road once been opened, than extension followed extension until town now vies with town, not which shall contain the smallest area and population, but which the largest. We can hardly believe that, when the work of amalgamation has been completed, the citizens of London will be content to be judged by any other standard.

DIFFERENCES BETWEEN LONDON AND OTHER TOWNS

The real point of difference between London and any other large town, viz., its huge area and population, makes it necessary that besides the over government of the future corporation, there must be subsidiary bodies to discharge local highway, sanitary, and other duties, and these are already found in the existing vestries and in the district boards created by the Metropolitan Management Act, 1855, which bodies now discharge in London the important duties of urban sanitary authorities. Some of our witnesses have indeed told us that they saw no other limits than those set by the geographical formation of the ground to the extent of a town which might be directly governed by a single municipality, and the experience afforded by the administration of large continental towns like Paris and Berlin lends some countenance to this view. But in the government of these cities there is an admixture of state control materially modifying the character of their administration.

In considering the government of the metropolis we must take note of existing facts, and London already contains within itself a large number of separate areas administered with varying but in many cases considerable success, and possessing attributes of local life which could not wisely be weakened or endangered. Whether the present areas of local administration are always those best suited for convenience of management is a question which we will not discuss at length; some of our witnesses have urged the creation of from six to fourteen municipalities, with wider powers and greater dignities, in lieu of the existing forty-one vestries and district boards; while others have advocated the retention of an area as small as that of the present parish of St. James, Westminster — containing no more than 164 acres and a population of 25,000 — as a separate unit of local government. Our opinion is that while some of the existing areas are of a convenient and suitable size, others might with advantage be grouped even more than at present.

QUESTIONS TO BE CONSIDERED

All our witnesses, even those most opposed to centralization, have admitted the necessity of having a central body charged with the duties of administering matters common to the whole of the metropolis, in this following the view of the commissioners of 1854. We think we may therefore start from this as a postulate, and confine ourselves to considering the following four questions:

1. What should be the constitution and functions of this central body?

2. How should the powers, duties, and property of the existing corporation be dealt with?

3. What should be the functions and constitution of the local authority of the City (and other local authorities in London)?

4. In what relation should it (and they) stand to the central body?

These questions cannot be kept altogether distinct, but such repetition as is necessary will not, we think, obscure the issues.

CONSTITUTION OF THE NEW CENTRAL BODY

The principle of indirect election of members of the central body in practice had the advantage of keeping the central body in touch with the local bodies, but something of this kind may perhaps be secured by other means; and as Parliament deliberately discarded the principle of indirect election in the act of 1888, we think we need not further consider it. In the same act, Parliament applied to London the machinery provided for other counties of a council with councilors elected all together every third year, the constituencies being the parliamentary constituencies within the metropolitan area; and in applying this machinery no consideration seems to have been paid to the fact to which we have called attention, that London is a town with town life, rather than a county. After hearing evidence on both sides of this question the commissioners do not feel called upon to suggest an alteration of the recent decision of Parliament — whether taken after much deliberation or otherwise (and it does not appear that the point was debated in relation to the metropolis) — until a larger experience has demonstrated the expediency of reopening the question.

[The commissioners approve of the present plan of electing county council aldermen, but think the suggestion that a change "which should secure in these coöpted members some representation in due degree of the divisions among the elected councilors, so that the election of aldermen should not operate as the addition of so many votes to the power of the majority," deserves serious consideration whenever the question of the election of aldermen is reopened. It was suggested that the aldermen of the London corporation should be elected by the local bodies, and this suggestion might have the advantage of keeping the central body more in touch with the local bodies, but this object may be attained by other means.]

NUMBERS OF ALDERMEN AND COUNCILORS

The existing council consists of 118 councilors and 19 aldermen. In view of the incorporation in London of the present City on the same conditions as the rest of the metropolis, it may be considered whether, remembering that its ratable value is about one eighth of the ratable value of the whole, there should not be an additional representation given to the City. If we combine the elements of population and ratable value, as is already done in the case of the division of parishes into wards under the Local Government Act, 1888, it would seem that this representation might not unfairly be doubled, so that the present City might have eight representatives; and it may be pointed out that this would cause an addition of one more alderman to the council. We recommend that, if at any time the council think fit, they may frame a scheme for altering the number of aldermen or councilors or either of them. It is manifestly convenient as well as economical to have one register of electors for both the central and local bodies, and we think that the electorate fixed by the act of 1894 should be taken for both.

AN "OLD CITY" CREATED, AND A NEW ONE

We recommend that the whole area of the present administrative county of London, including the present City, should in future be styled the "City of London," and should be a county in itself; while the present City should be styled, and we shall hereinafter also so refer to it, the "Old City."

The governing body of the City of London and its electors should be incorporated under the name of "the Mayor and Commonalty and Citizens of London"—the designation hitherto borne by the Old City—and this corporation should succeed to the present corporation of the Old City and the London county council, and should act through its council as already described.

A LORD MAYOR FOR ALL LONDON

The council should elect from the citizens of London a lord mayor, and he should be admitted in the same manner, and with the same ceremonies, as the lord mayor of the Old City is now admitted.

He should be the titular chairman of the council, but it should not be necessary for him to be present or to preside at its meetings. He should be the official representative of the people of London, and, except as otherwise provided in our proposals, he should exercise and enjoy all the personal rights, offices, dignities, and privileges which belong to the lord mayor of the Old City by custom, charter, or law.

He should be a justice of the peace for the City of London during his year of office, and, if not disqualified to be mayor, for one year afterward. His name should be included in the commissions of Oyer and Terminer and jail delivery for the district of the central criminal court.

We further propose that the council should have power to appropriate such sum as it thinks fit for the remuneration of the lord mayor, or the expenses of his office, and to choose a town clerk and other officers, and to pay them such salaries as it sees good, but that no member of the council, other than the lord mayor or sheriff, should hold any office of profit under the council.

At present the head of the staff of the county council is the deputy chairman, one of the elected members, who receives a salary. We have taken much evidence upon the relative advantages of this system and of that obtaining in provincial municipalities generally, under which the head of the staff is the town clerk, a permanent officer, usually possessing legal qualifications. We think it highly desirable that the head of the staff should be independent of the party divisions and conflicts necessarily found in the council, and we are impressed with the inconvenience that would arise if at a critical moment the corporation, through the chances of a contested election, were deprived of the services of its principal officer. We are, therefore, decidedly of opinion that the system provided by the Municipal Corporations Act is to be preferred.

FUNCTIONS OF THE NEW CORPORATION

We think the resettlement of the government of the Old City should be made on lines which are capable of being more or less rapidly adopted in the other component parts of London, so that its organization may be regarded as an example to be followed.

In developing this principle we think that everything possible should be done to maintain the strength, authority, and dignity of the local bodies of London, and that, in the partition of functions between the corporation of London and local authorities, the former should be relieved of all administrative details for which its intervention is not really necessary, and the latter should be intrusted with every duty they can conveniently discharge. In the case of doubt our inclinations would lean to the allotment of functions to the local bodies, and we believe that in cases where uniformity of action is necessary, this may often be best secured by giving to the corporation the authority to frame by-laws which should be locally administered; with provision, however, for the intervention of the corporation to secure their enforcement should they be neglected.

PRESENT DUTIES OF THE COUNTY COUNCIL

The proposals put before us by the London county council aimed at the extension over the Old City of the powers of the council which are now stopped at its boundary, and the transfer to them of such powers, duties, and property now vested in the corporation of the Old City as relate to matters in which the whole metropolis has an interest. In distinguishing these we are much helped and guided by the fact that the old corporation has in

practice, so far as the area of the Old City is concerned, delegated to the
commissioners of sewers the principal part of the functions usually exercised by a municipal town council; and this delegation suggests a distinction between central and local powers which, though not in all cases strictly
accurate or complete, still affords a good general indication of the division
that should be followed.

[The principal functions which the county council now discharges are
then described.]

As a rule these powers would naturally vest in the new corporation, but
we think that they should be reconsidered, with the view of seeing how far
any of these functions can be exercised by the local authorities without loss
of efficiency.

FUNCTIONS NOW EXERCISED BY THE "OLD CITY"

There are other functions exercised in other component parts of London
by the county council, but in the Old City by the corporation or the commissioners of sewers. These comprise powers exercised in the City by the
common council relating to bridges, locomotive traffic on highways, street
improvements, water-supply, infant life protection, storage, etc., of petroleum and explosives, contagious diseases (home animals), coroners, gas
(testing purity of), asylums, reformatory schools, shop hours, weights and
measures, and in relation to the following, exercised in the City by the
commissioners of sewers; dangerous structures, unhealthy areas, and provision of lodging-houses for the working-classes (under the Housing of the
Working Classes Act), licensing of offensive trades, and slaughter-houses
and sky signs.

These powers would, under the scheme of the county council, vest in the
new corporation for the whole of London. But while we approve of this
proposal, we do so subject to such reconsideration as has been already
recommended.

There remain a few matters, for which the existing corporation is the
authority for the whole of London, such as the provision of markets, supervision of foreign animals as imported, and the sanitary administration of
the port of London, the maintenance of Epping Forest, and other open
spaces. These, while arising out of, and dealt with under, special acts of
Parliament, are clearly administrative municipal functions, and their benefits extend to the whole of London. Accordingly they, with their appropriate revenues and debts, would naturally vest in the new corporation.
Bridges, which have already been included in this class, partake of the same
characteristics. The City corporation maintains out of trust funds appropriated to the purpose London Bridge, Southwark Bridge, Blackfriars
Bridge, and the new Tower Bridge; and it will be observed that the southern approaches of these bridges, and the whole of the Tower Bridge and its
approaches, are outside the ordinary jurisdiction of the Old City.

The other duties of municipal administration, which in an ordinary municipality are, as a rule, exercised by the town council, are, in London, now

vested in the Old City, partly in the corporation, but more generally in the commissioners of sewers, and outside the City in the vestries and district boards, in burial boards, overseers, commissioners of baths, wash-houses, and public libraries, and guardians of the poor. Many of these duties, including practically the local sanitary administration of London, are of the greatest possible importance, and will require special examination when we deal with the functions of the local authorities.

[Here follows a long section, devoted to the readjustment in detail of the powers, duties, and property of the old corporation.]

CEREMONIAL FUNCTIONS OF THE LORD MAYOR, ETC.

As the new corporation would inherit and succeed without breach of continuity to the powers and possessions of the existing corporation, and as it would be within its discretion to assign to the lord mayor such sums as might be thought proper to meet the expenses of his office, we may look for the maintenance in the future of all the useful and many of the stately traditions of the past; and in particular the lord mayor may be trusted to represent before the world the great community of which he is the head, with the splendor becoming his position. It may be noted in this connection that among the privileges which would be transferred, should our recommendations be approved, would be the right of special access of the corporation to the sovereign and of the presentation of petitions at the bar of the House of Commons.

OFFICERS

The officers of the old corporation should, as far as possible and convenient, be transferred to the new, on equitable terms of employment, remuneration, and retirement if necessary. As the functions of the commissioners of sewers would be vested in the new local authority for the old city, their officers would naturally remain attached to it, and it may also be convenient that some of the officers of the old corporation should remain connected with the Old City.

LAW AND JUSTICE

The sheriffs of London should be appointed by the council of the new corporation, as provided in the Municipal Corporations Act, 1882. The jurisdiction of the court of quarter-sessions and justices of the county of London should extend into the area of the Old City, which should cease to be a county of itself.

The justices by charter of the City of London should be abolished, but the names of the existing lord mayor and aldermen of the Old City of London should be included in the commission of the peace for the county of London. It would probably be ultimately found convenient to extend the Metropolitan Police Court Acts to the Old City, and to make the Mansion House and Guildhall justice rooms metropolitan police courts, as elsewhere; but pending legislation for the police courts of the whole metropolis we see no objection to the present aldermen continuing to serve these courts so long as they can furnish a rota.   The jurisdiction of the aldermen appears from the evidence given before us to be both efficient and popular with the classes which frequent the justice rooms, and the assistance of commercial men is not unreasonably claimed to be an advantage in dealing with commercial cases.

In the large provincial municipalities paid and unpaid magistrates not uncommonly sit together or in adjacent courts, and we think the same system might be usefully tried in London, especially if means could be found of allotting to separate courts the trial of cases not properly of a criminal character though involving penalties, such as summonses under the Education, Metropolis Management, Building, and other acts, which often require the attendance of respectable women and young children, to whom the contaminating atmosphere and companionship of the ordinary police court are an unnecessary evil.

We have proposed that the City of London court should pass to the new corporation, at all events for the present, and a similar course should be followed with regard to the mayor's court, the jurisdiction of which should be extended over the whole metropolis.   The new corporation would also take the place of the corporation of the Old City in relation to the London Chamber of Arbitration.   Obsolete courts and offices, such as the Court of Hustings, the Borough Court and Bailiwick of Southwark, and the judicial power of the city chamberlain over apprentices and masters, which is concurrent with that of the magistrates, should be abolished.

The recorder of London should be the chairman of quarter-sessions for the county of London.   The present chairman of quarter-sessions and the common serjeant should be deputy recorders, each with power to hold a court of quarter-sessions by himself subject to a scheme to be approved by a secretary of state.   Power should be taken for the new corporation to petition the Crown for the appointment of additional deputy recorders as required.   No sufficient reasons exist for maintaining the present anomalous mode of appointment of the recorder, and we recommend that he should in future be appointed, as in other boroughs, by the Crown.

The central criminal court should continue as at present, except that the aldermen should no longer be included in the commission.   In any legislation dealing with this court it might be well to restrict its area to the administrative county of London, apart from special removals under Palmer's Act.

FREEMEN AND LIVERYMEN

Freedom by patrimony, apprenticeship, redemption, and gift should be abolished with the exception that it should be lawful for the new corporation to grant the honorary freedom of the city of London to any person as a mark of distinction.   The existing freemen of the City, who are liverymen, would retain the Parliamentary franchise, and the freemen, their widows, children, or orphans, should retain such rights to charities and schools as they at present possess. We elsewhere recommend that the management of these schools and charities should be reserved to the local governing body of the Old City.

The power of granting and fixing the numbers of the livery of the City companies should be transferred to a department of the imperial government, probably the privy council, which at present deals with the grant of charters to such companies.

POLICE

The question of the police in the area of the Old City must be dealt with by itself. The City police is now under the control of a commissioner appointed by the common council, with the approval of the secretary of state, and removable for misconduct, either by him, or by the court of aldermen with his approval. The pay, clothing, and general equipment of the force are dealt with by a committee of the court of common council, but the commissioner is practically independent in all matters relating to the discipline and disposal of the force, the control of the corporation over him being much less than that exercised by the watch committee of an ordinary municipality over their chief constable. The expenses of the force are paid, one fourth — about £30,000 — by the corporation, out of their general estates and revenues, and three fourths out of the police rate, which is levied on the wards, together with the ward rate to meet ward expenses.

The county council have proposed that this force should be transferred on amalgamation to the new corporation, and that one fourth of its cost should continue to be paid by the new corporation out of their general revenues, the remainder, about £90,000, being raised, as at present, by rate. We cannot say that we concur in this proposal. Though we have no reason to suppose that any serious harm results from the present arrangement, the advantages of having the whole of the police of the metropolis under one administration are so obvious that we do not see that any counterbalancing advantage would be gained by vesting in the new corporation the control of a small part of it. It has been pointed out by the commissioner of metropolitan police that any control of the police within the area of the Old City by a body having general jurisdiction over the metropolis without the City would be a very different thing to, and might lead to much more serious inconvenience than, the control of the police within the Old City area by a body having general jurisdiction only within that area. With whom the control of the police of London, as a whole, should rest, it is not for us to discuss; but we can only say that, so long as it remains under the imperial government, the police within the area of the Old City should form part of it.

If the force within the Old City were thus fused with the metropolitan police there would result, on the present figures, an advantage to the London ratepayers of over £50,000 per annum, supposing that the metropolitan police force were correspondingly increased, and that the imperial exchequer contributed, as in the rest of London, four ninths of the cost of the pay and clothing of the whole, as follows:

Total present cost of City police force per annum (say)...£120,000
Of which there is paid by the corporation out of its general
    revenues 30,000

Leaving to be raised by police rate £90,000

As proposed:
Total cost of addition to metropolitan police to replace the
    Old City police force (say)............................£120,000
Contribution from imperial revenues (four ninths of whole)   53,333

Leaving to be raised by rate............................ £66,667

It has been urged on behalf of the Old City that if its area was policed by the metropolitan police force, there would be a danger lest the commissioner should assign to that district a number inadequate to protect the banks and warehouses, with all their valuable contents, which are often left entirely unoccupied at night, even by a caretaker. The experience of the manner in which the police is managed by the watch committees in large provincial towns with business quarters does not justify this apprehension, and it can hardly be suggested that the imperial authorities would not have the necessary regard to interests so important. In addition it may be remarked that there would apparently be no difficulty in arrangements being made for the assignment of a larger number of police than the commissioner thought necessary, so as to meet the views of the local authority, upon its paying for them, as banks, docks, railway companies, and other institutions pay for their own special police.

The chairman of the Essex county council, Mr. Andrew Johnston, has thrown out the suggestion that, in the event of the control of the metropolitan police being transferred to the new corporation, it might be convenient for the area in the southwest of Essex, now under the control of that force, to be separated from it, and given its own police jointly with West Ham. It may be remembered that this suggestion is in agreement with the report of the select committee of the House of Commons in 1867, to the effect that the remoter districts of the metropolitan police area might be annexed to the neighboring county districts where an efficient police had been established. So long, however, as the metropolitan police continues, as at present, under the control of the home secretary, no change is desired.

FINANCE

We propose that there should be one City or Borough Fund for London, and that there should be a rate levied by the new corporation, to be called the City or Borough Rate. So far as any functions may be intrusted to the council of the Old City which are at present vested in the London county council as regards the rest of London, it would be necessary to have a special fund and rate, as well as a general fund and rate; but we contemplate that the existence of the former should be temporary only. We think it of the highest importance that the relation of the central body to the local bodies should be uniform throughout London, and that the separate funds and rates should only exist until the functions of the district councils generally are assimilated to those assigned to that of the Old City, should the resettlement of the other districts not be contemporaneous with that of the Old City.

The county council have made detailed proposals for the management of this fund, and the incorporation in it of the several funds now managed by the county council and the old corporation, which seem to us, in the main, unobjectionable. These contemplate that a separate account should be kept of, *inter alia*, markets receipts and expenditure, with the provision that any net surplus receipts therefrom, after allowing for all contingent liabilities, should be devoted to the extension or improvement of market accommodation, the reduction of tolls, or otherwise for the purposes of markets generally throughout London. We approve of this proposal, but in view of the uncertainty of the receipts from many of the markets, we think that a considerable reserve fund should be built up out of these surplus receipts before they are applied as proposed.

The proposals of the county council contemplate the formation of a separate "Corporation Estates Account," into which all receipts in the nature of income arising from property transferred from the corporation of the Old City, except market receipts, should be paid, and upon which all debts and sums of money secured upon or payable out of any of those receipts should be made a first charge according to their several priorities. The proposals suggest that any surplus remaining after satisfying these charges should be divided according to its origin into portions under the following heads, viz.:

(1) Charity estates.
(2) Bridge-house and Blackfriars-bridge estates.
(3) Other trust and statutory funds.
(4) General estates.
And should be respectively applied to —
(1) Charitable objects.
(2) Other bridges and tunnels in London.
(3) Objects similar to those to which such portion is now applicable.
(4) Any purposes to which such portion may now be applied.

It appears to us that there would be great and unnecessary difficulty in working out this plan, and that it would be better to keep these four accounts separate — as we have already recommended with regard to the markets, and, in effect, to the bridges — until at least the obligations outstanding in respect to any one were satisfied, when the question of merging the assets of such account in the general estates might be reconsidered. Meanwhile, after allowing a sufficient reserve, the balance on the general estates account should pass into the City or Borough Fund.

If the City or Borough Fund is insufficient to meet the expenditure of the corporation in any year, the deficit should be made good by a rate to be levied for that purpose over the whole of the metropolis, subject to the provision as regards a special rate already referred to in respect of the Old City.

In addition to the purposes already specified, the county council has proposed that the council of the new corporation should have power to vote the expenditure of money out of the City or Borough Fund for the purposes of entertaining and of conferring the freedom of the City of London upon, and for making presentations to, distinguished persons, and of contributing to public charitable objects, and of making inquiries into any matter of municipal concern, and of illuminating and decorating the streets on occasions of public rejoicing, and of the purchase of works of art and books for civic galleries and libraries, and of maintaining the City of London School and the Guildhall School of Music.

In these recommendations we concur; but we think it necessary before any expenditure is incurred upon objects beyond these, that the consent of the Local Government Board should be obtained. We think also that the power of the new corporation to alienate corporate property should be made subject to the restrictions imposed by the Municipal Corporations Act upon town councils generally.

We think, also, that the corporation should be subject to restriction as to the amount of debt which they may charge upon future ratepayers, and that they should be bound to pay off their debts within a limited period. What such restrictions or limitations should be is a matter which we cannot undertake to settle, and must be left to be determined from time to time by the government and by Parliament. It may, however, be laid down as a general rule that the amounts to be borrowed, and the purposes to which they may be applied, should be strictly defined, as those of the present London county council are in the acts by which loans are sanctioned, and that the duration of any loan should never exceed the probable duration for any work for the execution of which it was raised.

The treasurer of the new corporation should, we think, retain the title of chamberlain, but he should be elected, as provided by the Municipal Corporations Act, by the corporation, and should hold office on the same conditions as a borough treasurer.

Besides the restrictions imposed upon ordinary boroughs by sections 139 to 149 of the Municipal Corporations Act, 1882, as regards payments out of the Borough Fund, the Local Government Act of 1888 laid upon the London county council further restrictions from which county boroughs were in terms exempted, viz. :

(1) That all payments out of the county fund should be made in pursuance of an order of the council, signed by three members of the finance committee present at the meeting, and by the clerk of the council. (Section 80.)

(2) That no order for the payment of money should be made, and no liability exceeding £50 be incurred, except upon a resolution of the council passed on a recommendation of the finance committee. (Section 80.)

(3) That three clear days before any meeting of the council a summons should be sent to every member, specifying the business to be transacted, and stating every sum of which payment was to be ordered, and the amount of every liability over £50 which was to be incurred, with the purposes for which they were to be paid or incurred. (Section 80.)

We have had evidence to show that some difficulty is experienced by large corporations in complying strictly even with the comparatively elastic provisions of the Municipal Corporations Act as regards finance, and the ingenuity of the London county council is taxed to find means of observing the letter of the more rigid requirements of the act of 1888. The result of these provisions is to load the agenda papers and weekly cash statements of the county council (of which we were shown copies) with an unnecessary mass of details, which serve no end but to provoke useless discussion. We are strongly of opinion that no sufficient reason exists for subjecting the finance of the new corporation of London to greater restrictions in this respect than those imposed upon the finance of other municipal boroughs.

AUDIT

It seems doubtful whether the machinery of audit provided by the Municipal Corporations Act would be well suited to the circumstances of the metropolis. Under it three auditors are annually appointed, two being elected by the burgesses and one (who must be a member of the council) nominated by the mayor, and the term of office of each is one year only. There is no provision in the act as to the remuneration of these officers. Under the reorganization of the Old City the City's cash and other principal accounts are audited by four persons serving for two years — two going out of office each year, and being ineligible for twelve months; and these gentlemen are elected by the Livery in Common Hall under a statute of George I. Under the general provisions of the Local Government Act, 1888, the accounts of the London county council are audited, like those of other county councils, by district auditors appointed by the Local Government Board. The act of 1894 provides that the accounts of parish councils and of urban district councils shall also be audited by the district auditors of the Local Government Board, but the construction of the act appears somewhat uncertain in relation to the accounts of London vestries. We think it expedient to maintain for the new corporation the machinery of audit provided for the London county council, and we would recommend that the latest legislation should be followed, by requiring that the corporation accounts shall be audited by two district auditors appointed by the Local Government Board, with whom, however, might be associated a third auditor appointed by the lord mayor.

FUNCTIONS OF THE LOCAL AUTHORITIES

As we have already said, we contemplate the establishment in the Old City of a local authority for the discharge of the functions of local administration at present exercised within that area by the common council and the commissioners of sewers, and outside by vestries and district boards.

These functions comprise amongst others:

(1) Sanitary administration generally, including the sanitary construction and drainage of new buildings, control over unhealthy dwellings under the Housing of the Working Classes Act, and sewers other than main sewers.

(2) Maintenance of highways other than main roads, including the regulation of locomotive traffic and tramways upon them, and small street improvements.

(3) Valuation and assessment and registration of voters (in cases where the vestries exercise the powers of overseers).

(4) The provision and maintenance of small open spaces and mortuaries.

(5) Powers as regards electric lighting and (as regards the four small companies only) gas-supply.

(6) The administration of the Overhead Wires and Sale of Food and Drugs Acts.

These functions, with their respective officers, buildings, sources of income, and debts, would, subject to the observations made elsewhere as to the partition of powers and duties between the central and local bodies, remain with the local authority of the Old City.

The powers of the corporation and commissioners of sewers in the city, however, extend beyond these, embracing in addition powers as regards

Dangerous structures;
Unhealthy areas;
Provision of lodging-houses for the working- classes;　}　Under the Housing of the Working Classes Act.
Licensing of offensive trades and slaughter-houses, and registration and inspection of dairies;
The administration of the Sky Signs and Weights and Measures Acts,

which are in the rest of London exercised by the county council. These powers, as well as all or most of those now exercised by the common coun-

I.— 24

cil in the area of the Old City, would, subject to the qualification already suggested, naturally pass to the new corporation.

The duty of inspecting common lodging-houses is now intrusted in the Old City to the commissioners of sewers, and outside it to the metropolitan police; but negotiations are, we understand, proceeding with a view to its transfer in the latter case to the county council. If this transfer should take place, the duty of inspecting these houses in the area of the Old City would naturally also pass to the new corporation, otherwise it should be confined to the police controlling the Old City.

We have already stated that we have taken much evidence on the subject of the partition of powers between the central body and the local bodies, to which we desire to call particular attention. We venture to repeat that we think it important for the sake of the dignity and usefulness of the local bodies, whose status should be enhanced as much as possible, as well as for the sake of the central body — where a continuous increase of work may be expected, requiring relief from needless administrative detail — that no duties shall be thrown upon the central body that can be equally well performed by the local authorities.

It must at the same time be remembered that there is often an administrative advantage in dissociating from local influences officers intrusted with the enforcement of penal statutes. This would apply, for instance, to the administration of the Weights and Measures Act, now enforced by the county council and common council, and the Food and Drugs Act, now administered by the commissioners of sewers and the vestries and district boards within and without the Old City respectively. In such matters as the licensing or inspection of cow-houses, dairies, slaughter-houses, and offensive businesses, and, no doubt, in many other cases of a similar kind, the central body should, to whatever hands the immediate administration is intrusted, have, in accordance with the general principle we have already enunciated, power to regulate the performance of the work by general by-laws, so as to secure uniformity of administration. The administration of the Petroleum and Explosive Acts, involving, as it does, the superintendence of their removal from place to place, as well as of their storage, should, we think, for convenience' sake, be in the hands of the central authority.

It might be well in any legislation to provide some machinery for such a repartition of functions between the central and local authorities as experience might prove desirable, without having recourse to Parliament in each particular case.

The commissioners of sewers also provide burial-grounds, a duty which outside the area of the Old City is intrusted to commissioners appointed by the vestries of the several parishes. Many of our witnesses have urged that the powers of the vestries and district boards should be extended so as to embrace these functions, and also the provision of public libraries — a duty which in the Old City rests with the court of common council, and outside the Old City with commissioners appointed by vestries and district boards adopting the Public Libraries Acts — and of baths and wash-houses, which is in the hands of commissioners appointed by the vestries both within and outside the Old City. In this recommendation we concur, and would desire that all these powers, as well as those of the present vestries and district boards, should, subject to the observations made above, be intrusted to the new local authority of the Old City. We think, however, that it might be well to retain a power of appointing on the libraries and, perhaps, the baths and wash-houses committee, gentlemen interested in these matters who are not members of the council. We think that it would be well if the registration of births, deaths, and marriages, and the enforcement of the Vaccination Acts, were intrusted to the same authority, under the control of the imperial government, as at present. Their present association with the administration of the poor-law is accidental, and may lead to misconception.

With the local authority of the Old City would remain the management of many charities and trusts, and the property belonging thereto, including some, if not all, of the following, viz.:

> The Freemen's Orphan School.
> The London Almshouses.
> The Gresham Almshouses.
> Wilson's Loan Charity.
> Emanuel Hospital (Pensions).
> The Mitchell (City of London) Charity.
> The City of London Parochial Charities.
> Russell's Charity.

Inasmuch as these, and other functions which we have not recommended should be transferred to the new corporation, involve an expenditure in excess of the income derivable from the trust and other estates applicable thereto, we have proposed that the new corporation should, on taking over the general estates and revenues of the old, assign to the local authority of the Old City suitable revenues or a fixed annual payment to meet such expenditures on these objects as could not properly be met out of rates, together with the appropriate buildings and officers. Some assignment is clearly necessary in respect of the Gresham almshouses, since the endowment of the Gresham trusts, out of which they have been sustained, would pass to the new corporation.

The council of the Old City should, like the local bodies of the other districts of the metropolis, have power to appoint officers and levy a rate, and should be subject to the same provisions as regards audit as district councils generally under the Local Government Act of 1894.

CONSTITUTION OF THE LOCAL AUTHORITIES

We turn now to the constitution of the local authority for the Old City area, in considering which we have again borne in mind the circumstances of the vestries and district boards, so that what we may say may apply with but slight modification to them.

The present common council of the City consists of no less than 232 members — viz., 26 aldermen and 206 common councilors — a number which we cannot regard as being in any way necessary for efficient administration. The number of the commissioners of sewers is 92, and even this number seems large. The maximum number of members allowed by the act of 1855 to a vestry or district board is 120, and most of the witnesses who were in a position to express an opinion on this subject thought this number unnecessarily and even inconveniently large, an opinion in which we concur. The largest number of members comprised in a provincial corporation is, we believe, 72, and this much exceeds the number found sufficient for towns far larger in size than the Old City.

In bringing the organization of the Old City into lines applicable, when not already existing, to other parts of the metropolis, some reduction in number in the governing body is necessary, besides other changes which may appear considerable; but the experience of the Municipal Corporations Act of 1835 leads us to believe that all of them may be accomplished without practical difficulty. The new governing body should be elected as elsewhere in the metropolis, and the right of election should be exercised under the enlarged franchises of the act of 1894. We think reasons of analogy as well as a large preponderance of advantage lead to the conclusion that the governing body should be elected in thirds every year, the term of office of each member being three years. A suitable number of members would, in our judgment, be 72, and the Old City should be divided into 24 wards each represented by three members. The present commissioners of sewers might be invited to frame a scheme for this division of the Old City; but, in the event of any difficulty arising, the work could be otherwise performed. We think the body thus elected should be called the council of the Old City, and the elected members should be empowered to choose annually from the citizens of the Old City a mayor, and the governing body should be styled the mayor and council of the Old City. As a transitory arrangement which would be useful in maintaining some continuity of administration, the existing aldermen should be entitled to sit as additional life members of this body. The mayor should be *ex officio* justice of the peace for the county of London, and, as we have already said, the existing aldermen who are now justices of the Old City would properly become justices of the county. We have not suggested that the aldermen should form permanently a part of the new governing body of the Old City. As we have intimated, we have had in view the other parts of London, and whilst it would be easy, and for many reasons desirable, to confer on these governing bodies the name of council, and to enable them to elect mayors of their respective districts, no element analogous to that of alderman is found in their present composition, nor have we met with any desire to adopt such an addition.

We may here recall a question to which allusion has already been made. Many witnesses have urged the propriety of establishing some personal connection between the local governing bodies and the central authority of the metropolis, and we concur in thinking this a desirable object. We believe it could be best secured by making, where the areas are conterminous, the members of the central body elected for any district *ex officio* members of the local governing body of the district. The four (or, if our suggestion is adopted, the eight) representatives of the Old City in the new corporation would then be members of the council of the Old City. We have been assured by many witnesses entitled to speak on the subject that there would be no jealousy on the part of members of existing vestries against the addition to their own numbers of the representatives of the same district in the central body, and in at least one vestry a formal resolution has been passed inviting their presence. We believe the same friendly reception would be generally experienced, and the reorganization of the Old City affords an opportunity of introducing an element which would bring the corporation of the whole City into touch with the councils of its component parts.

AREAS OF LOCAL ADMINISTRATION

The suggestion we have thus supported is intimately connected with the question of the rearrangement of the areas of local administration, which we have already said we would discuss in dealing with the reconstitution of the Old City. In order to adopt universally the proposal that the members of the corporation representing any given area should be *ex officio* members of the local governing body, it would be necessary that the areas for local administration should either coincide with the areas for electing members of the corporation, or should actually contain two or more of them. This condition would prevail in the City and in the following parishes, where the proposal might, therefore, be at once adopted:

St. Marylebone.	Paddington.
St. Pancras.	Bethnal-green, St. Matthew.
Lambeth.	Newington, St. Mary (Surrey).
St. George's, Hanover Square.	Clerkenwell, St. James and St. John.
Islington, St. Mary.	Chelsea.
Shoreditch, St. Leonard.	Hampstead, St. John.
Kensington, St. Mary Abbott's.	Westminster, St. Margaret and
Fulham.	St. John.
Hammersmith.	Poplar.
Mile-end Old Town.	Whitechapel.

It will be seen how large a part of the metropolitan area is thus ready for the immediate application of the proposal, and a very slight alteration of

I.—24*

present arrangements would extend its application so as to nearly cover the metropolis. It is beyond our power to make proposals leading up to this extension, and, if the principle be adopted, it would be necessary to provide other machinery to secure its complete application. We may, however, point out that the vestries of all the areas we have just specified might be at once styled councils and invested with the privilege of choosing a mayor, so that within each of these areas the mayor and council would be its governing body.

Considerations of local feeling and of historic development would have to be weighed in conjunction with those of administrative convenience in extending this organization to the rest of the metropolis; but we are much impressed with a sense of the expediency of attaining a result highly conducive to the simplification and efficiency of the government of London.

RELATIONS OF THE LOCAL AUTHORITY OF THE OLD CITY AND OF THE OTHER LOCAL AUTHORITIES TO THE NEW CORPORATION

There remains the final question of the relation which the new council of the Old City and the councils, if we may so describe them, of the other districts of London should bear to the corporation. The feasibility of a personal connection between them we have already discussed in dealing with the resettlement of the Old City; and we have only to indicate somewhat further than we have already done the administrative control to which the local authorities should be subject on the part of the central. The control at present exercised by the county council over the vestries and district boards is of three kinds —

(1) It frames by-laws under which they work — *e. g.*, for sanitary matters generally, for locomotive traffic on highways other than main roads, regulating the formation of new streets, drainage of buildings, etc.

(2) It has power to act in default, as in sanitary matters, and an appeal lies in some cases from the action of the local authority to the county council — *e. g.*, as regards the construction of drains, etc.

(3) Its consent is necessary in certain matters — *e. g.*, to the raising of loans, or closing streets for repairs.

(1) Most of our witnesses, even those who urge most strongly the aggrandizement and independence of the local authorities, recognize the practical inconvenience of having the administration of an act different in one locality from that in another, and are content that, to secure uniformity all over the metropolis, the central authority should frame by-laws under which the local bodies should work. In this we fully concur, and we think that if this were done, some of the functions now administered directly by the central authority might safely be intrusted to the local authorities.

(2) The power to act in cases of default and of appeal, especially in sanitary matters, is one that must be preserved. We would wish to see the direct administration by the central authority of such matters as are within the scope of a district authority lessened, as far as possible, and its action limited to general supervision and control in cases where it is necessary. The mere fact that such supervision, control, and appeal exist, with the power of taking action in default, is often sufficient to secure effective performance of a duty, without actual exercise of that power.

(3) As regards consent to loans and other matters, we do not find that as a rule it has been arbitrarily exercised, or is likely to be in future, and we think that in this respect matters may well stay as they are, at all events for the present. Apart from the fact that the council in most cases lends the money which the vestries seek to borrow, and thus gives them the benefit of its superior credit, it is well that, so far as possible, the currency of loans for similar objects should be alike, and the administration uniform throughout the whole of London. The principles of limitation which we have suggested as applicable to borrowing by the central body should therefore be made applicable to local borrowing.

The questions of rating and assessment remain, and are of the highest importance. There is much reason for thinking that they should not be left as entirely as they are at present to the local authorities. Assessments vary a good deal between the different localities, as well as within them, and the movement in the direction of uniformity of rating strongly points to uniformity of assessment as its basis, which the present arrangements for assessments cannot be said to secure. Local knowledge and experience are, no doubt, necessary for the purpose, but they should be associated with some representation of the central authority, so as to secure uniformity throughout the metropolitan area.

We cannot conclude without expressing our sense of indebtedness to our secretary, Mr. Gleadowe. He has brought the quickest and readiest intelligence to the discharge of his task, and he has added to this natural endowment an assiduity and industry commanding our highest admiration. We are satisfied that our labors would have been more prolonged and more difficult had we not enjoyed the advantage of his assistance.

All which we humbly submit to Your Majesty's gracious consideration.

LEONARD H. COURTNEY.
FARRER.
ROBERT D. HOLT.
EDWARD ORFORD SMITH.

G. E. Y. GLEADOWE, *Secretary.*
August 7, 1894.

INDEX

INDEX

379